The work you are holding began as a Bible study written for women by Angie Smith. This adaptation is our response to multiple requests that the study be made available to men.

Here is what others are saying about "James – Living a Life of Faith"

~~~~~~

Angie Smith has written an excellent study on the often misunderstood Epistle of James. Her 6-week study probes, with bulldog-like tenacity, the depths of this grand epistle. Students will find within the pages of her work biblical exegesis at its best.

Understanding the Bible isn't limited to the gifted few. Understanding the Bible is for everyone. Angie's study on James opens the door of understanding to anyone willing to roll up their sleeves and get dirty by digging deep into Scripture. Her helpful insights into Scripture can clear up many misconceptions and help one grasp the meaning of James and its application to your twenty-first century life.

~Mike Piburn, Director, Non-Traditional Studies, Calvary Bible College & Theological Seminary

To say that this study is exceptional would be accurate, yet much too vague. When it was announced that our new study would cover the book of James, most of the men responded favorably, "Great, I have been through James several times." As a pastor, I too shared this sentiment. We were a normal group of 14 guys, ranging in age from 27 – 81, varying in our life journey from new father to great grandfather. This is a vast age and experience gap, but 'the Word of God is living, active, and sharper than any two-edged sword' - it meets us where we are.

As we began this 6-week study (we finished it in just over 7 months) we all thought we were doing pretty well in our Christian walk. Yet, the study required us to answer questions that we, as men, are reluctant to ask of ourselves. Each day as the study opened up the Scriptures, we were prompted to allow the Spirit of the Almighty to use His Word and delve deeper into our lives. This wasn't easy. For a man, letting someone, even the Word of God, into our innermost being is terribly scary. BUT, let me tell you, you won't be disappointed. Through the sharing that was facilitated by this study, we have been made true brothers walking side by side, helping and encouraging each other as we grow in our relationship with our LORD.

I will leave you with the greatest truths that I received in this study. "Gentlemen, if there's one thing others need to see modeled better in us, it's a strength that is humble, restrained, and gentle."

James 3:13 "But encourage one another day after day, as long as it is still called 'Today,' so that none of you will be hardened by the deceitfulness of sin."

~Pastor David Andrews, Fairmont Bible Church, Golden, CO.

This study is the most powerful in-depth study I have ever done. It moved me from "knowing" to "applying" in many areas I thought I had already addressed. I can't even begin to describe its impact on my life!

~B. P.

Prior to the James study, I was leery of diving into this book. Having heard Scripture references in sermons, as well as in Bible study, I knew James did not mince words and was forthright on tough subjects. Angie Smith presents these passages in a manner that is easy to understand and without compromising God's word as written in its original language. Dave Vitt offers a male perspective on Angie's work. Both studies offer the learner an opportunity to grow in God's word without being a seminary graduate. This study stretched my mind, opened my heart, and strengthened my faith.

~P.P.

Part of a healthy, thriving life in Christ is relearning the Bible that we may have misunderstood with previous teachings. Not until completing this study did I realize I had misunderstood several things from the book of James, for example, "be quick to listen, slow to speak, and slow to become angry." I have known Dave and Angie for years, and have benefited immensely from being under their teaching in the classroom and in this book.

~R. I.

James

Living a Life of Faith

A Bible Study for men

Adapted for men by
Dave Vitt

Based on the original work by
Angie K. Smith

LIFE SENTENCE
Publishing, LLC

www.lifesentencepublishing.com

Like us on Facebook

Visit www.asiamministries.org

James - Living a Life of Faith – Angie K. Smith and Dave Vitt

Copyright © 2014

Printed in the United States of America

First edition published 2011

LIFE SENTENCE Publishing books are available at discounted prices for ministries and other outreach.

Find out more by contacting
info@lifesentencepublishing.com

LIFE SENTENCE Publishing and its logo are trademarks of

LIFE SENTENCE Publishing, LLC
P.O. Box 652
Abbotsford, WI 54405

Paperback ISBN: 978-1-62245-153-1

Ebook ISBN: 978-1-62245-154-8

10 9 8 7 6 5 4 3 2 1

This book is available from www.amazon.com, Barnes & Noble, and your local Christian bookstore.

Cover Design: Amber Burger

Contributing, Content Editor - Dave Vitt

Additional Editing by Mary Vesperman

CONTENTS

Foreword.. VII

About The Authors IX

Personal Note from the Author.. XI

Introduction XIII

James 1 (NASB)..XVII

James 2 (NASB)..XVIII

James 3 (NASB) XIX

James 4 (NASB) XX

James 5 (NASB) XXI

Week One: A Tried Faith

Day One - The Other Side of the Trees 1

Day Two – Endurance Training 5

Day Three - Wisdom for the Weary.. 10

Day Four - "Perspection"... 15

Day Five - A Crown Called Life 19

Week Two: A Tested and Triumphant Faith

Day One – The Blame Game 25

Day Two – One Choice at a Time 31

Day Three – The Soil of the Heart.. 36

Day Four – The Man in the Mirror... 41

Day Five – A Life of Worship 46

Week Three: An Active and Loving Faith

Day One – The Price of Partiality 51

Day Two – The Law of Love... 56

Day Three – The Law of Liberty 60

Day Four – Faith in Action 65

Day Five – A Life of Surrender... 70

Week Four: A Controlled and Gentle Faith

Day One – The Teaching Life 75

Day Two – Taming the Tongue 80

Day Three – What Goes in is What Comes Out...................................... 86

Day Four – The Power in "Prautes".. 90

Day Five – The Gentleness of Wisdom 96

Week Five: A Peaceful and Humble Faith

Day One – Conflicting Interests.. 101

Day Two – A Greater Grace 108

Day Three – Joy Comes in the "Mourning"... 113

Day Four – To Judge or Not To Judge 118

Day Five – Caution: Construction Ahead 124

Week Six: A Prayerfully Patient Faith

Day One – The Lord of Sabaoth.. 131

Day Two – Waiting… 136

Day Three – Let Your Yes Be Yes 142

Day Four – Restoration and Righteousness... 146

Day Five – The Power of Prayer 151

Leader's Discussion Guide 157

Appendix A 163

FOREWORD

The book you are holding is not a Bible study for those who are looking for fluff. In a day when so many Bible study materials are superficial, the church desperately needs materials that take Christians deeper into the Word.

James, being a book of applied Christianity, is such an important study for modern Christians. It challenges the disciple of Christ to walk in holiness in areas such as speech, business, personal relationships and suffering. James emphasizes the need to apply Scripture to one's personal life, demonstrating the reality of one's faith – for true holiness is demonstrated in the details of life. In an age when the Church shows so little difference from the culture that surrounds it, the message of James is vital.

In this study, author Angie Smith and contributing editor, Dave Vitt, consistently demonstrate excellent Bible study methods, making them accessible to all students – especially those who haven't done in-depth studies before. Word studies, historical context, and explanation of grammatical detail will lead the student into the heart of the text. Yet, this is not a dry, academic exercise. Personal illustrations and humor are also employed to demonstrate the relevance of the Word in a 21st century context, assisting in personal application. Study questions provide an opportunity for individual interaction with the Scriptures, but the homework is not overwhelming for working adults with multiple commitments.

It is also a privilege to recommend this study because of my personal knowledge of the authors. Both Angie and Dave are deeply committed to walking out the principles they teach, both in their homes and in the community. Together they founded "as I AM ministries," an organization that produces Bible studies, serves others by growing and distributing food for the poor, and sponsors local mission trips that extend love to underprivileged children. With strong marriages, and families deeply committed to Christ, Dave and Angie have actively enjoyed ministry within their local churches for over a decade.

I trust you will benefit from the study, just as I have, as you make your way through its pages.

In Christ,

Rev. Keith Gibson
Pastor – Word of Life Community Church
Director – Apologetics Resource Center, Kansas City, MO

ABOUT THE AUTHORS

Angela K. Smith, known to those who love her as simply "Angie," was raised in a loving Christian home, the youngest of three children, all of whom have devoted the entirety of their adult lives to serving their Lord. While a junior at Blue Ridge Christian High School, Angie genuinely fell in love with God's Word, and it was then that she first felt God's calling. After devoting the early years of her adult life to being a wife, mother, and then home-schooling mom, Angie took a step of faith by sending her children to school and beginning classes herself at Calvary Bible College in Kansas City. Soon after, Angie knew it was time to begin the ministry God had called her to 18 years earlier. The study you hold in your hands is the culmination of nearly 20 years of waiting, learning, studying, and finally writing.

Currently, Angie lives outside of the metropolitan Kansas City area with her husband of 19 years, and their two beautiful daughters. Over the years, Angie's anchor for all outside ministry has been her activity within the local church as a teacher, speaker, worship leader, and musician. In addition, her energetic work with children and youth groups has earned her the endearing title of "Momma A." Recently, she and cofounder Dave Vitt, launched *as I AM ministries* – a non-profit organization that produces Bible study curriculum, daily devotions, and provides service opportunities for those in their community who want to be the hands and feet of Christ. Such opportunities include working in their community garden, which produces thousands of pounds of food for the hungry each summer, and staffing weeks of summer camp that ministers to underprivileged children. A more devoted student of God's Word and lover of God's people would be hard to find. What Angie writes, she lives. I trust you will find traces of both as you enjoy your time in *James – Living a Life of Faith.*

~~~~~~

Dave Vitt wrote the Leader Guide, the "About the Author" description above, and contributed to this study as collaborator and content editor. He resides in Raymore, Missouri, where he has served in his local churches in the music and men's ministries, as well as being a respected adult Sunday School teacher for many years. He is the loving husband of his wife, Davina, and devoted father to his two daughters, Amanda and Amy. As a graduate of the University of Kansas, Dave received his Bachelors of Science in Pharmacy and later went on to earn his Masters of Arts in Christian Counseling and Psychology. After working in the pharmaceutical industry as a medical writer and editor for 25 years, having owned his own business (Advanced Response Management) for 10 of those years, Dave felt the Lord leading him to retire from a successful secular career in order to commit his life more fully to ministry. His passion for God's Word, his gift for writing and editing, and a teaching style similar to that of Angie's, led to the makings of their special writing team and made his work in this study invaluable. He has recently adapted James – Living a Life of Faith, for male audiences in order to reach men and their families with the life-changing messages found in the book of James.

~~~~~~

Angie and/or Dave are available to speak at your upcoming event.
For more information, or to schedule, please visit: www.asIAMministries.org

ACKNOWLEDGMENTS

Dave wishes to thank: *Davina, my wife, and our daughters, Amanda and Amy, for their support, understanding, and patience while I edited and re-edited the original James study and again while the men's adaptation was completed. Thanks for knowing that when Dad's door was closed, some serious writing and editing was goin' on!*

Thank you to my church family who has given me the opportunity to teach God's Word to a very loving but ornery group of adults, and has encouraged me to pursue these in-depth Bible study projects.

To the other Smith family members - Brett, Cassidy, and Charity. Thank you for doing anything and everything necessary to help us complete these projects. Thanks for the many meals around your table that nourished my body and soul. I thank you for sharing your "momma-unit;" you are all like a second family to me.

*Lastly, a sincere thank you that brings a huge smile to my face. Angie – thank you for taking me along on this fascinating, and life-changing, journey of laughter, joy, sweat, and tears. Thanks for continuing to refer to me as "the best darn editor in the world" despite my many "excellent" contributions such as "Are your words sweet music to others or clanging **bongs**? (as opposed to **gongs!**)" ☺ I can't thank you enough for allowing me the incredible privilege of editing your initial study and now entrusting me to adapt it for guys.*

Angie's thanks: *A warm thank you to my husband, Brett, and daughters, Cassidy and Charity, who have shown tremendous amounts of patience and support as my passion for God's Word consumes a great deal of my time and often covers our house with Bibles, commentaries, and scriptural research materials. Your acknowledgment of God's calling in my life and your understanding that His call sometimes demands sacrifices for our family is a gift and treasure.*

Thank you, as well, to my dear friends, the Vitt ladies – Davina, Amanda, and Amy – for your patience and support while Dave scrutinized my theology, rearranged my sometimes dizzying thoughts, and helped me to articulate on paper what was sometimes stuck in my heart and mind!

To my unsuspecting class of ladies who were willing to go out on a limb and walk through this study with me without a clue of what you were getting into – thank you from the bottom of my heart. Your support, encouragement, and devotion to digging into God's Word together blessed my socks off! God used you in my life in ways you can't imagine. Thank you for being willing to take the time to be His tools of encouragement.

Finally, a thank you that brings tears to my eyes. To Jesse Wesselink, my high school Bible teacher – there are not sufficient words to fully thank you for teaching me to study my Bible inductively and to fall in love with God's Word so many years ago. Never doubt the impact of your passion for God's Word; the effects of your teaching will continue to ripple into eternity. Bless you!

PERSONAL NOTE FROM THE AUTHOR

Gentlemen,

Welcome to *James – Living a Life of Faith*! This study was literally 20-years in the making. During those decades, the Lord was working in the lives, hearts and minds of your authors as the things of this world lost their luster and a genuine love for God, His Word, and His people grew. Over the course of the next 6 weeks, we will dig deeply into the challenging book of James, a book that can literally change your life as you study and apply its truths.

First, actually read the introduction below (that's right, don't even think about skipping this part guys, because it has important background information that will help you understand the book of James). After that, your study time will consist of 5 daily "homework" assignments each week for 6 weeks. Plan to spend 30 to 60 minutes each day in study; I can't say this strongly enough – please take your time and let God's Word soak in as you go. If you're like me, your busy schedule will creep in and you may be tempted to save all five days and try to "cram" them into one sitting before it's time for your weekly meeting. Let me just tell you from experience – don't even try, it won't work! This study was written with the intent of delving deeply into God's Word and deeply into the heart and mind of the reader. That just cannot be rushed. God's Word was meant to change your life – but you will have to give it the time and opportunity to do just that. As mentioned above, your authors have put in their time, now is the opportunity for you to invest yours.

I promise you, that despite the inadequacy of the words within these pages, you will get out of this study exactly what you are willing to put into it. I can say that with confidence because this study will immerse you in God's Word and His Word always accomplishes the purpose He has for it. The next 6 weeks will be challenging, and you will face times you want to set this book aside and give up. But, if you will commit to completing it, you will have developed a habit that can change your life forever.

While you are welcome to use your favorite translation of Scripture, we will be using the New American Standard Bible (NASB) in our text, as it is a word-for-word, literal translation of the original Hebrew and Greek texts. In some instances, slight variations in the English words used, make significant differences. Therefore, it is important that we have a common frame of reference as we discuss particular words and topics. Again, you may use your preferred Bible, but be aware that any "fill in the blank" exercises will be based upon the NASB. As such, we have included all five chapters of James from the NASB in the following pages for your convenience. Each chapter is spaced as widely on the page as possible to give you the opportunity to take notes in the margins and between the lines, which may help you recall your studies and insights more easily. So, if you prefer not to write in your Bibles, please feel free to write on these pages instead! Or, if you wish, use these pages as a "rough draft" and then copy them over into your Bible when your study is complete.

Whatever you choose, make your method of study just that – yours. Making it personal, leads to making it permanent; and permanent life-change is our goal. I pray that as you work your way through the study, His Spirit will lead you into a more genuine and practical relationship with our Lord. He has a wonderful purpose for our time together, and I can hardly wait for you to find what it is – so let's get started (with the introduction below of course)!

Good Studying,

Dave

*Note: Some individuals or groups may wish to extend the study over 12 weeks rather than 6. If so, we have provided a 12-week study schedule as Appendix A, on page 163.

INTRODUCTION

To get the most from any Bible passage or book, it is important to understand the historical background of both the writer and the readers. Most Bible scholars agree that the book of James was written by James, the half-brother of Jesus. Our look into the historical background of this book will begin with him.

Imagine if your brother started telling everyone he was the Messiah / God. James was **used** to Jesus; He was just another guy to him. Perhaps they hunted together, they'd undoubtedly played games together, and James would have even known Jesus' bathroom habits! ☺ When you are closely-related to someone, you can easily take their uniqueness for granted as you see their common qualities every day. Ever wonder how much Mary and Joseph shared with the rest of the family concerning Jesus' birth? We are left entirely in the dark on that topic. We know that upon Mary's pregnancy, she and Joseph KNEW that Jesus was God's Son, but somewhere along the line, as described in the passages below, there was apparently a disconnect of some sort with His siblings.

> *For not even His brothers were believing in Him. (John 7:5)*
>
> *When His own people heard of this, they went out to take custody of Him; for they were saying, "He has lost His senses." (Mark 3:21)*

As the above passages show us, not only did His brothers not believe in Him, His family (His own people) thought He was crazy. James was part of a group of brothers who thought Jesus had lost His senses. Can you imagine the confusion, frustration, and likely division within their family?

But, just as it should in our own lives, the death and resurrection of Jesus changed everything. The Brother, whom James thought was "just a man," conquered death and rose again. James' world was about to turn upside down.

> *After that, He appeared to more than five hundred brethren at one time, most of whom remain until now, but some have fallen asleep; **then He appeared to James**, then to all the apostles. (1 Cor. 15:6-7)*

…then He appeared to James… Notice that after Jesus' resurrection, He appeared to more than 500 people, and the apostles, but James was singled out by name. Imagine that moment. We often hear about the moment "doubting Thomas" saw Jesus and was humbled by his disbelief. Imagine this moment when the brother who hadn't believed all along, who'd called Him a lunatic, who'd thought He was an embarrassment to the family stood face to face with Him, his Brother – risen from the dead!

Many of us have experienced the pain of losing a loved one. There is a longing there to just be able to go back and talk to them one more time. I wonder if James wished he could apologize for the way he'd scorned Jesus. He hadn't had faith in Him yet, but I can't imagine he'd wanted Him dead. Jesus was, after all, still his Brother. I can't even fathom the moment when he saw Jesus resurrected. What a flood of emotion it must have been. Besides seeing a dead man alive again, besides having the chance to say the "if onlys" to his family member, this was the moment when all reality must have flooded in. He really had been who He'd said, the Son of God! What remorse must have rushed into James' heart. "What have I done? I thought I knew so much, but I've been such a fool."

You know what happens after something that has been hidden is finally realized. Little by little, past details fall into place. Surely James had a rush of those revelations; a lifetime of things that suddenly made sense, but had seemed so ridiculous before. Things Jesus may have said and done, even as a child, may have suddenly made sense. Sermons He'd preached that had seemed ludicrous at the time, all seemed clearer. We have no scriptural evidence for what the encounter between James and the risen Jesus entailed exactly, but James was human, and it's only human for the past to flood in when the present reality proves that we'd entirely misunderstood what we thought was so clear.

What remorse James must have felt as the realization of who Jesus was flooded in upon him.

Regardless of what his immediate reaction was, once James saw Jesus for who He really was, we begin seeing James in an entirely new light. He sat with the disciples in the upper room after Jesus' ascension into heaven (Acts 1:14), he received the Holy Spirit at Pentecost (Acts 2), and he became a prominent leader in the early church. While he may have doubted and denied before, what he'd now witnessed with his own eyes transformed his life, making him into a man who would faithfully follow his Brother even though the path would be dangerous. This is proven by his faithfulness to Christ even after Stephen was martyred (Acts 6 and 7). James had learned that the One who'd come to die for him was worth dying for.

It is not hard to imagine that James' passion and faithfulness to Christ was driven by indebtedness.

As mentioned, James became a prominent leader in the church. It's not hard to imagine that his passion was driven by indebtedness. His sorrow over his disobedience in the past must have inspired his obedience now. The example he'd seen in Jesus to present the truth without expecting accolades may have been what drove him to seek no glory for himself in the writing of this book. Jesus' only desire was to share the gospel; this was now James' message. Understanding his own previous blindness to the truth must have driven him to have compassion for those who did not yet believe. He could so easily relate with their doubt and skepticism. Knowing he'd lived with Jesus 24/7 and not believed may have given him a great compassion for those who had only heard and not believed. What a responsibility he must have felt to clearly present the truth. He'd been given the chance to see Jesus alive in order to change his mind – **others must now be able to see Jesus alive in him in order to do the same**. He suddenly realized that he had a message of life and death in his hands. As a result, his life became consumed with the urgency of conveying it to all who were dying because of the same stubbornness he'd once had.

Understanding the recipients is also important.

As previously noted, it is just as important to understand the recipients of this letter as it is to get to know the author. At the time James wrote this letter, the churches, filled with Jews who had converted to Christianity, were under a great deal of persecution and had been forced out of Jerusalem and surrounding areas. This group, known as the Diaspora (the Jews dispersed abroad), is precisely who James was writing to. We will look more closely at some of their trials in the weeks to come, but a broad overview shows us that being a Christian Jew invited trouble on all sides. Bearing that title could certainly cost them their life.

And he found a Jew named Aquila, a native of Pontus, having recently come from Italy with his wife Priscilla, because Claudius had commanded all the Jews to leave Rome. (Acts 18:2)

At nearly the same time that James wrote his letter, all the Jews were driven out of Rome under the Roman emperor, Claudius. So, the first wave of trouble came to them for simply being Jews. Their homes were taken, their property was looted, their businesses were boycotted, they'd lost all normal means of income, they were ripped away from family and friends, and their children were unwelcome in the schools. Dealing with these pressures alone, on a day-to-day basis, would have caused them to be weary and heavily burdened. But, their problems didn't end there.

Saul was in hearty agreement with putting him to death. And on that day a great persecution began against the church in Jerusalem, and they were all scattered throughout the regions of Judea and Samaria, except the apostles. Some devout men buried Stephen, and made loud lamentation over him. But Saul began ravaging the church, entering house after house, and dragging off men and women, he would put them in prison. Therefore those who had been scattered preached the word wherever they went. (Acts 8:1-4)

James wrote to Jewish Christians who had been dispersed from Jerusalem and Rome.

On top of being ostracized by the government, the Christian Jews were also hated by the Jews who did not share their newfound faith. The passage in Acts follows on the heels of the murder of Stephen. Saul, who would become a believer himself by the time James wrote his book, is shown looking on while Stephen is murdered, giving his hearty approval. This began a horrible season of persecution for Christian Jews by other Jews. People of their own former faith, who refused to accept the Messiah, were killing them, dragging men and women out of their houses in order to throw them in jail as public examples. To the unbelieving Jew, the Jewish Christian was committing blasphemy, and it was simply unforgiveable. Not only were these displaced Christians despondent due to the upheaval of their lives, they were now afraid for their lives, living in fear that at the least, they would be thrown into jail.

Now about that time Herod the king laid hands on some who belonged to the church in order to mistreat them. And he had James the brother of John put to death with a sword. When he saw that it pleased the Jews, he proceeded to arrest Peter also. Now it was during the days of Unleavened Bread. When he had seized him, he put him in prison, delivering him to four squads of soldiers to guard him, intending after the Passover to bring him out before the people. (Acts 12:1-4)

If these two sources of persecution weren't enough, there was still more available. Herod Agrippa I was appointed ruler of Judea under Claudius the emperor, and he was ambitious about pleasing his non-Christian Jewish subjects. This ambition led him to be a murderous persecutor of the Christian Jews. As we can see in Acts 12, he had James (the son of Zebedee, brother of John) put to death and sought to do the same to Peter at this time.

Life for these Christians who had stepped out in faith and accepted the Messiah was gruesome and lonely. Yet, James writes to them expecting them to hold fast to their faith and to grow in the Lord. If he could expect that from them in the midst of those circumstances, we believe he can expect the same from us today as well.

James became such a man of God that later in his life he was affectionately known as "Camel Knees" due to the calluses he developed from the many years spent on his knees in prayer. Eventually, he would give his life for his faith. Differing accounts of his death are given, ranging from being stoned, to being thrown from the temple and beaten with a club. Either way, he was martyred for his faith in 62AD and was joyfully reunited with his Brother once again. Until the day of our reunion with Christ in heaven, may we follow James' message of "*Living a Life of Faith*."

May God bless you as you study His Word.

JAMES 1 (NASB)

¹ James, a bond-servant of God and of the Lord Jesus Christ, to the twelve tribes who are dispersed abroad, greetings. ² Consider it all joy, my brethren, when you encounter various trials, ³ knowing that the testing of your faith produces endurance. ⁴ And let endurance have its perfect result, so that you may be perfect and complete, lacking in nothing. ⁵ But if any of you lacks wisdom, let him ask of God, who gives to all generously and without reproach, and it will be given to him. ⁶ But he must ask in faith without any doubting, for the one who doubts is like the surf of the sea, driven and tossed by the wind. ⁷ For that man ought not to expect that he will receive anything from the Lord, ⁸ being a double-minded man, unstable in all his ways. ⁹ But the brother of humble circumstances is to glory in his high position; ¹⁰ and the rich man is to glory in his humiliation, because like flowering grass he will pass away. ¹¹ For the sun rises with a scorching wind and withers the grass; and its flower falls off and the beauty of its appearance is destroyed; so too the rich man in the midst of his pursuits will fade away. ¹² Blessed is a man who perseveres under trial; for once he has been approved, he will receive the crown of life which the Lord has promised to those who love Him. ¹³ Let no one say when he is tempted, "I am being tempted by God"; for God cannot be tempted by evil, and He Himself does not tempt anyone. ¹⁴ But each one is tempted when he is carried away and enticed by his own lust. ¹⁵ Then when lust has conceived, it gives birth to sin; and when sin is accomplished, it brings forth death. ¹⁶ Do not be deceived, my beloved brethren. ¹⁷ Every good thing given and every perfect gift is from above, coming down from the Father of lights, with whom there is no variation or shifting shadow. ¹⁸ In the exercise of His will He brought us forth by the word of truth, so that we would be a kind of first fruits among His creatures. ¹⁹ This you know, my beloved brethren. But everyone must be quick to hear, slow to speak and slow to anger; ²⁰ for the anger of man does not achieve the righteousness of God. ²¹ Therefore, putting aside all filthiness and all that remains of wickedness, in humility receive the word implanted, which is able to save your souls. ²² But prove yourselves doers of the word, and not merely hearers who delude themselves. ²³ For if anyone is a hearer of the word and not a doer, he is like a man who looks at his natural face in a mirror; ²⁴ for once he has looked at himself and gone away, he has immediately forgotten what kind of person he was. ²⁵ But one who looks intently at the perfect law, the law of liberty, and abides by it, not having become a forgetful hearer but an effectual doer, this man will be blessed in what he does. ²⁶ If anyone thinks himself to be religious, and yet does not bridle his tongue but deceives his own heart, this man's religion is worthless. ²⁷ Pure and undefiled religion in the sight of our God and Father is this: to visit orphans and widows in their distress, and to keep oneself unstained by the world.

JAMES 2 (NASB)

¹ My brethren, do not hold your faith in our glorious Lord Jesus Christ with *an attitude of* personal favoritism. ² For if a man comes into your assembly with a gold ring and dressed in fine clothes, and there also comes in a poor man in dirty clothes, ³ you pay special attention to the one who is wearing the fine clothes, and say, "You sit here in a good place," and you say to the poor man, "You stand over there, or sit down by my footstool," ⁴have you not made distinctions among yourselves, and become judges with evil motives? ⁵ Listen, my beloved brethren: did not God choose the poor of this world *to be* rich in faith and heirs of the kingdom which He promised to those who love Him? ⁶ But you have dishonored the poor man. Is it not the rich who oppress you and personally drag you into court? ⁷ Do they not blaspheme the fair name by which you have been called? ⁸ If, however, you are fulfilling the royal law according to the Scripture, "YOU SHALL LOVE YOUR NEIGHBOR AS YOURSELF," you are doing well. ⁹ But if you show partiality, you are committing sin *and* are convicted by the law as transgressors. ¹⁰ For whoever keeps the whole law and yet stumbles in one *point,* he has become guilty of all. ¹¹ For He who said, "DO NOT COMMIT ADULTERY," also said, "DO NOT COMMIT MURDER." Now if you do not commit adultery, but do commit murder, you have become a transgressor of the law. ¹² So speak and so act as those who are to be judged by *the* law of liberty. ¹³ For judgment *will be* merciless to one who has shown no mercy; mercy triumphs over judgment. ¹⁴ What use is it, my brethren, if someone says he has faith but he has no works? Can that faith save him? ¹⁵ If a brother or sister is without clothing and in need of daily food, ¹⁶ and one of you says to them, "Go in peace, be warmed and be filled," and yet you do not give them what is necessary for *their* body, what use is that? ¹⁷ Even so faith, if it has no works, is dead, *being* by itself. ¹⁸ But someone may *well* say, "You have faith and I have works; show me your faith without the works, and I will show you my faith by my works." ¹⁹ You believe that God is one. You do well; the demons also believe, and shudder. ²⁰ But are you willing to recognize, you foolish fellow, that faith without works is useless? ²¹ Was not Abraham our father justified by works when he offered up Isaac his son on the altar? ²² You see that faith was working with his works, and as a result of the works, faith was perfected; ²³ and the Scripture was fulfilled which says, "AND ABRAHAM BELIEVED GOD, AND IT WAS RECKONED TO HIM AS RIGHTEOUSNESS," and he was called the friend of God. ²⁴ You see that a man is justified by works and not by faith alone. ²⁵ In the same way, was not Rahab the harlot also justified by works when she received the messengers and sent them out by another way? ²⁶ For just as the body without *the* spirit is dead, so also faith without works is dead.

JAMES 3 (NASB)

¹ Let not many *of you* become teachers, my brethren, knowing that as such we will incur a stricter judgment. ² For we all stumble in many *ways*. If anyone does not stumble in what he says, he is a perfect man, able to bridle the whole body as well. ³ Now if we put the bits into the horses' mouths so that they will obey us, we direct their entire body as well. ⁴ Look at the ships also, though they are so great and are driven by strong winds, are still directed by a very small rudder wherever the inclination of the pilot desires. ⁵ So also the tongue is a small part of the body, and *yet* it boasts of great things. See how great a forest is set aflame by such a small fire! ⁶ And the tongue is a fire, the *very* world of iniquity; the tongue is set among our members as that which defiles the entire body, and sets on fire the course of *our* life, and is set on fire by hell. ⁷ For every species of beasts and birds, of reptiles and creatures of the sea, is tamed and has been tamed by the human race. ⁸ But no one can tame the tongue; *it is* a restless evil *and* full of deadly poison. ⁹ With it we bless *our* Lord and Father, and with it we curse men, who have been made in the likeness of God; ¹⁰ from the same mouth come *both* blessing and cursing. My brethren, these things ought not to be this way. ¹¹ Does a fountain send out from the same opening *both* fresh and bitter *water*? ¹² Can a fig tree, my brethren, produce olives, or a vine produce figs? Nor *can* salt water produce fresh. ¹³ Who among you is wise and understanding? Let him show by his good behavior his deeds in the gentleness of wisdom. ¹⁴ But if you have bitter jealousy and selfish ambition in your heart, do not be arrogant and *so* lie against the truth. ¹⁵ This wisdom is not that which comes down from above, but is earthly, natural, demonic. ¹⁶ For where jealousy and selfish ambition exist, there is disorder and every evil thing. ¹⁷ But the wisdom from above is first pure, then peaceable, gentle, reasonable, full of mercy and good fruits, unwavering, without hypocrisy. ¹⁸ And the seed whose fruit is righteousness is sown in peace by those who make peace.

JAMES 4 (NASB)

¹What is the source of quarrels and conflicts among you? Is not the source your pleasures that wage war in your members? ²You lust and do not have; *so* you commit murder. You are envious and cannot obtain; *so* you fight and quarrel. You do not have because you do not ask. ³You ask and do not receive, because you ask with wrong motives, so that you may spend *it* on your pleasures. ⁴You adulteresses, do you not know that friendship with the world is hostility toward God? Therefore whoever wishes to be a friend of the world makes himself an enemy of God. ⁵Or do you think that the Scripture speaks to no purpose: "He jealously desires the Spirit which He has made to dwell in us"? ⁶But He gives a greater grace. Therefore *it* says, "GOD IS OPPOSED TO THE PROUD, BUT GIVES GRACE TO THE HUMBLE." ⁷Submit therefore to God. Resist the devil and he will flee from you. ⁸Draw near to God and He will draw near to you. Cleanse your hands, you sinners; and purify your hearts, you double-minded. ⁹Be miserable and mourn and weep; let your laughter be turned into mourning and your joy to gloom. ¹⁰Humble yourselves in the presence of the Lord, and He will exalt you. ¹¹Do not speak against one another, brethren. He who speaks against a brother or judges his brother, speaks against the law and judges the law; but if you judge the law, you are not a doer of the law but a judge *of it.* ¹²There is *only* one Lawgiver and Judge, the One who is able to save and to destroy; but who are you who judge your neighbor? ¹³Come now, you who say, "Today or tomorrow we will go to such and such a city, and spend a year there and engage in business and make a profit." ¹⁴Yet you do not know what your life will be like tomorrow. You are *just* a vapor that appears for a little while and then vanishes away. ¹⁵Instead, *you ought* to say, "If the Lord wills, we will live and also do this or that." ¹⁶But as it is, you boast in your arrogance; all such boasting is evil. ¹⁷Therefore, to one who knows *the* right thing to do and does not do it, to him it is sin.

JAMES 5 (NASB)

¹ Come now, you rich, weep and howl for your miseries which are coming upon you. ² Your riches have rotted and your garments have become moth-eaten. ³ Your gold and your silver have rusted; and their rust will be a witness against you and will consume your flesh like fire. It is in the last days that you have stored up your treasure! ⁴ Behold, the pay of the laborers who mowed your fields, *and* which has been withheld by you, cries out *against you;* and the outcry of those who did the harvesting has reached the ears of the Lord of Sabaoth. ⁵ You have lived luxuriously on the earth and led a life of wanton pleasure; you have fattened your hearts in a day of slaughter. ⁶ You have condemned and put to death the righteous *man;* he does not resist you. ⁷ Therefore be patient, brethren, until the coming of the Lord. The farmer waits for the precious produce of the soil, being patient about it, until it gets the early and late rains. ⁸ You too be patient; strengthen your hearts, for the coming of the Lord is near. ⁹ Do not complain, brethren, against one another, so that you yourselves may not be judged; behold, the Judge is standing right at the door. ¹⁰ As an example, brethren, of suffering and patience, take the prophets who spoke in the name of the Lord. ¹¹ We count those blessed who endured. You have heard of the endurance of Job and have seen the outcome of the Lord's dealings, that the Lord is full of compassion and *is* merciful. ¹² But above all, my brethren, do not swear, either by heaven or by earth or with any other oath; but your yes is to be yes, and your no, no, so that you may not fall under judgment. ¹³ Is anyone among you suffering? *Then* he must pray. Is anyone cheerful? He is to sing praises. ¹⁴ Is anyone among you sick? *Then* he must call for the elders of the church and they are to pray over him, anointing him with oil in the name of the Lord; ¹⁵ and the prayer offered in faith will restore the one who is sick, and the Lord will raise him up, and if he has committed sins, they will be forgiven him. ¹⁶ Therefore, confess your sins to one another, and pray for one another so that you may be healed. The effective prayer of a righteous man can accomplish much. ¹⁷ Elijah was a man with a nature like ours, and he prayed earnestly that it would not rain, and it did not rain on the earth for three years and six months. ¹⁸ Then he prayed again, and the sky poured rain and the earth produced its fruit. ¹⁹ My brethren, if any among you strays from the truth and one turns him back, ²⁰ let him know that he who turns a sinner from the error of his way will save his soul from death and will cover a multitude of sins.

WEEK ONE: A TRIED FAITH

Day One - The Other Side of the Trees

Over the centuries, the book of James has been fiercely debated due to its strong stance on works. The great reformer, Martin Luther, denounced it, claiming that it should be stricken from Scripture as he felt it contradicted the clear teachings of Paul concerning salvation through faith alone. What Luther apparently failed to see, at that time, was that the book of James does not clash with the rest of Scripture, but rather creates a harmony line to an already established melody.

Paul and James, the half-brother of Jesus, had a common goal, but they targeted different audiences. Because of this, their tone and emphasis varied from one another. Just as we find it necessary to address and discipline our children differently depending on their personalities, level of maturity, and individual situations, these two authors found themselves addressing audiences with different struggles, temptations, and needs. In the books of Romans and Galatians, Paul pressed the issue of salvation by faith alone, because the recipients were struggling with understanding that works had nothing to do with eternal security. His emphasis was on the Christian finding liberty in his or her faith. On the other hand, the original readers of the book of James needed to hear that although their salvation was secure through faith, that very faith needed to be *demonstrated* by an outpouring of works in obedience to the God in whom their faith was placed. Paul emphasized the *origin* of their salvation; James emphasized its *evidence*.

Recognizing who the recipients of the book of James are is imperative for understanding this difference.

Read James 1:1-2.

In these verses, James refers to the recipients in two ways. What are they?

_____

First, he refers to them as the twelve tribes who are dispersed abroad. You most likely recognize the twelve tribes as the tribes of Israel, the Jews, God's chosen people. This in itself is significant, but the second description completes our understanding. As James repeatedly refers to his recipients as "brethren," he is letting us know that these Jews are also Christians. Therefore, his message to them through this letter is equally applicable to us in our daily lives as Christians. It is important that we never take promises or instructions intended for a specific group of people within Scripture and claim them as our own, unless they are restated for us in Scripture elsewhere. For example – the promise of a land flowing with milk and honey (Ex. 3:8) is intended exclusively for the children of Israel. Through our study of James, though, we will discover that although distinct technicalities are addressed

Welcome to Day One of what promises to be a great adventure in God's Word! We pray you'll grow in your walk with Christ as a result of your time in the book of James!

Paul emphasized the origin of their salvation; James emphasized its evidence.

for the recipient's particular situations, every principle is valuable to us and meant for our instruction as fellow Christians.

Knowing that the original readers were Jewish Christians, we have more insight into the tone James used in writing his letter. The Christians that James addressed apparently already knew that their salvation was secured through faith, and we can conclude that this was not a point he needed to reinforce in the manner that Paul was compelled to on other occasions. Instead, James was able to write his letter with the intention of building upon the Christian's foundational understanding of saving faith, expounding on the works that demonstrate the faith of a true believer.

At times, topics such as faith and works found in books such as James and Galatians can cause doubt in the mind of readers, as the two books appear to say two different things. Remember, Scripture never contradicts itself. When it seems to, historical context and other Scripture will always reveal truth that may not be clear upon first glance.

As the overarching theme of James is the manifestation of true faith in a believer's life, he begins the book with an ultimate test of faith: trials.

When you hear the word "trial," what thoughts first come to mind?

_____

_____

Throughout life, our concept of the word "trial" evolves. Somehow through life's hard knocks, we go from stressing over not making the sports team or not having a date to the junior high dance to coping with cancer as an adult. What was once earth-shattering becomes trivial as we stretch and grow in our faith.

Read James 1:1-4, specifically noting the word "trial."

The word trial, as it is used in this passage, is the Greek word *peirasmós*, which has two meanings. The first refers to a testing that challenges the strength and integrity of one's faith. The second refers to temptations that challenge one's moral strength and integrity.[1] We will see both meanings used within the first chapter of James, but our immediate attention will be directed to the first. How we interpret life in full, its challenges as well as its joys, depends entirely on our perspective. **How we see things outwardly, fully affects how we receive them inwardly**. During our study of trials, it will be our personal challenge to all of us, that we learn to see trials and suffering in this life through new lenses, with a new perspective that allows us to recognize trials as tools in the hands of a loving God, rather than merely negative setbacks and tragedies.

In order to change our perspectives, it is important for us to identify our current view so we recognize our starting place while working toward our end goal. When you think of the trials in your life, past and present, what is your knee-jerk reaction to them?

_____

_____

Scripture never contradicts itself

The overarching theme of James is the manifestation of true faith

peirasmós – 1) testing of one's faith; and 2) temptations to one's moral strength and integrity

---

1   Charles R. Swindoll, *Swindoll's New Testament Insights, Insights on James, 1 & 2 Peter*, p. 25

Looking back to the introduction, what are some of the trials you can imagine that the Christian Jews who had been 'dispersed abroad' had to endure?

_____

_____

Because James, himself, was a Christian Jew, he was well-versed and experienced in the trials and sufferings his readers had endured. He understood the cruelties of life, even to the extent of having his own Brother, Jesus, die a merciless death on a cross. Make no mistake, when James used the word "trial," he wasn't speaking of getting stuck in traffic, being late to a ball game, not meeting a work deadline, or the fact that someone's wife yelled at him for refusing to put the toilet seat down or not squeezing from the right end of the tube of toothpaste! No, James knew that the trials his readers were undergoing involved life and death, fear and great suffering. Even so, he did not coddle his brothers and sisters in Christ with excuses to give up.

James knew the trials his readers were undergoing!

Certainly these Christians had their faith tested by their trials. What questions might you have had for God had you been among them during these years of early church persecution?

_____

_____

Do you think they could have endured such trials and suffering had they taken their faith lightly or considered it optional? Why or why not?

_____

_____

Reread James 1:1-4. How should we *consider* trials that come our way? _____

Joy seems like a pretty strange way to consider trials, doesn't it? Immediately, we see that James has called for a change in the perspective of his readers as they thought about their own trials. He made a pretty bold request of them that he realizes is going to seem like a hard pill to swallow. Instead of lambasting them with an outright statement such as, "Trials should bring you joy," he calls on them to change their thinking, their consideration, in order for them to absorb the profound truth that he is about to share; truth that can only be fully understood through a godly mindset. Are you ready to change your thinking? Are you ready to see your life through the lenses of God's sovereignty rather than with your limited vision?

We're called upon to change our thinking about the trials we face

In her original James study, Angie told the following story: "Nearly two years ago, I was driving on a cold winter afternoon after an ice storm had hit our city the night before. I need to preface this with the reality that I do not delight in winter, nor do I relish cold; when it's 80 degrees outside, I'm in hog heaven! This being the case, when ice not only lines every blade of grass, but the streets as well, I'm in no hurry to drive anywhere. I much prefer to hunker down in my home and keep the fire burning until spring! Nevertheless, necessity required that I run an errand, and I found myself with both fists clinching the steering wheel while driving on our ice-covered country roads. As much as I could handle eliminating the entire winter season, there is one thing about a Missouri ice storm I've always found breathtaking – the trees. As I drove along on this frigid day, I noticed the sun absolutely twinkling off the ice-laden trees as if they were diamond-crested visions of splendor; it was magnificent. I didn't mind driving slowly; I simply could not get enough of their beauty."

"Eventually, I reached my destination, accomplished my task, and began my journey home. I was anxious to get to the particular country road that had so grasped my attention, and yet when I got there, the view had changed. The trees that were dancing with light only an hour before were now dark, cold, and dreary. Their limbs that had broken under the heavy weight of ice were now readily apparent and to be completely honest, the new vision was quite depressing. My heart sank as I had so recently been praising the Lord for the beauty of His creation and had looked forward to basking in it once again. Like a child disappointed on Christmas morning, I wondered what had changed so quickly. I must have just caught the sun at the perfect time; my chance to see its beauty must have been over. A bit saddened by the whole account, upon coming to the end of the road, I turned around to look once more at the trees that had brought me such joy - as well as such disappointment. To my amazement, they were ablaze with light, dancing with beauty that now seemed to surpass any beauty they had provided before. The sun had not changed. The trees had not changed, nor their beauty. The only factor that had changed was the direction in which I was driving; my perspective had completely been altered. On my way, I had seen the same trees, burdened with the weight of ice, brittle and breaking under their heavy load, but beautiful in the midst of their trial as the sun shone so brilliantly upon their weakened branches and filled them with light. On my way home, as my perspective had changed, so did my focus. I saw only their burden, their brokenness, the devastation, and the darkness. In no way, though, had their beauty disappeared… it was simply my choice as to which side of the trees I would set my gaze."

There are always two sides to every trial; will you set your mind to finding God's perspective?

We've only just begun our look at trials, but we've begun in a place where we can decide which side of our trials we will choose to set our gaze. As the illustration above highlights, there are always two sides of every ice-covered tree. Men, the challenge set before you today is to set your mind on finding God's perspective in every circumstance – to look for the good that can come from the ashes of even the darkest trial. If we're honest, each of us can look back on a storm of life and see something of worth amidst the brokenness. The same is true of our current and future storms; **if** we'll choose to find God's hand moving in their midst.

Take time now to think back. Ask God to show you what He's brought you through that has made you a more usable tool for Him, a more unique creation, a greater reflection of His light.

Below, thank Him for bringing you through past trials, for helping you through current suffering. Use this space to talk to Him, to ask Him to help you to see the light in a trial that has so far seemed to provide only darkness. Ask Him to open your eyes to a new perspective, not only as you turn to look at the trees in your past, but as you drive into the seasons ahead.

_____

_____

_____

_____

_____

_____

Day Two – Endurance Training

We realize that asking you to delve into the deeper recesses of your minds and souls can be a daunting task. These are places that we find intimidating in our own lives. If given the choice, we all prefer to stay on "safe" ground where we can go about our daily business, not subjecting ourselves to potential vulnerability. May we ask, though, that for today, we remove our masks that we so often hide behind in order to learn from our past experiences and trials? For it is in our most honest, desperate moments that we often hear our Lord's voice the clearest. *Lord, open our eyes, and as You do, please speak to us.*

Read James 1:1-4 again.

If you're tempted to skip reading these verses again because of repetition, please don't. It is through the process of repeatedly reading passages of Scripture and focusing on a different facet each time that our eyes open to what the Holy Spirit desires to convey. It is through this process that the Word comes alive, providing everything we need.

Yesterday we discussed the fact that the book of James challenges us to see our trials with a new perspective, to consider them joy. If you're like most of us, you're not easily swayed by requests that seem unreasonable. Thankfully, we serve an entirely reasonable God, and He always supports His requests with sovereign wisdom. Knowing that the request in verse 2 goes against the grain of natural human thinking, James uses verse 3 to support it with logical rationale.

What are we to *know* about trials that test our faith? _____

When James says, "*knowing that the testing of your faith produces endurance*" immediately after his request to consider trials as joy, he is not commanding that they now learn that the testing of faith does so. Rather, he is presuming that the persecuted Jewish Christians already understand, through experience, that the testing of their faith brings about endurance; **therefore**, they can consider it joy when they encounter the trials that they do. Reversing the order of verses 2 and 3 may give us a better idea of what James had in mind - "…knowing that the testing of your faith produces endurance, consider it all joy when you encounter them." The assumption here is that the Christian actually desires to build endurance, even if trials are required to do so.

Can you look back on your life and recognize ways in which you have learned to endure greater burdens as a result of previous suffering? In what ways have you seen your endurance grow?

_____

_____

Although we would be willing to bet that you don't want to relive those trials, are you grateful for the growth they have brought you and the endurance they have built? That is what

In our most vulnerable moments, we may hear God's voice the clearest.

Reading passages of Scripture repeatedly opens our eyes to what the Spirit wants to convey.

James is seeking to convey here. He is giving a logical foundation for what seems to be an illogical request, laying out a reasonable process for us in regard to our trials. First, we see that we are to *consider* our suffering in a new way – as joy. It is therefore supposed to seem reasonable to do such because we *know* that the testing of our faith brings a positive result – endurance.

Read verse 4. What are we to *let* happen as we endure trials? _____

_____

Seeing our trials as tools in the hands of a loving God is not enough; we must let God accomplish what He desires.

This next part of the process is a daily challenge for all of us. We can learn to consider our trials as tools in the hands of a loving Father; we can know that it will eventually bring a positive result, but we often struggle to *let* God accomplish that task in us, by fighting Him during our suffering.

Angie's daughters both love swimming and participated in her town's swim team. During one particular year, they did endurance training all year long, early in the mornings before their school days began. It was hard for them to get up out of a warm bed that early in the morning only to jump into a cold pool. It was difficult swimming 2000 meters after just crawling out of bed, and it really wasn't much fun dragging themselves out of the pool only to get cleaned up and start a full day of school. One of her daughters is very compliant and constantly had her eye on the prize. She knew she was becoming one of the girls to beat in the pool, and although the hardship of training was just as difficult for her, she rarely ever voiced a word of complaint. Her other daughter, who really needs her proverbial cup of coffee every morning, did not find it as easy to bite her tongue. Every day she expressed her disapproval of the hardships of endurance training. She, too, wanted the benefit of the training in the end, but she didn't want to let the endurance do its work in her while it was stretching and strengthening her muscles.

We may miss out on the joy He has in mind for us if our attitudes during trials aren't correct.

We cannot have one without the other. We cannot grow spiritually without spiritual strength training and we cannot realize the effect of that training if we do not *let* it have its perfect result. As applicable as a swimming illustration is, the two stories diverge upon the end result. Both swimmers built their muscles and skills regardless of what their attitudes were, and they both happily claimed their medals at the end of the year. One daughter let endurance do its work; the other was made to endure under duress and both of their medals appeared the same. But, we do not have that option. We will suffer trials in this life, but depending on how we endure, our "medals" will look quite different in the end. God may reward obedience one way or the other; however, we will miss out on the joy He has in mind for us if our attitudes during trials aren't correct. If we set our minds to growing during our suffering, letting God use our pain to mold us and reach others, our endurance will have its perfect result. However, if we fight our heavenly Trainer and refuse to *let* Him work in us and through our trial, our reward will be bitterness rather than joy.

Considering the swimming illustration above, give other examples of what positive spiritual endurance might look like?

_____

_____

Why do we want to strive for positive spiritual endurance? Does it really matter?

_____

_____

The real answer to that question lies in another question. Do you want to live a life of peace and hope - or a life of turmoil? The answer to that question seems obvious, but we so often fight against the way God desires to bring us peace that we chose our own turmoil.

Read 1 Peter 1:3-9.

In what is our hope that causes us to rejoice? _____

Will this hope fade even in the darkest trial? _____

According to verse 6, how long will our trials last? _____

When distressed, what does our endurance prove according to verse 7? _____

What does that proof result in? _____

How we endure trials in our lives proves the genuineness of our faith.

Ultimately, how we endure the trials in our lives proves our faith; it is an evidence of our ultimate trust in Jesus Christ to adequately cover not only our salvation, but our daily needs as well. If our faith is the cornerstone of who we are, as it should be, then that in itself should spur us on to begin enduring our trials in a Christ-like manner. But, beyond proving our faith, God gives us additional practical, everyday reasons for positive, rather than negative, endurance.

Read Romans 5:1-5. Verse 2 tells us that we can exult in hope of the glory of God from whom we have obtained grace by faith. What does verse 3 also tell us to exult in?

_____

This passage in Romans 5 is similar to what we have been looking at in James. Just like James, Paul tells us that we can look on our trials positively because we *know* their result. Chart the progression of their positive result below.

_____brings _____ brings _____ brings _____

In our brokenness, we grow in grace and wisdom.

As much as we'd like for there to be at times, please note that there is no shortcut from our suffering to our hope. If we never have anything to endure, we will never learn endurance; if we are never forced to persevere, we will never grow in maturity. It is in the trenches of hardship that we learn the most; it is in our brokenness that we grow in grace and wisdom. If we were capable of living a perfect life, we would expect perfection of those around us. If, though, we are forced to live a life of hardship, exposing our own inadequacies and need for a merciful God, those very hardships give us the opportunity to receive grace from Him, which in turn makes us want to share it with others. Through this process, we are all given the opportunity to become more Christ-like as we give grace where it is not deserved.

Read James 1:4 again and finish the sentence: Let endurance have its perfect result, that you may be _____ and _____, _____.

Angie and I often call ourselves "recovered perfectionists." We grew up holding ourselves to such a high standard that it was eventually suffocating. We've since learned to enjoy God's grace and not have such unreasonable expectations of ourselves (and consequently of others). If you're anything like us, reading a verse that mentions a goal of perfection makes you cringe. We know we can't reach perfection, and it causes us stress to think that we need to attain a perfect goal.

What do you think this verse might be saying when it suggests that endurance will make us perfect and complete, lacking in nothing?

téleios – perfection toward a given end

_____

_____

Thankfully, we can understand more about this goal of perfection by digging into the meaning of the Greek word for perfect, *téleios*. *Téleios* implies perfection toward a given end. It is not as much about reaching an unattainable standard as it is reaching a maturity in order to fulfill a task. In other words, our endurance in trials will mature us into the servant of God we were born to become; it is up to us to allow that work to be done.

Remember, from yesterday, that this kind of testing challenges the strength and integrity of our faith. It isn't an easy road, but if we stand back and look at the big picture, what are our options? On one hand, we have the option of shaking our fists at God, expressing our disapproval at the trials He allows to come our way. We can tell Him that we don't want Him to use this trial for our growth and we really don't care to allow Him to use it for the encouragement or growth of others, we just want **OUT**! But, trials are inevitable and shaking our fist at God, or even sulking in the midst of them, only causes us to fight against the trial as well as God, Himself. As we have learned from our own experiences, this road is unfortunately paved with more suffering than healing. On the other hand, we have the option of endurance and surrender. It does not guarantee that the trial will disappear, quite the contrary, some of the most beloved of God have taken their trials to their last breath. What it does guarantee is that we can put our fighting gloves down and find incomprehensible peace in the midst of the darkest storm (Phil. 4:7). By surrendering to endure suffering in order to be used in a greater way that will bless us and others around us, we are allowing God to mature us in ways that we cannot imagine. The ripple effects in our lives and the lives of others will know no end. Trials will continue to hurt; they wouldn't be trials if they didn't. Wouldn't it be best to come to the point where we have decided to suffer peacefully in the hands of our Father than to hopelessly fight outside of them? Through this, we press on toward becoming *téleios*.

It is better to hurt peacefully within the hands of our Father, than to hopelessly fight outside of them.

The book of James is not intended for those who desire to remain "baby Christians;" it is a book of instruction concerning how to grow up in Christ, how to let our lives become molded to spiritual maturity, even when we don't feel like subjecting ourselves to the growing pains. It is at this point that we realize the choice is ours. We are confronted with two alternatives. Do we let endurance have its perfect effect, or do we tell God, "I don't deserve this! I want out of this situation and refuse to allow it to do a work in me!" It is our human nature to want to escape suffering; we aren't masochists. Suffering is inevitable, though, and it will inevitably plant seeds in our hearts. Will those seeds grow into something incredible that can strengthen others or into bitterness that will crush us and the spirits of those we come in contact with?

We cannot conclude this time without looking to the example of our Savior, after whom we are called to model our lives. As we are tempted to look on our trials and ask our God the question, "Why?" we need look no further than the cross to understand that suffering plays no favorites and knows no bounds. As our Savior walked this earth, He didn't deserve the ridicule or the scorn; He didn't deserve to be misunderstood by His own family or mocked by His own peers. He didn't deserve to be born in a manger; He didn't deserve to die on a cross. When He asked His heavenly Father if this cup might pass from Him, the answer didn't reflect what He deserved. The answer made it clear that there was a greater purpose and for that purpose, He needed to endure – to *let* endurance have its perfect result. There was amazing purpose that would come from His life and death of suffering, and His responsibility was to allow it to happen. The fact that He willingly did that for you and for me is what was undeserved. If in return, He asks each of us to find joy in our trials and let endurance through suffering do a work in our lives, we can justify no other answer than to say, "I will." Believe us, this is not easy; we will have to say it today, and we'll likely have to say it tomorrow as well.

Today, as you conclude your time, lay your trials out before the Lord and be very honest with Him about the way in which you've chosen to endure them thus far. Will you consider handing them over to Him, letting go of any bitterness their seeds have grown, asking Him for peace in the storm and for Him to use them in whatever manner He would choose in order to make you perfect and complete, lacking in nothing? Make any notes you'd like in the space below.

In every trial, we have two alternatives: to let endurance have its perfect effect; or to tell God, "I don't deserve this!"

The example of Christ shows us that suffering plays no favorites and knows no bounds.

_____

_____

_____

_____

_____

_____

Day Three - Wisdom for the Weary

You may be wondering how we are going to get through the entire book of James at the pace we are currently moving! Today, we will double the number of verses we have looked at thus far and we will eventually work at a more rapid pace. However, we believe it was necessary to take our time as we carefully stepped into the turbulent waters of trials and suffering, because James immediately presents us with a request that is so contrary to our human nature. A call to change our entire perspective concerning something that affects us so personally needs to be communicated and absorbed slowly. We will be well-served down the road for having invested the extra time upfront.

A call to change our perspective concerning trials needs to be communicated and absorbed slowly.

Trials continue to be the emphasis of James 1, but today we will shift our emphasis a bit. Before we do that, let's briefly revisit what we've covered so far.

With what perspective are we to *consider* trials and suffering?

_____

What are we to *let* happen through those trials?

_____

Read James 1:1-8. Pay close attention to the use of the word faith as you read.

Verses 1-4 have painted a best-case scenario for us. They have shown us the ideal way to see and meet our trials. Verse 5 begins with a word that lets us know that God understands our humanity and that it will be an ongoing struggle to accomplish the goals of the previous verses. Although some translations have excluded this word, the NASB, which has been provided for you at the beginning of this book, is a literal translation of the original Greek, and this word is included.

What is the first word of James 1:5? _____

Be assured as you go through your trials that God understands your humanity.

In other words, "There is a perfect way to handle trials, BUT you're going to need to ask a perfect God to not only help you see it that way, but to help you to live it out."

When working through our trials, what are we to ask of God? _____

When you personally ask for wisdom, what do you feel you are requesting of God?

_____

_____

We tend to see wisdom as an end – the answer or solution. We pray for wisdom as if it is the insight needed to solve our problems and end our suffering. Yet, wisdom is the vehicle needed for endurance and insight in the midst of the trial, not necessarily the way out of it. Wisdom is a goal that has no end but is characterized by an ever-growing, life-long process.

Ironically, it is often when we hit rock bottom and realize that we have no answers on our own, that we become our wisest and humbly choose to look up for guidance rather than focusing on ourselves and our circumstances.

Daniel 2:21 says, *"He gives wisdom to the wise..."* This may seem strange, as it would make more sense to us for God to give wisdom to the unwise in order that they might become wise.

Read Proverbs 9:10. What is the beginning of wisdom? _____

The fear of the Lord is a multifaceted thing, but for our purpose today, we will only focus on one aspect. A proper fear of the Lord acknowledges His position of sovereignty as well as our position of submission. The fruit of wisdom is born of its first seed – the desire for wisdom and the recognition of its need. The birth of wisdom occurs the moment one realizes his need for wisdom and his inadequacy to attain it on his own.

Wisdom is the vehicle for endurance and insight during a trial, not necessarily a way out of it.

Just as you will never find a truly humble person proclaiming his humility, you will never find the wise broadcasting their gift of wisdom or discernment. The wiser we become, the more we realize how weak we are on our own and how little we truly understand. A fool rushes in believing he has all the answers (Pro. 14:3), but the wise man recognizes his own need for further wisdom in every circumstance. In our context of trials, this is entirely applicable. How many times have you heard a fellow hurting Christian say, "I don't think God realizes that I'm not strong enough for this...?" We've all thought this at times; you may be in a circumstance where you're thinking it now. It is at this time, when we are on the edge of a breaking point, where healing begins and wisdom grows. This breaking point is exactly where He desires to bring us in order for us to recognize our inadequacy in contrast to His adequacy. It is from this point that we grow in maturity; and in future trials, we will call on wisdom earlier and it will multiply itself within us.

The wise man realizes his need for further wisdom in every circumstance.

We now know that God will give wisdom to the wise and that it takes true wisdom to realize our need for additional wisdom. What does James 1:5 tell us we must do in order to receive wisdom?

_____

Barnes' notes on the Bible states it this way:

> *"...no man can feel that he has a right to hope for the favor of God, who does not value it enough to pray for it; no one ought to obtain it, who does not prize it enough to ask for it..."*[2]

Rest assured – you are always within God's will when you ask Him for wisdom.

Simply stated, God is waiting to give us all the wisdom we can possibly have, but we have to ask for it. How great it is to know beyond the shadow of a doubt that every single time we ask for wisdom in the midst of our trials, He will give it. This verse doesn't say wisdom **might** be given, it says it **will**. On the days when we have no idea how to pray because we can muster nothing but groaning, and we can't begin to know how to pray God's will in a matter, we can rest assured that we are always within His will when we ask for wisdom. Life offers us very few guarantees, but we can know that He is always ready and willing to give us wisdom when we ask.

2   http://bible.cc/james/1-5.htm

How does verse 5 say that God gives wisdom to those who seek it in the midst of their trials?

_____

Guys - do you ever feel foolish asking for help? Of course you do; what man doesn't? We are taught to be self-sufficient. But, there is irony in that, isn't there? We've now been told that there is wisdom in humbly admitting that we don't have all the answers, and yet our human nature makes us feel weak and foolish for admitting such. It seems pretty clear that this is a ploy on the part of the enemy who has a goal of keeping us as foolish as possible. Foolishness isn't the only fear we often face when asking for help. Intimidation and shame come to mind as well. James is very clear in this verse concerning the confidence in which you can approach the Father when asking for wisdom in times of suffering. In the midst of a bold statement, he adds a much needed element of assurance. In your trial, no matter what it is, no matter its origin, no matter your level of responsibility in it, you can humbly come to your Father without shame in this request. He will not only respond with generosity, He will look on you with love without scolding. There will be no record of past wrongs held over our head; there will be no mention of ways that He knows you will disappoint Him in the future. A humble request for His wisdom in trials will always be met with an assuring "yes."

A humble request for wisdom during trials will always be met with a loving "yes."

Read Matthew 7:7-11. What do these verses explain about your heavenly Father and good things?

_____

_____

You need never feel foolish or ashamed when requesting wisdom.

There are times when we all worry about whether or not what we are asking of God is truly in His will. Read Proverbs 4:1-9. How does God esteem wisdom?

_____

_____

The description of wisdom in these verses is similar to someone just returning from vacation wanting to describe the wonder of something they just can't seem to find adequate words to describe! There are two things in Scripture that are promised to us upon our humble request: salvation and wisdom. Gentlemen, you can come to God with this request, never feeling ashamed or foolish, but with confidence that you are merely asking Him for the gift He is eager for you to receive.

The request for wisdom must be accompanied by faith.

At the beginning of verse 6, we find another instance of the word "but." It does not nullify anything previously said; it does not need to deflate the sails of confidence in what we've just discussed. It does, though, give us the stipulation upon which it all rests. There must be faith in the request for wisdom.

Read James 1:6-8 again. The one who doubts and lacks faith is likened to something in v. 6 and directly called something else in v. 8. List the two descriptions below.

_____

_____

Verses 1 through 5 have painted the picture of one who handles trials with unwavering consistency. That man has built a maturity that is only realized through a stable faith in God. Such steadfast trust is now contrasted with the man who is lacking faith. The reference to being like the surf of the sea, driven and tossed by the wind, uses the same language we find in one of the gospel scenes.

Read Luke 8:22-24. What was the source of the disciples' fear? _____.

Did you say the storm? On first glance, many of us would say that. But, was it the wind, or the waves threatening to drown them that caused their fear? There is no doubt the wind caused the waves, but the wind and the storm alone would not cause their demise. Their fear was worsened because of the waves that were tossing them about in the midst of the storm. The word in James 1:6 used for "surf" is *kludón*. This is the same word used for the waves in Luke. Simultaneously, the word for doubt in our focal passage is *diakrinó,* which gives a picture of disputing with oneself and wavering about. The image in James is not merely of a man burdened with a trial, but of a man wavering so much in his beliefs that he has a conflict of loyalties that prevent him from standing on his own two feet, as if tossed about by the sea. When the storms of life come his way, he has no foundation of faith or wisdom to stand on; consequently he creates his own waves, causing additional instability and detriment.

kludón – surf or waves

James 1:7-8 further develops this description by calling the doubting man *dipsuchos*, which transliterates as "double-minded." With the same basic theme of a wavering person, this description gives the image of one who simultaneously wants God's will but refuses to give up his own. He is entirely divided and unstable in all his ways. This man is told to expect that he will receive nothing from the Lord.

diakrinó – doubt represented by a man disputing with himself or wavering about

Now read Luke 8:25. What did Jesus ask them? _____

He promised them so much and only asked for faith in return. Had they not already seen Him raise the dead and heal countless others? Were they really fearful of the waves of the sea when they were with the Man they had witnessed doing miracle after miracle? Had they not seen enough?

What was the disciples' response to the calming of the storm?

_____

_____

dipsuchos – doubleminded

For one, they were fearful and amazed. What did we say was the beginning of all wisdom? The fear of the Lord. He'd done nothing to technically scare them; this was good, old-fashioned 'shock and awe', respectful and reverent fear. Sometimes we need to be reminded that although our faith is in a loving God, it is also in the Creator of the universe, and we need to bow our knee accordingly.

Secondly, they didn't take for granted the magnitude of what they had witnessed. They looked at one another in amazement and said, "Who is this?" Why this drove them to ask this question after they had already witnessed Him raise two people from the dead may seem amazing to us. But, may we ask you; aren't we often tempted to do the same thing?

We serve the God of creation, the God of infinite power, yet are we surprised when He provides for us in the midst of our storms?

We serve the God of creation, the God of infinite wonder, and the God of our daily provision, yet when we see Him step in and provide in the midst of our storm, we are so often surprised. It is often easier to trust the God of the universe to provide for the needs of others during their crises; but we wonder, will He truly come through for us in ours? Where is our faith? It was upon this experience that the disciples were given the opportunity to add to their wisdom. By hiding this experience in their hearts, their maturity would develop, their wisdom would increase, and perhaps the next time, their faith would trump their fear in the storm. We know they wouldn't be perfect, but they were growing in wisdom. Men, the question for us is, "Are we?" When trials come our way, are we willing to call on the Lord for wisdom and hand the details over to Him while we calmly rest in His hands? Or are we so convinced that we have to hold on to every detail, that we are like the double-minded man, unstable in all our ways? Are we creating our own waves in the midst of the storm by allowing our hearts and minds to be torn between loyalty to ourselves and loyalty to God? Do we, today, need to be reminded of the One who can calm the storm? If we stand back and allow ourselves to be amazed with the majesty of our God, saying, "Who are You really?" are we willing to hear His answer and accept Him for who He is?

Place your trials into the hands that are strong enough to handle them – and leave them there!

Faith is at the root of the effective prayer for wisdom in the midst of the darkest storm. As we conclude today, we challenge you to place your trials into hands that are actually strong enough to handle them, and guys, need we remind you, those aren't yours?! Also, resolve to set your feet on the firm foundation of wisdom rather than subjecting yourself to the raging sea. Below, list at least one trial that you will take out of your own hands and place into the hands of your Father. Then pray that you will leave it there.

_____

_____

_____

_____

_____

Day Four - "Perspection"

So far, we've discussed joy, endurance, wisdom, and faith in trials. Today we are going to try to find glory in them. Talk about an oxymoron! This is that sort of comment that makes the world look at us and call us foolish. It can only be by the indwelling of the Holy Spirit that we realize the difference between the faulty wisdom of the world and the infinite wisdom of our God.

Read Mark 3:20-22. What did Jesus' own family say about Him? _____

By the indwelling Spirit, we distinguish between the faulty wisdom of the world and the infinite wisdom of God.

It is interesting to consider this verse now, for it is likely that James, the half-brother of Christ, was among the family members reprimanding our Lord for His apparent insanity. James was not yet able to see the wisdom of Christ for what it was through the lens of the Holy Spirit.

Read 1 Corinthians 1:18-25. According to these verses:

What is the message of the cross to the unsaved? _____

What is it to those who have accepted Jesus Christ? _____

Was the world able to recognize who Jesus was in their own wisdom? _____

What "foolishness" was preached that pleased God, yet proved to be a stumbling block to the Jews and foolishness to the Gentiles? _____

Finish this sentence: The foolishness of God is _____.

If the means by which we are saved seems foolish to the world, it should be no less surprising that the way in which we are called to find peace and joy in the midst of life's storms seems equally foolish. But, because we know Whom we have believed and are persuaded that He is able to secure our salvation (2 Tim. 1:12), we can choose to trust Him in how to handle our trials as well.

Let's briefly revisit a concept from Day One. As we looked at considering our trials as joy, we discussed the need for a change in perspective. Fill in the blanks using the comment in **bold** on page 2 from Day One.

Every situation has a positive and negative side; human nature invariably gravitates toward the negative.

How we see things_____, fully affects how we receive them _____.

If you look long and hard enough, you will find that every situation in life has a positive and negative side. However, if you listen carefully to conversations around you, you will notice that human nature invariably gravitates toward the negative. When watching your new HDTV, 2 million of those glorious pixels could be perfect, and yet that one dead pixel in the lower left-hand corner catches your natural eye, holds our attention, and is internally processed as negative. Or consider this: You're outside on a brutally cold day in the midst of a winter storm. Your nose is running and frozen from the biting wind, your teeth are chattering, your breath has literally frozen in your mustache and your feet and fingers are

Your outward view (your perspective) changes your internal view (your perception).

numb. What you would give to walk into a warm house, with a roaring fire and thaw out while drinking a cup of fresh coffee. Upon entering your house, the fire is lit and there is a cup full of Joe waiting for you on the mantle. But, as you sit by the fire, thawing out with your coffee, the raging storm outside catches your attention through a nearby window and the moment is shot. All you can think about now is the fact that you have to return to the blasted cold at some point; so instead of enjoying the positive moment you've been given, your mind cannot escape the negative scene your eyes have just witnessed. Your perspective (your outward view) is changing your perception (your internal view) of the moment.

Because perspective and perception are intertwined, the process can be called "perspection."

I remember taking art class in junior high; poor Sister Julietta trying to teach art to a bunch of bratty pre-teen boys! One of the basic art skills taught was perspective – the effort to draw things in a realistic manner that is convincing to the eye. What we physically set our eyes upon is our **perspective**. On the other hand, how we internally receive and process that information is our **perception**. One process never happens without the other, for we always translate and internalize what we see in either a positive or a negative manner. We believe this entire process begins and ends with the heart. It is the heart that chooses what we set our gaze on, and it is also the heart that chooses whether to let the object of our set gaze affect us in a positive or negative manner. For instance, will we choose to be thankful for the blessing of the coffee or will we refuse to take our eyes away from the storm raging outside the window? Because perspective and perception are so inseparably intertwined, Angie calls the entire process our "**perspection**." As we look at these next verses, we will need to wisely alter our perspection in order to understand them with the eternal mindset that God desires.

Read James 1:9-11. In what is the brother of humble circumstances to glory?

tapeinos – means lowly.

_____

Because verse 10 speaks of the rich man, we might simply assume that the "brother of humble circumstances" in verse 9 concerns the poor. While this is correct, it's not exclusive. The Greek word describing this brother is *tapeinos*, also translated as "lowly." This sense of the word *tapeinos* is often used in the Old Testament.[3] Read the following verses and list the different ways the "lowly" man is described.

Psalm 10:18 _____

Psalm 34:18 _____

To glory means to boast; we are to boast in the things that God values.

Psalm 102:17_____

Words like oppressed, broken-hearted, crushed, and destitute, don't naturally lead us to think of things to glory in, nor do they sound like a high position! This, however, is exactly why God is requesting that we change our perspection. We need to see these words in the light of His purpose, and therefore respond to them accordingly.

In this context, to "glory" means to boast. This lowly person is to boast in his high position.

---

3   Douglas J. Moo, *Tyndale New Testament Commentaries, James*, p. 69

What is it about his position that he could possibly boast about?

_____

_____

When Scripture calls us to boast, it is never from a place of pride in our positions or our-selves. We are to boast in what God finds valuable. The English Standard Version translates James 1:9 this way: *"Let the lowly brother boast in his exaltation."* Exaltation here is *hypsos*, a word used to describe the heavenly realm.

Read Philippians 3:20. Where is our citizenship? _____

*hypsos –
describes the
heavenly realm*

Read Ephesians 1:18-21.

According to verse 18, what are our true riches? _____

According to verse 20, where is Christ now seated? _____

Now Read Ephesians 2:4-7. Finish this sentence using a portion of verse 6:

Our God, rich in mercy, gave us the riches of His grace by raising us up with Him, seating us

_____.

Guys, that is eternal security and riches beyond comparison! When we were saved, we were **seated** with Christ. That concept is mind-boggling, because God's ways are so much more complex than ours. But, this verse tells us that we are already seated with Christ, our *"body of humble state"* is simply waiting to be transformed *"into conformity with the body of His glory"* (Phil. 3:21). There is no greater richness to boast of than the inheritance of our salvation. Remembering James 1:5, though, it takes wisdom to recall this truth in the midst of a storm.

*We are already seated
with Christ; there
is nothing greater
to boast of than the
inheritance of our
salvation.*

Read James 1:10-11 again. What is the rich man to glory in? _____

What do you suppose is the rich man's humiliation?

_____

_____

*We are to see our
value in an eternal,
not earthly, sense.*

Because the rich man is used for so many negative illustrations in the Bible, it would be easy to assume the same is happening here – perhaps, that the negative rich man is being contrasted to the downtrodden poor. But, that is not the case. The two men, although con-trasted in their socio-economic state, are both Christians (remember the recipients were Jewish believers) being asked to see their value in an eternal, rather than earthly, sense.

Read Isaiah 40:6-8. Who is like grass that will fade away? _____

What endures forever?_____

The point of this illustration is not to emphasize the physical demise of the rich man, for all men are like the grass that withers, not just the rich. Instead, James uses this picture, to point out the volatility of riches and the fact that the rich man should boast in his eternal inheritance in Jesus Christ without concerning himself with the potential sudden loss of his earthly wealth. Although this sudden loss would seem humiliating to the secular world, he is able to 'boast' because he would lose nothing of any true value; his true identity is not in his wealth.

As men, we tend to measure our value by what we're able to accumulate or achieve. Where has your sense of identity come from? Is it consistent with what you've just learned?

_____

_____

Seeing each moment with an eternal focus will bring the peace of Christ into our lives and into the lives of those around us.

Both the rich and the poor man need wisdom, faith, and maturity to see their lives in the way God is requesting. No matter our economic status, we are asked to do the same. It takes an entire change of perspective to see each moment of our lives with an eternal focus. However, with daily practice it can become a life-changing habit that will not only bring peace to our own lives, but to the lives of those around us who learn through our godly example.

Read Colossians 3:1-3. What are we to seek? _____

Where are we to set our minds? _____

Where is our true life? _____

These verses are the prescription for our altered focus. They are the coffee sitting on the mantle while the blizzard rages outside the window. It isn't easy, but we can learn to focus on the blessings of the coffee and the warm fire even when the storm rages on. It is in this place where we allow God to show us a peace that we never imagined possible, and which is beyond description (Phil. 4:7). Remember, the peace Christ wants to give to us, is completely contrary to what the world would tell you to expect. But, hear Jesus Himself as He reminds us, *"Peace I leave with you; my peace I give you. I do not give to you as the world gives. Do not let your hearts be troubled and do not be afraid"* (John 14:27).

Day Five - A Crown Called Life

Have you ever had to humbly look back and admit that something you had adamantly argued against was indeed true after all – perhaps something your parents, a teacher, or a wise friend had tried to tell you that you refused to accept as true? James must have had many moments like that after realizing the Brother he had once called a lunatic was really his Savior. How humbled he must have been time after time, as he grew in wisdom and realized that the One he had so often considered a fool, was God Himself; it was he who had been the fool all along. Thinking about today's focal verse, it is not hard to imagine a light bulb coming on in James' mind during one of those humbling moments as his understanding of a truth he'd heard his Brother preach became clear.

We've all had to admit that something we had once argued against was indeed wisdom after all.

Read James 1:12 noting the word trial as you have before. Fill in the blank:

_____ is the man who perseveres under trial...

Now read Matthew 5:3-11, and fill in the blanks below.

v. 3 Blessed are the _____...

v. 4 Blessed are those who _____ ...

v. 10 Blessed are those who have been _____...

v. 11 Blessed are _____ when men _____,

and _____, and say _____...

Strong's concordance defines the Greek word for blessed, *makários*, as happy, blessed, or fortunate. This same word is used in James 1:12 and in the beatitudes found in Matthew, listed above. No doubt, James thought his Brother was crazy as he heard Him proclaim these things. Do the above descriptions sound like situations that would induce happiness or, on their own, make one feel fortunate? Of course they don't, and neither James nor Jesus was implying they *would*.

makários – happy, blessed, or fortunate

Let's look more closely at the beatitudes and see how they relate to our text in James.

Blessed are the:
Poor in spirit, gentle, merciful, pure in heart, peacemakers

Blessed are those who:
mourn, hunger and thirst for righteousness, have been persecuted for the sake of righteousness, are insulted, persecuted, and falsely accused on account of Me (Jesus).

Theirs is:
The kingdom of heaven (listed twice)

They shall:
Be comforted, inherit the earth, be satisfied, receive mercy, see God, be called the sons of God

For you visual learners, we have used two separate columns in order to separate two themes in our minds. The beatitudes are not "cause and effect" statements. Look at the "blessed" column in the chart. Everything listed there describes characteristics and situations that are consistent with the Christian life. It is true that unbelievers will go through trials, but in His Sermon on the Mount, Jesus was contrasting the humble Christian walk to the pious and self-righteous way of the Pharisees. "This sermon showed how a person who is in right relationship with God should conduct his life."[4] This way of life sharply contrasts the way of the world, and therefore generates misunderstanding and persecution of followers of Christ, as it did for Christ Himself.

Now look at the right-hand column that lists the things Christ promised. These give the Christian the hope of their eternal inheritance beyond the hardship of their persecuted experience. In other words, Christian, you are blessed, fortunate, and can be genuinely happy even though you suffer in this life *now*, **BECAUSE** you will reap an eternal reward *later*. Christ was offering eternity to the masses. We tend to get so caught up in what seems to be the "trial" part of the beatitudes that we can miss the fact that this part of Scripture is not about the trials, but about the hope that lies ahead; hope that we can claim today! It's a passage of encouragement to get us through our trials by teaching us an eternal perspective, not a passage that demands delight in persecution or suffering. Plenty of Scripture assures us that we will have to take up our cross and endure pain for the sake of Christ; we're not suggesting that is not the case. What we are suggesting is that this passage describes the Christ-like humility of a Christian and then declares, "There is hope!" And oh how important hope is; Paul reminds us that greater faith in Christ and love for one another spring from our hope that is laid up for us in heaven (Col. 1:4-5).

Christian, you are blessed, fortunate, and can be happy even while you suffer now, because of your eternal reward later.

Read Matthew 5:12. Rejoice, and be glad, for your reward in heaven is _____!

The beatitudes offer encouragement in trials by teaching an eternal perspective; they do not demand that we delight in them.

While it may have been a short rabbit trail, a review of the Beatitudes lays the right foundation for today's primary verse.

Read James 1:12. This time, read it using the corresponding word for blessed: fortunate.

According to this verse, why is the one who perseveres under trial considered fortunate?

_____

_____

hupomenó – to stay behind, to await, to remain, to endure under

There is great eternal promise in this verse, and we will soon explore it further, but first, we need to examine the phrase "*when he has been approved.*"

Let's clarify something important before moving on - this is not a stipulation for salvation. By grace you have been saved; it is Christ's blood that has been approved in order for you to receive this grace, there is nothing further you can do to deserve or attain it. The approval described in 1:12 refers to a refining process, a progressive withstanding and endurance in the ongoing trials of life.

The Greek word for perseverance here, *hupomenó*, is a compound word comprised of "*hupo*," meaning "under/by," and "*menó*" – "to remain, not flee, to abide." Together, it means "to stay behind, to await, to endure under the pressure/heat." Its meaning works in tandem

---

4   John F. Walvoord and Roy B. Zuck, *The Bible Knowledge Commentary, NT edition*, p. 28

with the translation of the Greek word for approved, *dókimos*, which is translated "tested, tried, acceptable." This word is used elsewhere to describe the refining of precious metals and the testing of coins in order to prove them genuine. If we plug these definitions into the context of verse 12, we can see that our testing allows us to be tried, and successful endurance gradually refines us, so that what is left (what "stays behind") is acceptable, genuine, and pure. The goal is an enduring steadfastness that proves itself in trial after trial. This is similar to Romans 5:4, where we saw that perseverance brings proven character, and proven character, hope.

We all endure in different ways. What does endurance look like to you?

_____

_____

dókimos – tested, tried, found acceptable

A few years ago, I (Dave) had the hare-brained idea that I wanted to complete a triathlon. Whether it was the first signs of gray in my hair or a spare tire beginning to inflate around my gut, I'm not sure, but I decided it was time to get off the couch and prove to myself that I wasn't all washed up. For months, the triathlon motto of "swim, bike, run" filled my mind. I could picture myself crossing that finish line (perhaps on a stretcher), with arms raised high in victory. But, I quickly learned that I wasn't going to be able to reach that line without first developing a truckload of endurance. Apparently, completing the race and being equipped to finish the race are two completely different things! I had always been a runner and cyclist, so those parts of the event didn't scare me too much. But the swim? I must look like a wounded turtle swimming; I refuse to put my face into even the cleanest of pool water. So, half a mile in dirty, muddy lake water? No way. The idea of holding my head out of water that long, and then climbing out of the water for a grueling bike ride, followed by a long, hilly run was overwhelming. While there must be a million different ways to train, I chose a regimen that looked like it would work for me. So, over the course of the late spring and early summer, I followed a very detailed daily routine. Some days I just swam circles in my small pool in the back yard – first 20 laps, then 40, then 60, and eventually 100. Other days I biked – first 5 miles, then 10, and eventually 50 miles. Still, other days I just ran – first 1 mile, then 2, working my way up to 7. Closer to the day of the triathlon, however, I had to start combining the three components together. There were times, as I was in the middle of the run on a hot, humid Midwestern afternoon, that I was sure I was going to be ushered into Paradise on the spot. It was the most physically grueling thing I'd ever put myself through. There were many times when I thought to myself, "Why are you doing this to yourself, Dave? You're not getting graded or paid; nobody cares if you do this or not. Why endure this pain? Why not just quit and go home." There were days I'd return from a workout and crash on the living room floor and members of my own family would question my sanity. There was no applause. There were no cheerleaders in the stands encouraging me on. This had become a personal battle – a war against my will and my mind. I discovered how quiet it was swimming alone in the pool, how quiet it can be on a bike alone, how quiet it is to run alone. I spent much of that time talking to God – praying, singing, and trying to listen to Him. I also found that it was in those quiet, alone moments that I had to determine

Personal endurance is a battle of the will and mind. It is in the quiet, alone moments when you will decide to either give up or press on.

While we may want to "go home," for now He asks us to remain and trust Him while He refines us into His image.

whether or not I would give up or press on to attain my goal. (By the way, on July 7, 2004, I crossed that finish line – and not on a stretcher!)

That's endurance gentlemen. It's painful and grueling, yet if we determine to press on, and if we will quiet our hearts and souls while we endure our trials, it will be possible to hear from God during them. It's funny how much better we can hear His voice when we lower our own. While there may not be a stadium of people watching your progress as you endure, His eyes are always looking on your pain, and He is never helpless. He may not see it fitting to change the course of the trial as we would hope, but His everlasting arms are always available to hold us securely and bring us peace when there is no easy escape. There will even be times when we look to Him and cry, "I want to quit and go Home…" He knows that and He's anxious for us to be there as well, but for now He asks us to trust Him while we are being refined into His image. Our responsibility is to stay steadfast and keep our eyes on the finish line, our eternal hope.

We've come to the end of a week-long look at trials, trials that will one day end in a crown.

Read James 1:12 one more time.

Once he has been approved, he will _____.

When the refining process is over, when all our enduring is done, we will come to an end beyond our greatest dreams and receive the crown of life.

Read Revelation 2:10.

In this passage, the church of Smyrna was being asked to endure persecution that most of us can't even imagine. During a time when martyrs were being gruesomely tortured and killed because of their faith, the Lord asked them to endure until death, for they would receive the crown of life.

The word used for this crown is *stéphanos*, and is traditionally thought of as the laurel wreath given to a victorious athlete. It can also apply to a crown worn on occasions such as feasts and weddings, a crown worn in authority, or victory, or one that symbolizes honor and glory. Regardless of whether one or all of these are implied in this passage, they all seem fitting for the beautiful eternity that awaits us. It is very easy to jump to the conclusion that this crown is literal, as are some other crowns referred to in Scripture. We are accustomed to thinking this as we have been told of crowns that we will lie at our Savior's feet. Yet, this crown is different. Unlike literal crowns with formal titles, this crown is literally the crown *of* life – in other words, our eternal life is this crown. Once we have endured, when our weary days are done, we will receive our crown – life – life free of sorrow, free of tears, and free of pain, life with our God. We will come to the end of our journey and have the opportunity to hear, "Well done, good and faithful servant." Therefore, be steadfast, Christian, for your crown will be life.

It's so hard to think that way on a daily basis as the waves of life pound us and knock us down. Our daily life crowds in and threatens to steal our focus; it happens so easily. Before we end today, hold this paper up in front of you. Read a few lines from it entirely focusing

stéphanos – a crown of victory, honor, glory, or authority

When our weary days are done, we will receive a crown of life – life free of sorrow, tears and pain; an eternity with God.

your attention on the page in front of your face. Without altering your focus, notice that the things in the room outside of the paper are blurry. Now, keeping the paper in the same spot, raise your eyes and focus on something across the room that seemed blurry a moment ago while you focused on the paper. As it becomes clear, notice that the paper is now blurry. No matter how hard you try, it is simply impossible to achieve clear focus on both at one time. You must choose to focus on what is right in front of your face or on what is in the distance. Our perspective is like that. When we set our gaze on the here and now, we cannot have an eternal perspective. What is in front of our face will crowd in on us and we will not be able to view it in the context of God's bigger picture. But, when we set our minds to have an eternal perspective, eternity becomes clearer as we take our eyes off of our situations and learn to focus on God's greater plan.

Read Ephesians 1:18a. I pray that the _____ may be enlightened.

It is not possible to focus clearly on more than one thing at a time.

This way of looking forward to what lies ahead and finding peace in it even during the darkest storms is about heart focus, and it never happens by chance. This takes training and practice; it's an intentional choice to look to God for how He can use our trials in our lives and in the lives of others. Our endurance not only refines our own lives, but becomes a large part of our testimony as well. As those around watch how we endure, we have an opportunity to reach them and bless the Lord. Our trials are not only useful to us once we reach the other side of them. Sometimes, right in the middle of our own storms, we can be the brightest light of hope to others as they go through storms of their own.

Read Philippians 4:5-8 below. Digest these verses and meditate on them in the context of everything we've learned this week.

> *Let your gentleness be evident to all. The Lord is near. Do not be anxious about anything, but in everything, by prayer and petition, with thanksgiving, present your requests to God. And the peace of God, which transcends all understanding, will guard your hearts and your minds in Christ Jesus. Finally, brothers, whatever is true, whatever is noble, whatever is right, whatever is pure, whatever is lovely, whatever is admirable—if anything is excellent or praiseworthy—think about such things.*

Take some time now to ask the Lord to help you to endure and to be your strength. Ask Him to give you an eternal perspective when this life doesn't make sense and to give you peace in the chaos. Be honest with Him; He knows your every thought, tell Him what's on your mind and ask Him to open the eyes of your heart to truths that only He can bring. Be still and quiet; allow Him to speak.

Our ability to endure refines us and becomes a part of our testimony.

_____

_____

_____

_____

WEEK TWO: A TESTED AND TRIUMPHANT FAITH

Day One – The Blame Game

TEMPTATION! Now that I have your attention guys, let's review the two definitions of the Greek word for trials mentioned on Day One of the first week. Looking back to page 2, fill in the blanks below:

As mentioned there, the Greek word *peirasmós*, has two meanings.

The first meaning refers to a _____ that challenges the _____

_____.

The second refers to _____that challenge one's

_____.

Today's verses use the second meaning. Read James 1:13-14.

The beginning of verse 13 includes something significant that we might miss initially. It reads, "*Let no one say **when** he is tempted…*" (emphasis added) In other words, we are **all** going to run into temptation, it's just a matter of when. 1 Corinthians 10:13 says, "*No temptation has overtaken you but such as is common to man…*" We are all susceptible to temptation; there is <u>no one</u> above <u>any</u> temptation, no matter his or her position in life.

We will all be tempted, it is just a matter of when.

Notice that this portion of James, emphasizing the second meaning of "trials," follows immediately on the heels of the section that highlighted the type of trials that challenge the strength and integrity of one's faith. The trials we've studied in verses 2-12 are not born of temptation to sin; they are the hardships of life that inevitably come our way. God allows and uses these trials to test, refine, and strengthen our faith, while maturing us in wisdom. There is no sin or malice in Him as He does so; in the end, trials are for our good, even if they seem unbearable as we go through them. In our humanity, we naturally ask God why He allows these hardships which we feel inadequate to handle. Our same human nature can lead us to question God concerning temptation.

Our human nature can lead us to question God about our temptations.

Have you ever found yourself asking God why He would tempt you with something you feel completely unable to resist? Have you felt He was tempting you with a proverbial carrot? If so, explain:

_____

_____

Finish the sentence using James 1:13: "*Let no one say when he is tempted, 'I am being tempted by God'; for God cannot be tempted by evil, _____.*"

It is very important to keep the two meanings of the word *peirasmós* in context, for one *can* originate with God for our good, whereas the other never comes from the Lord. For a quick summary, we will boil the two definitions down to a few words. The first is a **testing** of faith; the second is a **temptation** to sin.

If temptation never comes from God, where do you think it comes from?

_____

Peirasmós – a testing of faith; or a temptation to sin

Using James 1:14, fill in the blank: "*But, each one is tempted when he is _____*

_____."

Most of us find it much easier to think that there is something or someone to blame our temptations on besides ourselves! We know that it isn't God, because we've just seen His Word tell us that very clearly. If it isn't God, then we know it must be something else, and one of our favorites to blame is Satan! But, here's the unwelcome reality. While Satan and his legions of demons are tempters, this verse clearly tells us that oftentimes, Satan does not even have to enter the picture for our own sin nature to be tempted.

Satan does not have to enter the picture for our sin nature to be tempted.

Gentlemen, like it or not, we need to take personal responsibility in the matter. To be responsible for anything, we need to be educated on the subject so we can understand it. So, let's break down the process of temptation in order to learn how we can reasonably withstand it.

All of humanity has been tempted from the dawn of time, so we might as well start at the beginning.

Read Genesis 3:1-7. Who tempted Eve? _____

It is easy to see that Satan, himself, played an active role in this temptation. Looking closely, though, we see that there is more to the picture. The Greek word for entice used in James 1:14 is *deleázō*. It is a fishing term, used to describe the bait that lures in the catch. Satan was baiting Eve, but she apparently wasn't tempted at first.

deleázō – a fishing term describing bait that lures

It is reasonable to presume that Adam and Eve had seen this tree time and time again. We know that it was located in the center of the garden. Unless they lived in the suburbs of Eden, they probably passed it most every day as they walked the dogs. Obviously, we're kidding, but the fact is, the "bait" of the tree had been there all along. Even when Satan first asked Eve about the tree and its fruit, she apparently wasn't tempted by it at all.

There are things in this world that tempt some, but not others; not all bait looks the same to each of us. For instance, if you place a worm on a hook in front of a hungry fish, you've presented that fish with its greatest weakness, and it's going to have trouble resisting. On the other hand, that same worm is perfectly safe when dangled in front of one of our dogs. There is no way you're going to get Fido to chomp! A dog is simply not going to be tempted. You may have baited him, but you didn't tempt him.

Eve knew that the fruit of the tree of knowledge of good and evil was not good for her to eat. Not in the sense of its flavor or satisfaction, but because she knew her God had told her not to. Initially, she wasn't tempted by its presence in the garden, or by Satan bringing it up. She even explains to him why she doesn't intend to eat from it. It is at this point, though, that Satan sprinkles sugar on the bait and it appears different to her than it ever had before. Suddenly, Eve is tempted. But, what has caused that temptation to begin to burn within her? Yes, Satan provided the bait, yet in order for her to be tempted by it, a lust, a longing for what she didn't yet have, had to awaken her desire for getting it. According to James 1:14, "Each one (even Eve) is tempted when he is carried away and enticed by his **own** lust." As much as we may want to, we can't even blame the bait.

According to Genesis 3:6, when did Eve decide she wanted to eat from the tree?

_____

_____

Each is tempted by his own lust; we can't blame the bait.

That verse lists three reasons she desired to eat from the tree, all of which can be summarized in one statement: She suddenly saw it would bring her something she didn't have and she **decided** she wanted it. That's where temptation is conceived. Men, we live in a fallen, sin-filled culture, and there is bait all around us every day. But it isn't until we desire the bait and are carried away by **our own** lust that we are tempted. We are the ones who carry a great responsibility to guard our hearts against temptation. We may be tempted to blame the tempter or the bait, but no one can physically force lust to take root in our own being.

Understanding where actual temptation originates is important, but it is equally important to understand that temptation, in and of itself, is not a sin. We do need to guard against getting into situations where we know we will be easily tempted, because we want to prevent ourselves from succumbing to it. If Eve had only been tempted, yet turned away from the tree just as she approached it, she would not have sinned.

When we see something we don't have and decide we want it, temptation is conceived.

Read Matthew 4:1-10. Who was tempted in this situation?_____

It is so hard to imagine the level at which Jesus was tempted. Look back to the final paragraphs of Week One, Day Two and all we discussed that Christ didn't deserve. Temptation was still another, and yet He willingly endured it for you and me.

Temptation, in and of itself, is not sin.

We often use the old cliché "the devil made me do it," but the truth is, Satan has far greater targets to set his radar on than us. If there is any influence tempting us outside of our own selfish desire, one of his depraved minions is likely behind it and not Satan, himself. Jesus, though, was taken on by *"the commander of the powers in the unseen world"* (Eph. 2:2, NLT). Not only was Evil, himself, the tempter, he came to the desert with both barrels loaded. He knew whom he was facing and he hated Him more than anything in heaven or on earth. He'd waited for this moment for thousands of years, and this was his chance for revenge. After 40 days of fasting, Jesus was famished, starving for food, and endured perhaps the most intense season of temptation known to man. Christ knew who He was and the power He possessed, yet He resisted the temptation to succumb to the bait, and probably the temptation to throw Satan from the top of the temple as well!

The temptation of Christ was not meant to be a dramatic moment in the story line of the His life only. The valuable lessons we can learn from it are endless. Among them is the understanding of the love He showed for us while enduring temptation, as well as the compassion He now has due to His own understanding of the experience.

Read Hebrews 2:17-18. Because Christ suffered temptation, what is He able to do for those who are now tempted? _____

Read Hebrews 4:15.

What can our High Priest, Jesus, do in respect to our weakness? _____

Christ has compassion for us due to His own experience with temptation.

How many things was He tempted in?_____

Are there any temptations you face that you feel you simply cannot withstand? _____

We've all heard, "I just can't help myself;" we may have even said it ourselves. If you ask your children why they aren't obeying what we've asked them to do, you may hear, "Because I can't!" when the truth is they have just chosen not to. We know what they are physically capable of; they have just entered into a battle of the wills. Temptation is like that. Sure, there are some temptations that are small and easily avoided, but we need to be honest here – there are some serious temptations out there that can all but destroy us! It's when faced with seemingly overwhelming temptation we are likely to tell ourselves and God, "I can't! I can't withstand this! I can't help myself!"

There is as much temptation not to do the right thing as there is to do the wrong thing.

Temptation comes in all shapes and sizes; there is just as much temptation not to do the right thing, as there is to do the wrong thing. Yet, when we feel overwhelmed and defenseless against temptation, are we justified in meeting it with an attitude of, "This is just who I am. I can't change. I can't fight this. God, I can't do what you're asking?"

Read Romans 6:1-14.

Our relationship to God and our relationship to sin were both changed at the cross.

Let's look closely at the victory this passage promises us as Christians. These verses tell us that believers are dead to sin; **we died at the cross**. It wasn't only our relationship to God that changed at the cross; our relationship to sin was altered there as well. Sin's power is dead in our lives; it is no longer the controlling factor. Verse 6 tells us that sin used to dominate us and we were enslaved by it, but verse 7 tells us that by being crucified with Christ we have been freed from it! This doesn't mean we are free from the desire for sin or the temptation toward it, it means that **we have been given the power to deny it**!! When we were unsaved, we were slaves to sin. We literally had an "excuse" to sin because it held us in bondage and we did not possess the power of Christ necessary to resist it. But, when we surrender our lives to the Lord and submit to a new Master, we have the power of the resurrection alive in us to conquer the patterns of sin in our lives and live in the freedom of the power of the cross. We now have a new life!

We possess His power, but how can we apply it in practical ways? When searching for a specific example of a temptation that I have faced and successfully overcome, I had trouble narrowing it down to just one. Not because I have been successful in every area, but because I have been tempted in so many! You see men, I'm really no different than any of you. I have been tempted by sex and success; by power and possessions. My commitments to God and family have been tested, just as yours have been; at times very seriously. But regardless of which area of life the temptation showed up in, the practical way out - the victory - came through determining beforehand where my lines were drawn, and relying on God's strength to stay within them. During the calm seasons of life, when the temptations were held at bay, I had thankfully studied and memorized Scripture, I had spent time in prayer, I had made myself accountable to other men for years. Did those efforts keep temptation from arriving on my doorstep? Absolutely not. However, when they came knocking, I was prepared to look each one in the eye and say, "You are not welcome here; you will not control me."

When the temptation to "fudge" on an expense account or tax return entered my mind, I remembered the pictures in Scripture of the man I wanted to be where money was concerned. I'd ask myself, "Where is your treasure? Is that where you want your heart to be, too, Dave?" When the temptation to climb the corporate ladder by telling a half-truth in order to gain an advantage over a coworker entered my mind, I recalled Jesus kneeling beside His disciples, washing their filthy, stinking feet and saying that the greatest among them would be a servant of all. I remembered that the way up in His Kingdom is to choose to stay low in humility here. While I've thankfully never had a serious struggle with porn, I have been tempted to think of other women at times or to view explicit materials online or on TV. At those times, I have reminded myself of the father I want my daughters to look up to and respect, and that those women were somebody's little girls, as well. If I couldn't shake the temptation immediately, I would put down the remote and pick up the Bible, or I would literally go for a run until the temptation passed. Guys, I ran a lot as a younger man; I still have to run today. My knees hurt, but I'm a lean, mean running machine! ☺

Read 2 Corinthians 5:17. Write it in the blank below:

_____

_____

To claim freedom from the domination of sin, we must KNOW that sin is powerless against us.

What old things are passed away? Our bondage to sin, our excuse to sin, our defeat at the hands of sin! What new has come? Power to face our worst temptations square in the eye and say, "YOU HAVE NO CONTROL OVER ME!" Three times in Romans 6, Paul uses the word "know" (vv. 3,6,9). Repetition in Scripture is never coincidental; it's always to drive a point home. Paul recognizes that in order for the believer to claim his or her freedom from the domination of sin, they must KNOW that sin is powerless against them; otherwise they walk into the ring already defeated. When we say, "This is just who I am," he says, "KNOW that you are not who you once were; you can walk in new life!" (v. 3-4). When we say, "I can't change," he says, "KNOW that you are no longer enslaved to sin, you can do this" (v. 6). When we say, "I can't fight this," he says, "KNOW that just as death has no mastery of Christ, sin has no mastery over you" (vv. 9,14). You are free; you are free, indeed (John 8:36).

How we meet temptation will be determined by what we have resolved to do ahead of time.

Temptation is going to knock on our door, guys; it always does. The way we meet it will be determined not only by what we know about our new life in Christ, but by what we have resolved ahead of time to do when we answer the door. Are we resolved and committed to meet it with, "You are not welcome here anymore," or have we conceded to defeat before it ever comes our way? If we are going to be resolved, we must have something greater we believe is worth the fight. We must ask ourselves what is more important to us, the temporal satisfaction of getting hooked by the bait, which always leads to heartache, or the commitment we've made to our God who promises peace, even when what we temporarily deny brings us such pain. It's hard; there's no getting around that. But, when we seek a way out, He will provide. The physical tempting agent may not disappear, but when we cannot change the bait, we can ask God to change our mind, our heart, and our will. You may have experienced the stronghold of fear that you will never escape the way in which temptation consumes you, but we've seen Him work miracles even in the midst of the storm. Still, your heart has to be willing to lay down your own desires in order to accomplish His.

We must be willing to lay down our desires in order to accomplish His.

Fear and temptation are quite similar in their attack. They consume the mind and heart and squeeze out all reason. When Angie's daughters had nightmares as young girls, they would come to her in the dark of the night and ask her to pray over them. They were consumed with fear and they needed to be reminded that they were safe. She would whisper prayers over them, asking their heavenly Father to bring them peace by replacing the thoughts that had flooded their minds with new thoughts; thoughts of His protection, thoughts of all of the ways He'd provided for them in the past, and thoughts of the way He wouldn't leave them now. She would ask Him to wrap His loving arms around them and give them a sense of having a bubble of protection around them, as He would peacefully guide them back to sleep. Most nights, they were back to sleep by the time she had finished praying. They needed to be reminded of what was real and who their "Daddy" was. Their fears weren't of something real, but they were consuming. Their heavenly Daddy was bigger than their fears, He was real, and He provided the stability they needed when their peace was lost.

If anything we are drawn toward is not pleasing to the Lord, our sin nature is playing us for the fool.

Temptation lures us toward something we convince ourselves is a source of real satisfaction – and much like fear – that can be consuming. Do we need to be reminded of what's real? If anything we are drawn to is not something pleasing to the Lord, we can rest assured that our sin nature is playing us for the fool as it tries to convince us otherwise. Do we need to remember who our "Daddy" is? We are accountable to Him to make the right choice, and out of **His strength**, He has given us the power necessary to withstand the temptation. Remember, being tempted itself is not a sin, but are we prepared to stand strong when temptation strikes or have we admitted defeat before the attack?

The power of sin was conquered in your life when you surrendered to Him.

Is there one or more temptation in your life that burdens you time and time again? Some of them may be a temptation to do wrong, others may be temptation to not do what you know is right. If so, believe me guys, you are not alone. Will you take time to ask the Lord to fill your mind with new thoughts that remind you that you are a new creation because of Him? You **have** been given the power to resist as the power of sin was conquered in your life when you surrendered to Him. Will you give Him your weaknesses and temptations and ask Him to show you the abundance of His blessings awaiting you when you choose to turn from the old and move forward to the new?

_____

_____

_____

Day Two – One Choice at a Time

We've studied some pretty intense things over the last 6 days, and the forthcoming light at the end of the tunnel will be a welcome relief. We will look at one more verse completing the temptation process we spoke of yesterday, then we will contrast it with the light of God's hope. Just a bit more darkness before the light shines through.

Read James 1:13-15. We're backing up a bit in order to highlight the sin process. Fill in the blanks according to these verses.

Each one is _____ when he is carried away by his _____,

when _____ has conceived, it gives birth to _____; and when _____

is accomplished, it brings forth_____.

When tempted, we have to make a choice; to turn from it or walk toward it.

As these verses indicate, sin doesn't just happen, it's a process. Our desires tempt us and we have to make a choice. Are we going to turn from temptation or walk toward it? When we turn away, we employ the power of the resurrection to claim our new life in Christ, having been freed from the bondage of sin. When we walk toward it, which we all do in thought or action on a daily basis, we've given birth to sin, which brings forth death.

What is meant by the "death" brought forth by sin is a matter of differing opinion. We will briefly touch on it and move on.

"Jewish Christians saw people as either traveling the path of life (walking with Christ by the Spirit) or the path of death (walking apart from Christ in the flesh). To be "dead" was often a description of the poor quality of life rather than the cessation of being."[5]

"Lust can lead to physical death in a believer, and it can lead to physical and spiritual death in a non-believer."[6]

Thus, death may be an eternal, spiritual death for the non-believer, a physical death for the believer who refuses to turn away from habitual, unrepented sin, or "death" which is symbolic of not living the "life" Christ intends for us. Regardless, we can see that its effect prevents us from being able to live a surrendered life, fulfilled by proper service to our God.

Unrepented sin prevents us from living a surrendered and fulfilled life of service to God.

Let's draw a practical comparison between the sin and death described above and something we may all find easier to relate to. Like my grandfather and my father, I enjoy gardening. Unlike Angie, I prefer to grow veggies and fruit, not flowers. If you can't eat, why plant it – right guys? A couple of weeks ago, I spent several hours removing the remnants of last year's garden, turning the soil with a shovel, etc. After waiting several days, I then went over the entire area with my tiller. Ah, a freshly-tilled garden plot is always a welcome sign of spring. Because it was only late March, I waited to plant most of the seeds that I had purchased.

---

5   Swindoll, *NT Insights*, p. 37

6   Thomas L. Constable, *Notes on James, 2010 Edition*, p. 15

Unfortunately, it was at least two weeks before I could give any more attention to the garden due to rain and some family travel. When I returned home, I went out to the backyard and was amazed to find that my "garden" was already beginning to produce a bountiful crop - of weeds! What a hideous monstrosity. Are you kidding me? I hadn't even had the chance to plant the things I wanted to grow. Apparently, the soil of my garden was already full of "weed seeds." And merely treating the surface of the ground was not enough to remove them. Gentlemen, I have work to do in my garden before I can even begin to hope to see fruit grow. Our sin nature is like that; it festers deep within, providing the perfect environment for temptation to plant a seed, and for that seed to grow. My job is to prepare the soil to the best of my ability in order for it to receive the seeds that will eventually produce fruit. Even after the good seeds are planted, I know that I must battle throughout spring and summer to pull weeds that will threaten to choke out my crop. If I hope to have anything good to show, I must intentionally spend time weeding out the evil and watering the good. In the end, what I feed will be what grows.

Like weeds in a garden that choke out what we want to grow, sin prevents us from becoming what we could be for God.

Read Romans 7:15. What does Paul **not do**? _____

What does Paul **do**? _____

It was only the chapter before in Romans where Paul had declared that we are no longer captives to sin; that we have the power to overcome its mastery in our life. Here, Paul is showing his frustration with the **knowledge** that he has the power to resist temptation; yet, due to the sinful nature which constrains him while trapped in his physical body, he finds himself committing both the sins of doing what he shouldn't do, as well as not doing what he should.

Knowing that even Paul shared this struggle gives a sense of relief. While it does not in any way give us the freedom to use our human nature as an excuse to sin, it does show us that we are not alone in the battle against our own flesh and blood. Paul was an amazing man of God, striving to live the most Christ-like life possible, and yet he identified with the never-ending war to do so this side of eternity. Our goal needs to be the same as his, but we must not get bogged down when we fail.

You are not alone in the battle against your own flesh and blood. None of us can make it a full day on our own.

I used to be a long-range planner. Having spent years in the corporate world, I had the "pleasure" of attending countless departmental meetings. I had fully bought into the wisdom of 3 and 5-year plans. However, in my personal life, I've come to the point where I realize I can't successfully live in 1, 3, or 5-year increments. In fact, I can rarely make it through a full day successfully on my own strength. Life to me is now broken down in choice-by-choice, moment-by-moment bites. Regardless of what has occurred in the past, I can choose to do the next right thing in the next moment. Let me try to explain by comparing this concept to a failed pattern of exercising. Like so many people, we may set a goal for a new exercise program saying, "I'll start Jan 2nd." That day rolls around and we have a successful day at the gym. That pattern continues for the rest of that first week. But then, lactic acid begins to build up in our muscles and our motivation breaks down. By the 3rd week of January, we find ourselves saying it's too dark and cold to crawl out of bed, and before long, what used to be our workout time has passed with several easy punches of the snooze bar. What many of us may do at this point is throw up our hands and throw in the towel concluding that it is a lost cause for the year. "I'll try again next January," we may say. We allow defeat to set in for the rest of the year, and after multiple cycles of the same defeat, we just may not begin again at all. Guys, wouldn't you agree that a few days in the gym during the months of February through December would beat nothing at all? Yet, we often tend to live in similar defeat in our Christian walk. We resolve to stand against temptation and sin and when we fail, we imprison ourselves with walls of guilt and shame, convincing ourselves we are unworthy of the grace that says we can begin again. By living one choice at a time, we can give Christ our current moment in full. When we do fail, He looks at us with grace-filled eyes saying, "Give me the next moment; we can do this together. You don't have to wait for a new day to enjoy a new beginning." In living this way, the power of defeat has no victory; mercies don't have to wait until morning.

Do you have a pattern of defeat in your life? Can you identify areas where you have allowed the weeds to choke out the life you know you were meant to live?

_____

_____

Are you willing to begin removing the weeds, committing your next choice to moving toward new life and hope? _____

It is tragic to hear a brother or sister in Christ comment on their own sin, stating that they've ruined everything, that their testimony is beyond repair. However, **that can never be!** Yes, our testimonies can be tarnished, but thanks be to God, they can also be polished again. As I write this from a swing on my front porch, I'm looking at my car, sitting in the driveway a few feet away. My ride of choice is a 2006 Hyundai Sonata that my daughters named for its once spectacular paint job. What a driving machine it is - 162 of the tamest horses ever assembled under one hood! But, what my car may be lacking in the area of performance, its appearance more than makes up for. For under that 2-year layer of grime is the high quality exterior for which my car is named. To be honest though, right now, it looks pretty pathetic, completely dull and dingy. However, I know that with some time, elbow grease, soap, water, Turtle Wax and Armor All, it can shine as if she were new. Not only will she appear new again, but her luster will actually be much more impressive when I recall the condition from which it came. Likewise, our testimonies, though temporarily tarnished but never destroyed, cannot only be restored, both our successes and failures can become an integral part of who we are and how God can use us. He will use our failures, shortcomings, and seasons of defeat to reach people we never would have been able to relate to before, people who would have never been able to relate to us! We who have been forgiven much, have a greater capacity to understand and have compassion on others. Will you let Him use you? It is never, never too late…

What are the first 4 words of James 1:16? _____

Let's be very clear, our enemy, Satan, wants nothing more than for us to be deceived. He wants to deceive us into believing we must continue to walk in defeat, and in this verse specifically, we see that he wants us to be deceived concerning God's intentions toward us. The father of lies would have us believe that our temptations to sin come from God. If he can get us

When we fall, Christ simply asks for our next breath. His mercy need not wait until morning.

Our successes and failures become a part of the testimony of who we are and how God can use us.

Satan wants nothing more than for us to be deceived.

to fall for that lie, he can convince us that God is a tyrant enticing us to fail so that He can squash us like a bug. James now contrasts that lie with the reality of God's true intentions.

Read James 1:16-18.

Rather than temptation, what comes from God? _____

What characteristics of God are pointed out at the end of verse 17?

_____

Because God is good and pure, what He desires for us is also good and pure.

Our God is the "Father of lights," the Creator of the heavens and all they contain; the sun, moon, and stars are at His bidding. Note the contrast James gives between the Creator and His creation. Unlike the constant moving of the cosmos, with its shifting shadows and full eclipses, our God has no variation within Him. He is good and pure, and therefore He only desires what is good and pure for us. We do not serve a fickle God who reacts and responds to us with emotional shifting; we do not serve a God who tempts us with a desire to watch us fall.

Read Matthew 7:11.

In His love, God allows us to fall, but He never trips us causing us to fall.

This verse speaks to our hearts as fathers, because we know how deeply we want what is best for our children. Yet, God in His holy perfection wants good for us on a much deeper level, because His love is not tainted, it is not moved, and it does not vary during the storm. This love does not keep us from trials, for a loving parent knows they must **allow** their children to fall as they learn to walk. However, that loving parent never intentionally trips their child in order to deliberately **cause** them to fall.

As James concludes his defense of God on the issue concerning temptation, he wraps it up with a reminder of God's ultimate gift of goodness toward us, the message of truth.

Read Ephesians 1:13 and Colossians 1:5.

What is the message of truth?_____

According to James 1:18, fill in the blank.

In the _____ He brought us forth by the word of truth.

Far from tempting us to sin, God chose first to create man, and then to save him.

In other words, it was His will to initiate our salvation. God didn't have to create the heavens and the earth; but He wanted to, so He initiated it. He didn't have to create man; but He took the initiative to do so. Just as He had no obligation to create him, neither was He obligated to save him. But, because He loved him, He chose to, and He initiated the process that would cause His Son to die a grueling death on a cross. When we are tempted to blame Him for enticements He would never send our way, He wants to remind us that such evil is beyond Him and what He **did** choose to give us, was the best He had to give.

Men, you understand thankless sacrifice; some of you watch your wife do it all the time from your vantage point on the couch! But, seriously, some of you give more than it seems you even have to offer. You understand the pain of giving so much and having it questioned, or even ignored by others, whether by a child, a spouse, or a friend. Imagine the pain it must cause God when we forget that He gave us everything He had to give, and then question whether or not He wants what's best for us.

According to verse 18, why did God choose to gift us with salvation?

_____

First fruits are often referred to as something superior in excellence – the choice fruit, picked fresh from the vine at the perfect time, rather than the ones left rotting and neglected. The first fruits in Israel were used as sacred offerings to God. They were not only first in order, but first in honor.[7]

We have been given a position of honor and excellence in God's Kingdom.

What a great reminder of our position in Christ. In an effort to remind us that He loves us so much and gave us His very best, God also reminds us of what that fully entails. Being His first fruits, we have been given a position of honor and excellence in the Kingdom; never forget, you are a son of the King. You have been chosen and never neglected, loved and not discarded. You are the crowning achievement of His creation; the masterpiece of His hand. Some of us may even want to tattoo that on our forehead to remind ourselves every morning! At the same time, even in our position of honor, our lives are to be a sacred offering to our God; we are not our own – He has bought us at a tremendous price (1 Cor. 6:20, 1 Cor. 7:23). He has chosen us, He delights in us, He has given us eternal life with Him, and in return, we are to turn our lives over to Him as an offering of the best we have. He gave us His best and He asks the same of us in return.

He gave us His best and He asks the same of us in return.

Take time today to thank God for His gift of salvation that we so often take for granted. Perhaps spend time confessing the times you may have questioned His love. Thank Him for His steadfast holiness that does not respond to us in variation or shifting shadows. Thank Him that the reminder of His promise of love found in our passage today came after His description of a pattern of sin. Even knowing that we are going to continue to sin, He reminds us of His love, His choice to save us, and our place of honor in His eyes. We are never broken beyond repair, never tarnished beyond restoration. Don't know about you, but I've got some weeds to pull and a car to wash and wax – I don't need to wait for a new day – neither do you. So get to it.

_____

_____

_____

_____

---

7   James B. Adamson, *The New International Commentary on the New Testament, The Epistle of James*, p. 77

Day Three – The Soil of the Heart

I wonder how many of you have done as I have and greeted someone in the hallway at work or church and asked, "How ya' doing?" only to keep right on walking without waiting for a response. Or how often has someone asked you the same question and you automatically answered, "Fine," when things were anything but fine? Somewhere along the line, we have bought into the lie that "real men" are always "fine." We are strong; we are capable; we are knights in shining armor – and by golly, there are no chinks in that armor either! To ensure that no one ever discovers otherwise, we keep people at a safe distance. We lace our conversation with such vital things as the weather, the local sports teams, or if we're feeling especially "vulnerable," we'll tell others about the stress we encounter at work. (We are strangely proud of the stress we live under, aren't we)? But under no circumstances, do we reveal the real conditions of our heart. Heart? Vitt, you write as if I'm supposed to have one. Yes sir, and today, we're going to ask you to take an honest look at it.

As first fruits we are both excellence among His creation, and living sacrifices for Him.

It is important for us to examine our hearts, because its status determines what we choose to do with what we've already learned.

Read only the first three words of James 1:19. Write them here:_____

What did they know? What is James referring to that we know? They knew, as we do from vv 17-18, that Christians are the first fruits among His creation as a result of the good and perfect gift of salvation given to us. As first fruits, we are excellent among His creation; however, first fruits were also sacrifices to God. Likewise, we are to be living sacrifices for Him; our lives are to be an offering for Him to use as He sees fit. James is now going to ask his readers to understand that the condition of their hearts must be analyzed in order to respond accordingly to what they know.

The rest of verse 19 tells us there is a contrast between what they *know* and what they still need to fully *understand*. Admittedly, when reading the next few verses, they seem a bit disjointed. They don't seem to reflect back to the previous thought, nor upon first glance, do they necessarily seem to blend with each other. But, there is a uniting word that runs a cord of purpose through them all, if we are willing to find it.

What we are to do with the Word is the theme that binds these verses together.

Read James 1:18-22. Use one word to fill in the following three blanks:

James 1:18 – What were we brought forth by? _____

James 1:21 – What are we to receive? _____

James 1:22 – What are we to prove ourselves doers of? _____

What we are to do with the Word that has brought us forth is the binding theme that gives a sense of unity to these verses. As mentioned above, it seems that James has a sudden break in thought after declaring our position in Christ in verse 18. From there, he seems to elaborate on what nice characteristics Christians should strive to have. Yet, verses 19 through 21 don't seem to complement each other in that manner which should prompt us to look deeper for a cohesive meaning. Verses 19 and 20 seem to elaborate on anger, and while verse 21 begins with "therefore," a word that tells us it is referencing the previous thought, it then goes on to speak of *all* filthiness and all that remains of wickedness, not merely sinful anger.

There is an old saying when it comes to the word "therefore." When we read it, we should ask, "What is 'therefore' there for?" These verses begin by telling us that we **know** the Word of truth, **but** we need to have a proper response to it so we can **therefore** proceed to handle the Word in the way James further prescribes in this passage.

Based on the fact that we have been brought forth by the Word as a new creation, what three instructions do we find in verse 19?

_____

These verses are often simply used for life application in guarding the tongue and keeping our temper. While these instructions hold great truth when it comes to those topics, in its original context, they apply to how we respond to <u>the Word,</u> not how we respond <u>to others</u>. Verses are so often plucked out of their context in order to prove a point, that we lose the intent of the original message. Historically, these verses have fallen into that category. Because we are accustomed to hearing them taught as truths for personal relationships, seeing them in a different light may initially seem unusual, but stick with us and we will see it all pull together in the end.

When verses are taken out of context to prove a point, we often lose the intent of the original message.

Keeping the end in mind is so important when trying to understand these verses in context. Someone once said, "If you don't know where you're going, you'll get there every time." When planning a trip, we have to know our final destination before we can understand how to get there. Such is the case with verses 19-21. As we move forward, let's set our eyes first on the destination, then we'll plug in the practical tactics for getting there. First, fill in the next 4 words of James 1:21.

dechomai - to take, receive, accept, welcome

Therefore ...in humility _____ .

The destination of verses 19-21 is for the believer to **humbly receive the Word implanted**. We have the saving knowledge spoken of in verse 18. We are now being asked to absorb its truths with a ready and humble heart. The word "receive" here is *dechomai,* which means "to take, receive, accept, welcome." The word "implanted" is used to describe how we are to receive God's Word in our lives and appears only here in Scripture. The Greek, *emphutos,* means "inborn or natural"; figuratively, it speaks of what is planted and hence, natural. In other words, we are to welcome the Word of God in our lives in such a way that it becomes planted in our hearts; imbedded so deeply that all that grows from it is naturally glorifying to God.

emphutos – inborn or natural

Therefore, knowing that this is the intent of this section of verses, we can now go back and look at the preceding verses in the context of their end goal. In order for us to ever come to the place where we receive God's Word in such a way that we are not only accepting it, but welcoming it into our lives, the soil of our hearts has to be properly prepared for its planting.

We've already listed the three instructions given for properly receiving the Word, but now that we've identified their unifying goal, let's look at them one at a time.

According to verse 19, what is the first instruction for receiving the Word implanted?

_____

What do you think it means to be quick to hear?

_____

The word used in this verse for "quick" is *tachus,* which means "prompt, ready, swift." In order for us to adequately receive and absorb the Word of God in a manner that can effectively change our lives, we must be **ready** to hear it because we are eager to understand.

tachus – prompt, ready, swift

Perhaps more than the finer gender, we men struggle with being ready to hear from anyone. Never am I more aware of this than when I'm standing in front of the adults I teach in Sunday School. For over a decade now, I have spent hours each week researching the focal passage, then writing up a lesson plan. By the time I walk into the classroom, I literally have every thought I intend to convey and every word I hope to say written down. While this has proven to be a very effective way to teach, it is equally a very ineffective way to be prepared to listen. When others interject questions or comments during class, I am often only half-listening because of fear I'll lose my train of thought as well as my place on the page. In essence, I am so concerned with what I want to say next, that I pay little attention to what others are contributing. I am simply too pre-occupied with my own thoughts to be ready to hear theirs. Yet after class, when those same precious people are making plans for lunch, they have my full attention with my eyes locked into theirs. At that point, I am eager to hear every detail, anxious to learn how what they're saying is going to affect my tummy, and I'm quick to share these plans with others. The latter is the kind of hearing we are called to by James in this verse – a quickness to listen and a readiness to absorb rather than forget.

When approaching the Word of God, we are to have a quickness to listen and a readiness to absorb.

Read Matthew 13:1-23. According to verses 14-15, why did they hear but never understand?

_____

According to verse 15, what would God do for them if they would only listen?

_____

Verses 20-21 explain the seeds that landed on the rocky places. What happened to them?

_____

According to verse 23, who represents the seed that fell on good soil?

_____

Greet the Word with eager anticipation of truth you need to hear.

What sort of a crop does this seed produce?

_____

God is so anxious for us to listen to Him, because the seeds He desires to plant in our hearts will bring forth a harvest of fruit for Him and abundant peace and joy for us. It is our decision, though. Will we read through Scripture as if we are reading the dictionary, glazed over and uninterested? Or will we greet the Word with eager anticipation for the truth we need to hear? Will we quiet our minds enough to listen, or will we remain distracted with our own thoughts and worries –always hearing but never understanding? It is ultimately up to us. But, just as it was with all of us during our school years, when testing time comes, the measure of our listening is always revealed.

According to James 1:19, what is the second instruction for receiving the Word implanted?

_____

_____

No matter how you slice it, it is impossible to listen while the sound of your own voice drowns out the voice of the one speaking. Our heart cannot be still enough to hear the voice of God while our tongue is flapping in the wind. We cannot learn and grow if we cannot hear God; we cannot hear Him if we will not be quiet. Remember, the desire of a wise man is to grow in more wisdom. The wise bite their tongues in order to allow for that.

What is the third instruction for receiving the Word implanted, found in verse 19?

_____

_____

To hear the voice of God, we must silence our own.

When we are still and listen to the Word, allowing it to shape our lives, it will convict us. God's Word shows us a perfect standard, and as the light of that standard shines on us, it will reveal areas in our lives that we need to correct. Although we may want to, we must not respond with defensiveness and anger toward what we hear.

When you are in a situation where something personal or important to you is being questioned, what is your first inclination?

_____

_____

Did you say it was to sit quietly and listen, or did your answer reflect more of a natural tendency to defend yourself? If we are perfectly honest, we will admit that our human nature wants to defend ourselves. Because of that reality, when God's Word is the catalyst for conviction, we can, at times, want to turn away from it, defending our right to proceed as we wish, rather than heeding what we've read. Some may tend to avoid a certain passage of Scripture because it makes them uncomfortable, while others may try to twist the meaning of a passage to give them license to do as they choose rather than conform their will to the Lord's leading. Lastly, as verse 19 says, some may respond in outright anger, offended by the Word of God and desiring to hold on to their "rights" to live as they choose.

It is human nature to want to defend ourselves when God's Word brings conviction.

Verse 19 says that we are to be slow to this sort of defensive anger. Why? (verse 20)

_____

_____

This verse is another example of why it is important to interpret these instructions in the light of their context. If we don't understand what kind of anger is being addressed here, it would appear that of all sin universally known to man, James chose anger to point out as not meeting God's righteousness. True, it doesn't, but neither does any other sin. In its proper context, we see that the righteousness of God cannot be achieved in a believer who has a defensive anger against the convicting Word of God.

The righteousness of God cannot be achieved if we have a defensive anger against His convicting Word.

Read Romans 12:2. Do not be conformed to this world, but be _____ by the _____ of your mind.

We absolutely cannot achieve the righteousness that God desired us to strive for when He "brought us forth by the word of truth" if we keep our defenses high and refuse to allow that truth to transform and renew our minds. God's righteousness here does not refer to the righteous part of His character, but to the way of life that He requires of us. This righteousness will become ours, if we genuinely accept His Word.[8]

We have finally made it full circle back to our word "therefore!" Hopefully, all of the puzzle pieces fit together now, and you can see how the beginning of this verse fits perfectly with everything we've studied today.

Read verse 21. What are we to put aside? _____

Surrender to the Lord is a daily process and a constant battle against our pride.

If we are quick and eager to hear God's Word, slow to speak our own mind, and slow to defend our sinful nature in anger against Scripture, we put ourselves in a position to submissively follow James' next directions – namely, to surrender to the Lord everything that remains in our sinful nature. This is definitely not easy; it's a daily process of surrender and a constant battle against our inborn antagonist, pride. That is why special emphasis is put on **how** we are to receive the Word in the following section of verse 21.

In _____ receive the word implanted.

The safest and most blessed place to be is under the mighty hand of God.

There's no getting around it, asking the Lord to identify every area of sin in your life and allowing Him to ask you to change what He reveals requires extreme humility. But, placing yourself under the mighty hand of God is the safest and most blessed place you can ever be.

What do James 4:10 and 1 Peter 5:6 promise the humble?

_____

_____

Our circle around these verses has brought us back to our hearts. The question we are left with is whether or not our heart is in a place where we will allow it to be still, quiet, and humble enough to receive the Word implanted in the way in which God is asking us. As we conclude our day, let's revisit the Greek words used for "receive" and "implanted." *Dechomai* not only meant to receive, but to accept and welcome. *Emphutos* gave the image of one thing being imbedded so deeply that something else grows from it naturally. "The soil of the heart must be hospitable, if the seed of the Word is to grow."[9] How's your soil, guys? Do you greet God's Word with a welcoming eagerness for it to transform your life or with drudgery? Are you allowing what you take in from the Word to transform you, to become so deeply imbedded in your heart that what grows from it is a natural overflow? So, how's the soil of your heart?

"The soil of the heart must be hospitable, if the seed of the Word is to grow."

Use the space below to record the most meaningful point you'd like to remember from today's reading.

_____

_____

_____

_____

_____

_____

---

8   Adamson, *NICNT, James*, p. 80

9   Ibid., p. 81

Day Four – The Man in the Mirror

Yesterday, we left off in the middle of James 1:21.

Fill in the blank: Therefore, putting aside all filthiness and all that remains of wickedness, in humility receive the word implanted, _____.

For the benefit of review, who were the recipients of this book? _____

Because they were Christians, we know that James was not presenting them with the plan of salvation for "saving their souls." He had already established that they were a kind of first fruits among God's creation. His instruction to them to receive the word implanted was an exhortation to allow the Word of God to grow them into the type of mature Christian who permits Scripture to mold his or her heart when the Word has convicted them. If the putting off of sin and the receiving of the Word implanted is not his way of explaining salvation, then we are left asking why it is followed with the clause *"which is able to save your souls."* The term *"save your souls"* is not a term used anywhere in the New Testament to describe a conversion to Christianity.[10] Rather, "by obeying God's Word, the believer can save his life, himself, from the consequences of sin."[11] Our eternal security is certain; we need not worry about losing our salvation. Neither do we need to fear that this passage puts conditions on our salvation. Yet, it does tell us that there are consequences, both good and bad, in this life, based on how we respond to the Word on a daily basis.

"Save your souls" refers to saving oneself from the consequences of sin by avoiding sin in the first place.

The next verse could easily be the theme verse for the entire book of James. As we saw on Day One, James' greatest focus was on **demonstrating** one's faith through an outpouring of observable evidence.

Read James 1:22.

If we have humbled ourselves and received the word implanted in our hearts, what should naturally happen as a result?

_____

Again, James begins another verse with the word "but." What do you suppose he is contrasting from the previous verses?

One's faith should be accompanied by an outpouring of evidence.

_____

_____

James has written very important instructions for the way in which we **must** prepare our hearts to effectively hear from, and respond to, God and His Word. Yet, this next verse, in essence, says, "But, don't stop there!" Our families live in Missouri, the "Show-Me State."

---

10   Idem, *The Gospel Under Siege,* p. 24

11   Constable, *Notes on James,* p. 19

In many ways, the book of James is the "show-me book" of the Bible. The emphasis of his entire book is to reinforce truth that the reader already knew, as well as give new guidance and direction for the Christian walk, all of which he sums up with, "You understand the gospel, now show me."

Using verse 22, fill in the blank: But prove yourselves doers of the Word,

_____.

paralogizomai – to cheat or deceive by false reasoning

Have any of you had the "privilege" of raising a stubborn child? I know many of you have. While there are times when they can be compliant little angels, there are other times when we could give them clear directions to do something and have them look at us and say, "I'm not gonna, and you can't make me!" Even if the task could have been over and done with in a manner of minutes, it is apparently more satisfying to such a child to argue than it is to comply. You know they have heard you and understand your instructions, yet they somehow think that having their own way is going to bring them more satisfaction than complying with an absolute directive they have been given. In reality, most times it causes them more frustration and pain due to consequences than the argument was worth, yet they choose to stand their ground. And oh how exhausted a willful and wrong child can leave a parent.

Warning: Objects in the mirror are reflections – of YOU!

We often do that as Christians. We hear the Word, we understand the Word, and yet we look at God and foolishly say, "I'm not gonna, and you can't make me!" When we do so, we have deluded ourselves. The Greek word for delude is *paralogizomai,* which means "to cheat or deceive by false reasoning." How often must God shake His head in wonder, knowing that what He has chosen for us is so much better than any plans we could devise ourselves. Yet, our pride deludes us into thinking that ignoring the Word and going our own way will somehow lead to satisfaction. This fits the description of the man portrayed in our next few verses.

Read James 1:22-24.

The one who hears, but does not "do" is compared to what kind of man?

_____

_____

God's Word is a mirror for our souls.

From the context, what kind of man do you suppose he saw in the mirror before he turned away?

_____

_____

This verse isn't describing someone who looks in the mirror, sees perfection, and then quickly forgets how ruggedly handsome they are after turning away. This is a person who sees the imperfection of their reflection, realizes the changes they need to make, but forgets as soon as they walk away.

Read Hebrews 4:12-13.

The Word of God is like a mirror for our souls. If read openly and honestly, it will cut to the heart of our thoughts and intentions and fully expose our innermost being to the eyes of the Lord. For those of us who go to it wishing to grow, it lays us wide open before our eyes like a mirror that does not lie. At this point, we have a decision to make. Will we turn away from our reflection and forget what we've seen, or will we begin addressing what we see by applying what we've heard from the Word?

We **are** to hear the Word, but we are also to seek to hear it in such a way that we crave it like we do air to breathe or food to eat. I love the way Jeremiah described his approach to God's Word, even in the darkest of his hours. *"Your words were found and I ate them, and Your words became for me a joy and the delight of my heart; for I have been called by Your name, O LORD God of hosts."* (Jer 15:16). The Hebrew word for eat in this verse is *"akal,"* and it was used to describe an animal tearing apart and devouring its prey. To hear the Word in the way James asks is to devour it and absorb it so that it becomes such a part of us that it saturates our very being. Hearing without the intention of living out what we've heard is merely hearing without listening. Knowledge that goes in one ear and out the other does no good.

We are to crave God's Word like we do air and food.

In almost any bookstore, you will find aisle after aisle of self-help books or videos on nearly every topic imaginable. I've wondered at times what becomes of most workout DVDs that are purchased. Do the discs make it out of their cases? If so, does the typical viewer watch from the couch, or do they frequently and consistently follow the workouts presented on the video? If we're honest, many of us purchase these things thinking that having them in our homes is going to provide some sort of solution to our fitness needs. Yet, we somehow don't understand why we're not losing any weight as we watch from the couch eating chips and ice cream. We're taking in the information needed to improve – so why is there no improvement? Oftentimes, instead of getting off our duffs and exerting the effort the video presents as necessary to actually change our lives, we simply find another video as if it will have the magic "easy button" that the previous one obviously didn't possess. Many times, we approach Scripture the same way. We may "give it a try," reading it to see if it will really make the difference in our lives that others tell us it will. But if we don't see an instant change through a purely academic reading of the text, we may assume that it just doesn't "work" for us.

'akal – to eat, devour, burn up, or consume

Read James 1:25. Fill in the blank:

The one who _____ at the perfect law, the law of liberty,

and _____, not having become a _____

but an _____, this man will be blessed in what he does.

parakuptó – to stoop sideways to examine

We must approach the Word as a tool that the Lord can effectively use in our lives, but being the gentleman that He is, God will not force that tool upon us. The word used for the **intent** way we are to look upon God's Word is a compound word derived from *para*, meaning "from beside or by the side of," and *kuptó*, meaning "to bend, stoop down, or bow the head." Together, *parakuptó* means "to stoop sideways to look at." This makes me think of times I've sat in seats at a sporting event, movie, or concert and have gotten stuck behind some dude who's 6'6" and 300 lbs. Try as I might, I really have a hard time seeing around (or through) such a mountain of humanity. Yet, because I'm spending my valuable time and money, by golly, I'm going to find a way to see what I came out to see. I may stand on my tiptoes, crane my neck in every direction, lean to one side then the other, or stoop down to peer through a tight spot just to get a glimpse. We don't go to these events just to read the programs. We go looking for an up-close encounter with something that is outside of our everyday experience. The athletes or performers are there for us to see, but when they're not right out in the open, we must decide whether or not the benefit of finding them is worth our effort. Are we willing to "*parakupto*" to see them? Guys, I know the answer to that. Eighty thousand men will arrive 4 hours before game time, grilling in a smoke-filled parking lot, and then stand for 3 hours as 22 men battle it out on the gridiron. There is definitely a lot of worship on Sundays; unfortunately, more of it may occur in domes than in sanctuaries.

When the Word requires a change, do you make it? If so, what's your motive?

This brings us to our intent. Why do we come to the Word? Is it to check it off of our "to do" list because we know we should be spending time in it, or do we approach it as Jeremiah did, with an eager desire to tear it apart in such a way that it opens our eyes to truths we've not yet known? Do we hope to allow it to change our lives, or do we glance through it, hoping there won't be anything that makes us uncomfortable? When it does show us something that needs to change, will we actually make the change? If we do, what is our motive for doing so? For some, there is academic enjoyment in reading the Word, combined with a sense of superiority, as personal flaws are peeled away one by one in order to attain a higher level of "righteousness." Such was the goal of the Pharisees; they went to the Word regularly, but it was for their own self-exaltation. They were hearers of the Word, and they appeared to be "doers" of the Word, but with wrong motives. They did not absorb the Word correctly, as we'll see.

In Matthew, we find several "woes" Jesus speaks over the Pharisees. Read a sampling of them here – Matthew 23:23-28.

These verses emphasize the fact that the "cleaning up" the Pharisees were doing was for the benefit of their outward appearance and not a change of the heart. They were hearing the Word and doing **something** with it, but boosting one's own piety was never the intention of the law.

Reread Matthew 23:23. What three things had the Pharisees neglected while they emphasized tithing?

God's Word is meant to change our hearts first, then our actions.

_____

This passage doesn't condemn tithing, but it does condemn the Pharisee who only focused on acts of self-righteousness. Note this important contrast: tithing can be done by oneself, for one's own glory. However, justice, mercy, and faithfulness are actions learned by the Word that benefit others and often call for self-sacrifice. A genuine response to the gospel changes more than our actions; it changes our hearts in such a way that it overflows from us and benefits others in a way that draws them to the gospel. If we are selfish in our Christian walk, allowing it to only impact our own lives, we are not living out the Word; we have not become effectual doers, and we, therefore, have not allowed it to change our hearts in the way God intends.

Jesus put great emphasis on "doing" the Word. Read Luke 6:47-49.

To whom did Jesus liken the man who listens to His words and puts them to practice?

_____

To whom did He liken the man who hears His words but does not practice them?

_____

Let's revisit our Greek word for the intent way in which we are to look at the Word. *Para* meant "from beside or by the side of." The meaning of this word actually stresses a closeness that implies intimate participation. In other words, the one who looks intently at the Word is one who stoops down, cranes his neck, or does whatever he can to closely observe the Word that he is already faithfully abiding in. When he looks into the mirror of the Word, it is not for a quick glance to see if he has something stuck in his teeth or to check for bats in the cave. No, he studies the Word and absorbs it until it is so much a part of him that he can't look away from it. It has become the foundation of his life; without it, he knows that there is no hope.

Scripture will form a firm foundation that helps us stand when the storms of life come.

For many of us, it's nearly impossible to read the above verses in Luke without thinking of the children's song about the wise man who built his house upon the rock and the foolish man who built his house upon the sand. From the mouths of babes comes the lesson concerning what will happen to each of us when the storms of life assail. As life puts pressure on us, what comes out of us will be evidence of what we have chosen to absorb. Those who hear the Word and yet walk away will have no firm foundation to stand on and will more easily crumble under the burdens of this life. On the other hand, those who allow themselves to be changed by it will have the ability to stand firm on their foundation of the Word.

When we make the implanting of the Word the priority of our lives, putting ourselves in whatever position necessary in order to see its truths, we will see our lives transform before our very eyes and what we've **heard** will naturally become what we **do**. Just as we have to work to reposition ourselves to see the athletes at the stadium, we must put forth whatever effort necessary to see the Word for the powerful tool it is meant to be in changing our hearts and lives. What extra effort are you willing to make today to be more available to its changing power? As we wrap up today, let's look at our Greek word *parakuptó* one last time. *Kuptó* was the portion of this word that emphasized the need to reposition ourselves in order to intently focus on the Word. The positions included in its meaning were not only to bend or stoop down, but also to bow the head. May we suggest that to begin seeing the life-changing power of the perfect Word, we must first begin with a humbly-bowed head and an honest prayer? In the space below give to the Lord whatever is hindering you from placing full priority on both hearing and "doing" the Word as a natural outpouring from your life? Oh, and down in front big guy! ☺

To receive God's Word with humility, begin by bowing your head and knee to Him.

_____

_____

Day Five – A Life of Worship

Congratulations men, we've made it to the end of Chapter One! By this point, we've seen that it takes great faith to endure trials and temptations in the manner we are required to. We've learned that our faith is strengthened by an evolving relationship with the Word of God, which helps us grow in grace and wisdom as it deepens in our hearts. From this deep-seated implanting of the Word, comes a natural growth of Christ-like action as we begin to "do" the Word.

What does "doing" the Word look like to you?

James chose a sin of the tongue to represent a lack of sincerity in one's religion.

_____

_____

Read James 1:26-27.

Before answering that question for us, James shows us what "doing" the Word does not look like.

According to verse 26, whose religion is worthless?

_____

James spends a lot of time discussing the dangers of the uncontrolled tongue in Chapter 3, so we will not camp here for long now. But, it is undoubtedly significant to note that of all of the sins he could have pointed out as evidence for a lack of sincerity in one's religion, James chose a sin of the tongue. Whether the constantly running tongue is drowning out the sound of the Word as it needs to speak personally to us, or carelessly spouting off in pride or selfishness with others, it is a hindrance to what the Word needs to accomplish in our lives.

Read Luke 6:45. From what does the mouth speak?

_____

Hypocrisy – when our actions don't match our words.

We read previously about the Pharisees and their misguided self-righteousness. James 1:26 speaks of vain religion; the Greek implies a sense of "piety denoting the scrupulous observance of religious exercises – in action or words – …performed in the guise of devout religion."[12] Even in the "show" of their religion, the hearts and the hypocrisy of the Pharisees were revealed by actions that did not match their words. They spoke openly of their own religious superiority, while freely pointing out the faults and shortcomings of others, censuring and strangling them with legalism. "When we hear people ready to speak of the faults of others, that they themselves may seem the wiser and better, this is a sign that they have but a vain religion."[13]

---

12   Adamson, *NICNT, James,*p 85
13   Matthew Henry, *Matthew Henry's Commentary in One Volume*, p. 1932

The Greek word for religion used twice in this passage is *thréskeia*, which refers to worship expressed in ritual acts. So, when James talks about their "religion," he is really speaking to them concerning the sincerity of their worship. He warns that knowing the Word, speaking academic knowledge of the Word, and yet having no evidence of the Word in one's life is nothing more than vain worship and deception of one's own heart.

Read Matthew 6:1-8.

Although the Jewish leaders sought to give the appearance of worshiping through charitable acts and lofty prayers, Jesus saw the intent of their hearts and questioned the sincerity of their religion.

What is your own personal definition of worship?

_____

_____

thréskeia – worship expressed in ritual acts

Time spent in music and praise within a church service is often labeled the "time of worship." Sometimes, we can get caught up in the emotion of a particular song that really "gets us worshiping." But, to limit the meaning of worship in this way is to grossly limit the understanding of how we are to daily relate to our Lord. Worship occurs **any** time we put our focus onto God and off ourselves. When we give God priority in any moment, we are worshiping Him. Music does not have to be involved, although we can certainly worship our God through song. The emphasis is the intent and focus of the heart. Worship is an outpouring of selflessness in obedience to God in order to honor Him simply because He is worthy of honor. In fact, the English word, worship, is a contraction of "worth-ship." We are called to live a lifetime of worship, not to merely enter into worship in the sanctuary of a church one day a week.

When we give God priority in any moment, we are worshiping Him.

According to James 1:27, what is pure and undefiled religion (worship)?

_____

_____

Interestingly enough, not one single translation of this verse, defining what God accepts as pure and undefiled religion, mentions singing. Our religion is not a set of rules; our worship is not a book of hymns. We are to have an ongoing and "ongrowing" relationship with the Father who is worthy of the devotion of our every moment. When we wake up in the morning and choose to surrender our actions of the day to the Lord rather than focusing on what we think will bring us personal satisfaction, we are committing ourselves to worship. When we choose to alter our own plans in order to help someone in need, because that is what the Word in us has conformed us to do, we are choosing to worship. When we are in the midst of a trial and the world would tell us to turn our backs on God and run, yet we give Him a sacrifice of praise while our very lives may be shattering apart, we are choosing to worship.

Our religion is not a set of rules; our worship is not a book of hymns.

When we encounter a person who is living out the pure and undefiled religion described above, it is very obvious to us, for the type of mindset that leads to these actions never comes from our own human nature; it is only possible through the indwelling power of the Holy Spirit. For to sacrifice self – our time, energy, desires, opinions, and expectations – is unique to the life sold out to serving the Lord. Yes, we are to **reach up** to God in verbal worship, proclaiming His holiness, sovereignty, power, and provision, but James makes it clear to us that this sort of worship is only acceptable to God when it flows from the heart of one who is also **reaching out** to love his neighbor as well. "Worship is empty and idle unless it sends a man out to love God by loving his fellow men."[14]

We are to reach up to God in verbal worship and reach out in love to our neighbor in practical worship.

Although Scripture clearly points out that God has a heart that cares for the orphan and the widow, this is not an exclusive list of requirements for the "ideal level" of Christianity. In the context of James, it is important to note that these two social concerns were prominent within the 1st century church. But, we can see these two examples as opportunities for serving the sick, ministering to the downtrodden, and weeping with the wounded – all of which would include, but not be limited to, the orphans and widows.

It may seem easy to set aside a few hours on Sunday to devote to God and His people. It may be a little harder to carve out time to commit to Him every day in prayer and Bible study. But, if our religion is to be pure and undefiled in God's eyes, our worship must go beyond these personally-enriching worship activities and translate into actions that benefit others. Our worship must not have an "on / off" switch.

When you come in contact with others throughout your day who need someone to talk to, an extra hand with a project, or a word of encouragement, do you think of it as an opportunity or an inconvenience? What is your initial, honest response?

_____

_____

These are the opportunities we're given to prove ourselves "doers" of the implanted Word. It is at these times that the true content of the heart overflows and becomes evident. It is during these opportunities that we can bless the Lord with the worship of our lives, giving tangible evidence of the work He is doing in us.

Our worship should not have an "on / off" switch.

There is almost nothing as rewarding to a parent as when our children finally show an understanding of a difficult life truth that we have been desperately trying to teach them. Words can hardly describe the moment we see them **act** on the truth that we've doubted they've really even heard. Could that be how God feels with us? He's given us His Word, told us over and over to reach out to those in need, and yet we often get so wrapped up in our lives that we forget that one of the most significant avenues for obedience to Him lies in caring for others. How much it must bless His heart when He can finally look down on us as we put someone else's needs in front of our own and say, "I taught him that. I've been working on this lesson for quite some time now. I'm so proud of him; he listened." That, my friend, honors God, and in honoring Him in this way, we worship.

It's not easy to focus on the needs of others in our society. Even when we try, there is great emphasis on doing things quickly, conveniently, and efficiently. In addition, marketing and

---

14   William Barclay, *The Letters of James and Peter*, p. 62

ad agencies make sure their commercials convey the message that the needs of the consumer should be put first, conveying the message that we all need to look out for "Number One." As a result, we often try to selfishly minimize what it will cost us when we actually do care for others. Yet, the Lord tells us a different story.

Read Matthew 25:34-46.

Describe how seriously God takes reaching out to those in need.

_____

_____

Again, acts of mercy toward others are not requirements for salvation, but a tree is known by its fruit. We all need to seriously search our hearts and ask ourselves if the fruit of our lives is demonstrating the salvation we profess.

What is the final description of pure religion in James 1:27 and what does it mean?

_____

What did James 1:18 call us? _____

First fruits are holy and set apart for a holy purpose. Not only does pure and undefiled religion reach out to those in need, it strives to be unstained by the world. The one who seeks to set his heart on God, sets his mind to living his life in a way that does not compromise the standard which the Lord sets before him. But, maintaining this steadfast character does not happen on its own; it takes concerted effort to live a life that resolves to be set apart for the gospel. This does not imply that Christians should live their lives excluding all contact with non-Christians, for we are directly commanded to go into **all** the world with the gospel (Matt. 28:19-20). It does, though, recall a reference to the "double-minded man" of James 1:8, who wants to trust God's will, but refuses to give up his own. Surrendering our own will is tough business; we are naturally drawn to selfish desires. However, using the Greek word *aspilos,* which means "without spot or defilement," James asks us here to live a life above reproach, unstained by the things of this world, which God has rejected for our own good.

In order to live this sort of life, we have to consciously guard our hearts and minds, because this way of life is contrary to our human nature. Not long ago, I visited a Titanic museum near the 100th anniversary of its sinking. I was struck by the confidence that the ship's designers and builders had in their own creation. "God Himself could not sink this ship," some were recorded as having said. Talk about a false sense of security! They had built a ship that could accommodate over 3,300 passengers; however, they allowed for enough lifeboats to hold only about 1,100 of those travelers. Due to their pride and arrogance, they left two of every three passengers at unparalleled risk in the event of "the impossible." As fate had it, this false sense of security resulted in the deaths of over 1,500 souls that April day in 1912. Like that ill-equipped vessel, we are vulnerable to the intrusion of sin in our lives if we do not allow the Word of God to be our lifeboat in absolutely **every area**. We cannot live like the double-minded man, unstable in all his ways. The areas of our lives that we cling to are the chinks in our armor that the enemy will use to take us down. We may have a lifeboat

Society tells us to focus on "Number One;" yet God thinks differently.

aspilos – without spot or defilement

for some areas of life, but if we leave ourselves unguarded in any area, we are inviting trouble. The world is prone to stain us; it is hard to live within it and have to deal with it while remaining undefiled by it, but this must be our constant endeavor.[15]

If we leave ourselves unguarded in any area, we are inviting trouble.

To what areas of your life do James 1:26-27 speak? Does the way your worship **appears** match what your worship **does**? Are you living a lifestyle of worship or is worship something you choose to turn off and on depending on the day of the week? Does your worship include loving those who God loves, even the "unlovable?" Are you able to live a life of worship that is uninterrupted by the intrusion of the "stains of the world" due to unguarded areas in your life? Take time today to speak with the Lord concerning these things. Be honest with Him; He already knows your heart. He wants us to worship Him in Spirit and in truth (John 4:24); the truth of who He is, and the truth of who we are. Remember, it is only when we are fully honest with ourselves and with Him that He can do the greatest work in and through us.

Does the way your worship appears match what your worship does?

_____

_____

_____

_____

_____

_____

_____

_____

_____

_____

---

15   Henry, *Commentary in One...*, p. 1932

WEEK THREE: AN ACTIVE AND LOVING FAITH

Day One – The Price of Partiality

Ah, junior high. The changing skin, the changing voice, the changing body – oh yeah, good times! For many of us, junior high was a tumultuous season of extreme awkwardness. A time of acting like a jerk to some and having others act like jerks toward us. One of my clearest memories of junior high was choosing teams for any sport we played. Mark B. and I were always captains; just once I would have liked to have been on his team and actually won a game! I'd like to tell you that I was mature well beyond my years back then – mature enough to have randomly chosen kids of all ability levels to be on my team. I'd like to tell you that I intentionally selected the nerdy kid who literally put his jock on backwards the first day of practice. I'd like to be able to tell you that's what I did – but I'd be lying to you. I also wish I could tell you that the playground at school was the only place I sized people up and decided if they were "good enough" to be on "Team Dave." Sadly, I freely employed my infallible people-gauging skills and placed nearly everyone I knew into nice, neat categories. If you were smart, cute, popular, athletic, could make neat armpit noises or belch the alphabet – welcome to Team Dave; if you weren't any or all of these things, you could forget it. Such were the harsh realities of junior high.

Faith in Christ and personal favoritism cannot coexist.

As much as we may like to believe that such "team building" is limited to junior high, our next passage of Scripture shows that although we may grow up and out of a junior high mentality, our predisposition toward hurtful, careless discrimination may not altogether disappear. We may have only learned to polish it up, making it look more mature and acceptable. Recently, we had the chance to reconnect with a friend visiting from South Africa where he and his family are serving as missionaries. He described to us the very real distain that occurred between the Christians of different races, living in areas of the city physically separated by a single bridge. Not indifference. Not mere dislike. But, very strong animosity toward brothers and sisters in Christ based only on the color of their skin. Our friend stated that the Christians on one side of the bridge will at times send money "across the bridge" to help the other church, but they themselves will never physically cross that bridge, themselves. And sadly, they feel very justified in refusing to do so. Remember, there can be as much temptation not to do the right thing as there is to do the wrong thing.

As I learned from countless chemistry classes on my way to completing pharmacy school, "like dissolves like," meaning liquids with similar characteristics are compatible with one another. For example, oils mix with oils and water-based substances mix with one another, etc. But, liquids with dissimilar properties just don't mix. Unfortunately, we tend to apply the same principles to our relationships with people as well. We like (mix nicely with) those who are most similar to us and we're repelled by those whom we see as different.

Read James 2:1-7.

*Even those who should
have a sensitivity to
others are susceptible
to prejudice.*

Using three phrases within one sentence, James describes concepts that simply cannot coexist: my brethren, faith in our Lord Jesus Christ, and personal favoritism. By calling them brethren, he reaffirms their position as Christians, which establishes a sense of accountability in the matter. He then reminds them of their faith in the Lord Jesus Christ, the high and lifted up exalted name above all names, who lowered Himself so far as to become a poor man. There is irony on both sides of this coin. On one side, they were discriminating against the very kind of man their Savior had become in order to save their own souls. On the other, that Savior was and is the King of Kings and Lord of Lords who judges all of mankind according to His righteousness. In comparison, we all stand lowly and poor. A helpless beggar should have no right to discriminate against another beggar, and this is how we all come to the cross.

Just as the poor in spirit should be sensitive to those equally poor in spirit, it would also seem that a feeling of camaraderie would naturally bond those who are burdened with the weight of literal poverty. Unfortunately, that was apparently not the case in this early church.

*Do the poor find
sanctuary and hope
among us?*

Read Acts 11:27-30. What did Agabus prophecy was coming? _____

Not only were these early Christians enduring fierce persecution, they were suffering the effects of worldwide famine. Remember, these were not churches you would see on TV every Sunday morning. These congregations were persecuted by Rome for being Jewish, despised by the Jews for being Christian, and were suffering the hardships of famine. You would think that in such a setting, there would be an understanding for each other's burdens. But no, we see here that even those who should have a sensitivity to others, born from their own suffering, were susceptible to the blindness of prejudice.

What contrasting treatment of the rich and the poor did James give in his example?

*katadunasteuo –
to deny someone
their rightful high
position or blessing
by overpowering,
treating harshly, or
tyrannizing them*

_____

How devastating to consider the one who walked into the "sanctuary," equally persecuted and starving, looking for solace and comfort from those who were said to have a message of hope, and yet was asked to sit on the floor because of his haggard appearance. It may seem easy for us to look at this example and think, "I would never do that to someone!" But, before we pat ourselves on the back, let's consider the rest of the picture.

Why do you think the rich man was given preferential treatment?

_____

*Christ associated
with those we may
tend to avoid.*

The rich had discriminated against them, robbed them of their land, dragged them into court, and blasphemed the name of their God! The Greek word for oppression used in verse 6 is *katadunasteuo*, which means "to overpower or treat harshly." It also speaks of denying someone the higher position or blessing they should enjoy, literally tyrannizing them. It would seem ludicrous to show them favoritism when it was at their very hands that the Christian suffered. Yet, it must have occurred in the church, because this is precisely the type of action James is chastising.

According to James 2:4, what did these Christians have?_____

When something seems entirely illogical, it is helpful to consider the possible motives behind the action. Perhaps they were fearful of the rich man. They'd suffered at his hands; might giving him preferential treatment have lessened the severity of his future oppression? He was rich and they were poor; could the rich man have possibly benefitted the congregation financially if he found their treatment of him appealing? No matter their motive, James tells us it was inherently evil, although they likely felt it justified. Consider this. These rich people have your life in their hands; they hold the power over whether or not you have a home to live in, food to eat, or a means of income, and all you're doing is giving them a special spot in the sanctuary in order to perhaps lessen your burden. It's potentially life and death, your own and your family's. It seems reasonable to grease the gears just a little – is it really that big of a deal?

In order to answer that question, let's look at several examples Christ gave us. As you read each of the following passages, ask yourself, "To whom did Christ give the priority of His time?" List each name or description of the person by their corresponding Scripture reference in the **first** blanks. Instructions for the 2nd and 3rd blanks will follow.

Those we may see as horrifying or scary, Christ looks on with love.

John 4:7-29 _____ , _____ , _____ .

The woman at the well was a "questionable character" for Jesus to associate with on many levels. The Jews did not associate with Samaritans whatsoever, and of all possible Samaritans for Jesus to choose to be seen with in public, He chose one that even her own people most likely labeled as "trash." Some of the descriptions we're going to use today may seem harsh. We may think, "Oh, I would never call anyone trash!" and you are correct, most of us would never say such a thing aloud. But, we may think it – even without realizing it. For instance, would the woman at the well be on your list of people you would actively seek to make contact with if she entered your sanctuary on any given Sunday? Why is that? On the **second** blank by her description, write "the questionable."

Do we pretend we don't see those who make us feel uncomfortable?

Mark 5:1-20_____ , _____ , _____ .

Strong enough to break through shackles, insane enough to scream among the tombs night and day, and wild enough to gash himself with stones, this demon-possessed man was the epitome of "scary." It's not hard to imagine that no one went near him for fear of their lives. He was undoubtedly the talk of the town, shunned by all who lived in the vicinity; certainly they all wished that he would just go away, perhaps even going so far as to wish that he would die so he would stop inconveniencing their lives. However, whom they saw as horrifying, Christ looked on with love. We read those words with gratefulness for the work that Christ did in the life of this man, but how would you feel if you found him sitting in your pew next week? Why is that? On the **second** blank by his description, write "the scary."

How do we deal with others who interrupt or inconvenience us?

Luke 18:35-43_____ , _____ , _____ .

For us to actually run into a literal demoniac would be an extremely unusual occurrence, although we do cross paths with people who can scare us. We may not come in contact with a large number of blind beggars either, but he provides for us an example of something we come in contact with, or perhaps avoid, on a regular basis, "the awkward." Sitting on the corner of the street, the beggar was an eyesore who rarely ever shut up. Those who had to go in his direction might have walked on the other side of the street, hoping he wouldn't come in contact with them that day. Or perhaps they'd learned the skill of looking straight forward as they passed, pretending they didn't even see him. When Jesus came by and he cried out to Him, they hushed him and tried to put him back in his place. "You be quiet and sit there on the ground, don't bother Jesus… and don't bother us, either." The truth is, he doesn't have to be a beggar or a leper to make us feel awkward. She can be the woman at church that we know will talk for an hour if we make contact (and we just don't have time for that). He is the man in the pew near us that smells different, looks peculiar, or just acts "weird." Do we make a special effort to spend as much time with them as we do others we've looked forward to seeing when we get to church? Why is that? On the **second** blank by his description, write "the awkward."

Mark 2:1-5,11-12_____, _____, _____.

When others fail, do we extend grace or condemnation to them?

How rude. They were already crammed tightly into a hot room trying to hear Jesus speak and suddenly roof material is crumbling onto their heads, and this group of disrespectful friends had the audacity to interrupt the assembly in order to lower one man down on a pallet! Couldn't they see Jesus was teaching and they were trying to learn? We may not avoid them entirely, but how put out do we get with the parent who lets the baby cry through the entire church service, the class member who interrupts with input that we don't feel applies to the lesson, or the one who takes thirty minutes to give a prayer request about her Great Aunt Zelda's dog's flea infestation? Obviously, these are exaggerations, but the concept behind these examples is common enough that we all understand. Why is that? On the **second** blank by his description, write "the rude."

Mark 14:66-72_____, _____, _____.

Those we may tend to discount, Christ counts as valuable.

He's been zealous, a die-hard leader for the Lord, yet you just watched him fall. He had seen the example of Judas, who also failed. Should Peter end his life as well? Coming back to the other disciples was going to be humiliating, he had been so bold when he said he'd never do such a thing, and yet he did. Will they accept him? Should he even try? He's no stranger to us; if we're honest with ourselves, we see him in the mirror every day. But, when we see him in the congregation, do we greet him with compassionate understanding, or do we condemn him because he let us and God down? Do we extend grace and mercy to him, or do we avoid him because, although we're glad he's come back, we're not sure what to say? Or do we possibly fear what others may say if they see us associating with him? Why is that? On the **second** blank by his description, write "the failure."

No matter how low we are, we can be fully restored!

The list of those we may find ourselves avoiding could go on and on. However, for time and space constraints, we'll stop here. From each example, we see that Jesus spent most of His time showing His love and grace with those who were far from perfect. Those we may tend to discount, Christ counts as highly-valuable. But, the question we were addressing was whether or not it's really that big of a deal to show preferential treatment to those who enter our sanctuary who might be of some benefit to us, especially in the case of potential life and death, as was the case in James 2. Perhaps that question can be answered with another question. What's the cost? What price does the poor man have to pay at the expense of elevating the rich man? What price would all of the above examples have had to pay had Jesus spent all of His time with the Jewish leaders? What price would the entire Kingdom of God have to pay if we did not have the testimony of the miracles done in their lives?

We've labeled each of the characters above with words that should make us stop in our tracks because, like it or not, many of us relate to everyone. At some point, each of us has been the failure, each has been the rude. In our own awkwardness, we have made others uncomfortable, and we each have just as much capacity for being the questionable and the scary as anyone else who walks this earth. But, because Jesus came to save the sick and not just reach an elite few, He was able to rescue each dark and desolate sinner.

What's the cost of partiality within our churches? Life. Real, eternal life is available for those who are searching for hope, but we have to be willing to share it with any and all. If Jesus hadn't come to spend his time among the broken, we wouldn't have the hope of their testimonies to call upon in our own broken lives. Most of us, no doubt, would feel hopeless knowing that we cannot measure up to some standard that we simply can't obtain had He only ministered to the elite. Jesus showed us the restoration from deep sin in order to show us in His Word that we, too, no matter how low we are, can be fully restored.

Showing partiality can send a message that another's soul is not worthy of restoration.

On the **third** blank after every description, go back and write "restored."

The cost of partiality is to send the message to a broken soul that their life is not worthy of being restored and the ripple effects of that message are catastrophic. Each person above was not only restored, but went on to proclaim their story to all who would listen. Jesus left His "comfort zone" of heaven and came to dwell among us who were all hopelessly lost. Are we willing to leave our own comfort zones and extend His love to all we come in contact with, realizing that many of the most amazing testimonies begin in the most unlikely places, and we may have a part in that?

It is impossible for us to show this kind of selfless love to others without first humbly seeing ourselves as their equal. It is only when we realize our own former hopelessness, that we become sensitive to the fact that we needed the hope of Christ as much as they do. When we remember the reality of where we've come from and are overcome with gratitude because He was willing to restore us, we want nothing more than for others to experience the same hope and relief that our own restoration brought us.

Read the passage below (even if you have it memorized, read it fresh today). Fill in your own name, a label of some sort that applies to your own life without Christ, and finally fill in the last blank with "restored."

John 3:16. _____, _____, _____.

When we remember our own hopelessness, we will be passionate about sharing the hope of Christ with others.

Thank Him today that He showed no partiality when extending His love to you, and ask Him to give you a sensitive spirit to do the same for all others you come in contact with. Below, consider writing the names (or initials) of those you've perhaps labeled as trash, scary, awkward, rude, or failure – those who have never been invited to join your team. Ask God to show you how you can begin to extend His love to them this week. Junior high is over, gentlemen; it's time we grow up.

_____

_____

_____

_____

Day Two – The Law of Love

Yes, I said <u>love</u> gentlemen. Now don't roll your eyes at me just yet. I know this may not be everyone's favorite topic, but as I sometimes tell my girls, "You'll live – get over it!" Since God is love and "love" appears in God's Word nearly 500 times, it's apparently an important topic to Him, and what's important to God needs to become important to us as well.

For his visual learners, James uses a word picture (the rich man who enters the assembly) to illustrate his point about partiality in verses 1 through 7. Just in case the emphasis of the illustration doesn't make it across to everyone, he summarizes his point in two concise statements in verses 8 and 9! In a pointblank manner, he states both the positive and the negative aspects of the situation. If you do "this," you do well, if you do "that," you don't.

The "royal law" is to love your neighbor as yourself.

Read James 2:8-9.

What are his readers doing well if they do?

_____

If they don't, what are they committing? _____

basilikós - royal; to be connected with a king

James 2:8 calls the command to "love your neighbor as yourself" the royal law. Why do you suppose that is?

_____

Read Romans 13:8-10.

How are all of the commandments summed up?

_____

The greatest command – to love the Lord with all your heart, soul, and mind – cannot be fulfilled if the royal law is not kept.

The royal law is a repetitive theme throughout Scripture. It was originally stated in the Old Testament (Lev. 19), but Christ, as well as the New Testament writers, reaffirmed its importance many times, not only restating it, but adding gravity to its meaning. *Basilikós* means "royal; to be connected with a king." This law is royal as it was decreed by the King of Kings, demands a level of obedience due to the King by his subjects who will inherit the Kingdom, and it is considered the king of all laws concerning human relationships. As the above passage in Romans points out, all laws are summarized within this one command. Guys, we need to recognize that the greatest command – to love the Lord with all of your heart, soul, and mind – cannot be fulfilled exclusive of the royal law, for to love God in full, is to obey Him in full. Full obedience to Him cannot be accomplished without showing His love to others.

Fill in the blank: Love your neighbor as _____.

What is it to love oneself?

_____

It might be easier to define what self-love is not.

Read Philippians 2:3.

This verse dispels any misconceptions concerning the level at which we are to love ourselves. "*Love your neighbor as yourself*" does not imply that we are to have a vain conceit of ourselves and that we should strive to love others that much as well. In fact, it instructs us to regard others as more important than ourselves.

"Self-love" as the world defines it, is actually "self-destruction." We are constantly fed the lie that whatever "feels" good will make us happy. Yet, we are consistently shown in Scripture that instant gratification brings us nothing but sorrow in the end.

Read Matthew 26:14-16, 47-50; and 27:3-5.

Granted, the example of Judas is extreme, but it is a picture of the downward spiral our selfishness can lead to. Between our own sin nature and the fact that the enemy knows our greatest weaknesses to tempt us with, selfishness that may begin very small, can snowball out of control. When small self-indulgences do not lead to any immediate consequences, we can become desensitized to the fact that there is anything wrong with them. But, as we become addicted to the drug-like effect of their temporary fulfillment, the desire for more and more grows until it's out of control. Judas' greed, fed by a desire to feed his self-love, didn't start where it ended; he let it grow until it consumed him.

Let's consider a practical example that might have occurred in your home at some point. You've decided it's time for a small TV for the kitchen. That small desire for having a new TV leads to its purchase and a small sense of satisfaction. While there is usually nothing wrong with that single purchase, while you are searching for that small TV, the desire for a much bigger TV for your man-cave is awakened. You remember how good it felt to buy the little one, so this time you'll get the 55" plasma screen. You get that beautiful new Sony home and soon realize that you can't fully enjoy all it has to offer without a 7-speaker, 1000-watt surround sound home theater system and Blu-Ray player. Once you have all that nice, new equipment in place, it is almost a crime not to have 250+ channels to choose from on demand, so your "need" for a satellite subscription is now completely obvious for all to see! Before you know it, your little TV for the kitchen has turned into thousands of dollars in new electronics and an ongoing monthly satellite bill. While the world would tell us not to deny ourselves that pleasure and to find any way to make it happen; in the end, we may find ourselves drowning in debt, wondering how we ever got there, and wishing we could get out.

Now back to Judas. Ironically, Judas' self-love ended in self-hate. Satan does that to us. He convinces us that we **need** what we **want** until we can't see straight. We allow ourselves to become consumed as we feed our love for ourselves and then he drops us, leaving us feeling helpless to get out of the situation we find ourselves in. This pattern can be applied to every single sin; no fire begins as a raging inferno. The need to feed self-love in the way the world would prescribe will ultimately lead us all to self-loathing. This is **not** what Scripture is implying by loving yourself.

We are, though, created with an innate sense of self-love that is critical to our human survival. This is a fundamental love of self that protects our life and health out of natural reaction, that finds joy as good comes our way, and hurts when we suffer. It enhances life as we

We are to regard others as more important than ourselves.

The world's sense of self-love can consume us and end in self-hate.

We were created with an innate self-love critical to our survival.

learn to forgive ourselves and it wants us to learn and grow. This inborn love of self is what we are asked to freely share with our neighbor.

This type of love for our neighbor is not a tolerance beyond their faults, but an actual love for who God has created them to be. It is a love that seeks what is best for another, just as we would do for ourselves. **It is a love that puts us in the place of others in order to understand and love them better**. This love will not give up on them when they fail, and will ultimately spare no expense to ensure that they have the opportunity to know the Savior.

When done genuinely, this sort of love is difficult to share on a daily basis with even those we care about the most. But, God does not limit whom this sort of love is to be shown to.

Love for our neighbor goes beyond tolerating their faults.

Read Matthew 5:43-48.

Who are we to love? _____

Let's make the word "enemy" really practical. You are to love those who weigh you down, annoy you, intentionally hurt you, stress you out, cause you pain, or consistently bring you trouble and sorrow. As you read those words, are there specific people in your life who come to mind? In thinking about being commanded to love them in the way described above, what is your first reaction?

_____

_____

Our "enemies" include those who burden and hurt us, cause us stress and sorrow.

We tend to read passages like this a bit light-heartedly. But, when Christ told those gathered to love those who persecuted them, it wasn't a light command. When we gloss over the depth of its meaning, we are unconsciously minimizing the level of love the martyrs were being asked to give to those who were taking their lives, the level of forgiveness a father is asked to have for someone who has harmed his child, the level of grace asked of a husband who's been left alone, or a friend who's been betrayed.

It may be tempting, at this point, to think that this request is just too much for us, that there are some that we simply cannot love and could never forgive. But, let's look again at the example of Christ, whom we are asked to be like in every way.

Loving others as ourselves involves loving them at their worst.

Yesterday, we looked at a list of people with whom Christ chose to spend His time. They might have seemed "unlovable" to others, but none sought to do Him actual harm. Today, though, we've already looked at the example of Judas, the man who sold Christ right into the hands of the executioners. Jesus had loved him all along, just as He had loved His other disciples. When Jesus washed the feet of the disciples at the Last Supper, He did not skip the feet of Judas, even knowing what was to come. With proper self-love, we innately care for ourselves, even when we are at our worst. Likewise, in loving others as ourselves, we continue to love them when they are at their worst, just as Jesus did for Judas.

Read Luke 22:47-51.

In verse 51, what did Jesus do for the very man who came to do Him harm?

_____

The man whom Peter couldn't imagine looking on in love during that moment, was loved, touched, and healed by the One who shows us how to truly love our neighbor. This extraordinary example of love not only shows us **how** to love our enemy, but **when**. Jesus didn't wait to see if he would come and ask forgiveness, He loved Him right there and then, whether it was reciprocated or not.

Read Luke 23:33-38.

During the ultimate act of love, what did Jesus request of His Father for those who were executing Him? _____

He not only asked for the forgiveness of those present, but for you and me.

Look at the sentence in bold near the top of page 58 and fill in the blank:

True, selfless love is a love that _____

in order to understand and love them better.

Love is to be given freely; whether it is reciprocated or not.

When we are tempted to think that the kind of love we are asked to give to others, whether they seem deserving or not, is more than we should be expected to give, we need look no further than the cross. In an effort to put Himself in our place, to be tempted and tried as a human as we would be, He came to show us how deep His love truly goes. As He looks at us and sees how little of ourselves we are willing to sacrifice in order to show love, does He shake His head, remembering all He sacrificed in order to teach us true love? Are we ready to learn? Will we humble ourselves and follow His example?

Read Romans 12:9-21.

Loving others as ourselves requires great strength, grace, and wisdom.

Here we find the prescription for loving our neighbor as ourselves. As our time comes to an end today, use these verses in a time of prayer, asking the Lord for the strength, grace, and wisdom needed to love in each way described throughout this passage.

As you pray, consider these things: Our verses in James today had their emphasis in partiality. They tell us that the royal law, love your neighbor as yourself, cannot coexist with partiality in any way. But, this royal law does not end with a simple lesson on not showing favoritism. It challenges us to stretch our willingness to love, and it encourages us to search our hearts and question our motives regarding when and where we choose to show love. Do we extend love based on how it will affect us, or the good it will do for others? Do we interact with others based more on what they can do for us or how we can serve them? If others have no apparent benefit to us, will we take the time for them? The recipients of the book of James clamored over the rich man and neglected the poor. May we ask you, who is worth clamoring over today? Where is the line between those who are worthy of our love and those who aren't? If we're honest with Scripture, we must admit, there simply is no line. If you've drawn one, it needs to be erased, for we all stand equal at the foot of the cross. No one's sin is more worthy of punishment than yours or mine; no one deserves grace any less than you or me. If God in His perfection can find a way to put Himself in our place in order to show us love, we must do no less for everyone He places in our paths. Help us, Lord, to learn to naturally want what is best for others in the same way we naturally want what's best for ourselves.

We all stand equal at the foot of the cross.

Day Three – The Law of Liberty

Yesterday we left off with loving our neighbor as ourselves without showing partiality. James 2:9 tells us that if we do show partiality, we are sinning. What does the rest of verse 9 tell us?

you are committing sin and are _____.

The Ten Commandments, as well as the many other Jewish laws, were collectively known as "the law."

To understand this portion of James, we need to delve into some good, old-fashioned theology. Don't run! If you're a Christian, what we will look at today is at the core of your faith and it will be a welcome reminder of God's mercy by the time we finish.

Read James 2:9-11.

When you hear the word "law" in the Bible, what do you think of?

_____

Some of you likely said the Ten Commandments, others might have made reference to the hundreds of ceremonial Old Testament laws the Jews were required to live by found in the first five books of the Bible, also known as the Torah. Either way, you would be correct. The Ten Commandments, as well as the many other Jewish regulations, were collectively known as "The law."

What do you think was the point of the law?

_____

When we think of our own laws, we know that they are passed in order to promote structure and safety. The Old Testament law, no doubt, was practical in this manner as well, but God's intent in giving it to man was far more than imparting a set of safety guidelines. In fact, the law did the exact opposite of providing safety, at least in the eternal sense.

Read Romans 7:7. What did the law reveal to man? _____

The primary purpose of the law is to show us our sin.

The fundamental purpose of the law was to show man his sin. A toddler doesn't know not to stick his finger in a light socket until someone tells him not to. After being told, however, he must choose whether or not to obey or disobey what he has been taught. The law didn't create the sin; like the light socket, sin was already there and was inherently dangerous. But, the law did shed light on the fact that there was a right and wrong decision surrounding the light socket.

Read Romans 3:19-20.

The book of Romans tells us that God gave us the law, which shows us our sin, and at the same time, reminds us that keeping that law in its entirety is completely impossible. Why in the world would God want to reveal the fact that we have constant decisions to make between right and wrong concerning the law, and then turn around and tell us that there is absolutely no way we can fully succeed? Why give us a law that condemns us to failure?

In your opinion, does this seem unfair, making the law evil and vindictive? _____

The law, itself, is not evil. In fact, it is perfect. The fact that it is so perfect is what makes keeping it unattainable. **The Old Testament Law revealed the character of God and set His perfect standard for living**. This standard is so high that even our wrong thoughts cause us to fall short of obeying it.

According to Galatians 3:10, what is the word used for the man who cannot follow **everything** required in the law? _____

Holy Catfish, Batman! From our birth, until the day we die, if we cannot follow every single standard required by the law of God, 100% of the time, we're cursed.

What are we cursed to? Romans 6:23? _____

The law revealed the character of God and set His perfect standard for living.

No, we will not drop dead the moment we sin; well, not usually at least. But, we are cursed by the law to an eternal death, separated from God in hell, by committing only one infraction of the law. Seems pretty hopeless, doesn't it? That is **exactly** what God wants us to see by showing us His perfect standard. He needs for us to understand that there is no way that we can attain perfect submission to the law, no matter how hard we try. It is only when we realize this hopelessness that we become aware of our desperate need for THE hope He has to offer us.

Read Romans 5:1-2.

The hopelessness of ever fulfilling the entire law perfectly makes us desperate for the ONLY hope we have.

Is there any way that we can have peace with God and hope for our eternity even though we are unable to achieve the standard of the law?_____

Through whom do we obtain that peace and hope? _____

Romans 3:24-25 tells us that even though the law condemns us to death, we can be **justified** through faith in Jesus Christ. To be justified, *dikaioó*, is a judicial term meaning "to declare righteous." It sounds the echo of the gavel in a courtroom after the verdict "not guilty" has been declared by God, Himself. But, how can we be declared "not guilty" if the law condemned us to death, and we know we've fallen short of meeting its requirements?

dikaioó - a judicial term meaning to declare righteous

Many translations remove some of the key words in this passage that we need to look at, so a literal translation is provided below:

> ...being **justified** as a gift by His grace through the **redemption**, which is in Christ Jesus; whom God displayed publicly as a **propitiation** in His blood through faith. Romans 3:24-25a

We've seen that God justifies us, but how is He able to do that? Does He just decide one day to go easy on us if we will tell Him that we'll do our best? No, it is absolutely impossible for God to look on sin (Hab. 1:13), and when there is sin in our life that hasn't been "paid" for, He cannot look on us. This is the foundation of our faith, the cornerstone of our salvation.

God is only able to justify those who have been **redeemed** by the death of Jesus Christ on the cross. Redemption, *apolutrósis*, means "a release effected by payment of ransom; deliverance." When you redeem a coupon, the value stated upon its face is accepted as cash by the merchant, being applied toward payment in full; once redeemed, you owe no other amount toward the purchase. The **ONLY** way the debt incurred from breaking the law could be paid was with a perfect, spotless, blameless sacrifice; a requirement that only Jesus Christ could pay in full. His payment for our ransom became our deliverance out of the debt that would have cost us our lives.

apolutrósis – a release effected by payment of ransom; deliverance

What was required by the law is called **propitiation**. The word, *hilastérion*, describes "a sin offering, by which the wrath of a deity shall be appeased." In other words, propitiation is the appeasement of God's just and holy wrath through Christ's worthy sacrifice. His perfect life and sacrificial death appeased the perfect law and allowed Him to redeem **any** of us who would choose His gift by placing our faith in the adequacy of what He did on the cross. Once we accept Him as our Savior, when we commit an infraction against the law and Satan accuses us before our God, He looks at him and says, "It's been paid in full once and for all. Step aside. You have no argument against this one; he's mine – case dismissed." Thanks be to our God!!

hilastérion – a sin offering, by which the wrath of a deity is appeased

I know that was a lot to take in, and you may be wondering if we are still studying James! We are, so let's now tie it together with our current passage. Read James 2:9-11 again.

Christ's perfect life and death appeased the perfect law.

Based on what we've seen concerning the strictness of the law, what does verse 10 mean?

_____

In the context of these verses concerning partiality, this verse tells us that even the "little" sin of favoritism fully condemns us under the law. One sin, no matter how unimportant it may seem, is all it takes for us to entirely violate the whole law, which mandates our need of a Savior. But, we know that James was writing to Christians. Why would he need to tell them this if they were no longer condemned by the law?

Read James 2:12.

God justifies man. Christ redeems man. Christ propitiates God.

James wanted his readers to grasp the gravity of the sentence they were saved from so that they would appreciate the way they were to live in response to that salvation. This verse gives the command to speak and act as those who are judged by the law of liberty. This leaves us with two unanswered questions: 1) What is the law of liberty? and 2) Why are we still judged by a law when we've established that our sentence has been paid in full and the case against us in court has been closed?

Following Christ's death, God's character and His standard did not change.

Christ came to fulfill the law, and He did just that. We are no longer condemned by the law, yet the law itself never disappeared. God's character didn't change; His standard did not lower. We are still to live as if He expects such a standard. **Our freedom is not from the expectation of the law, but from the fear of the penalty of its infraction**. We are judged under a law for which arrangements have already been made to satisfy. We have the liberty to live at peace with this law, for it cannot condemn us with a penalty that Christ has already paid.

Has your liberty tempted you to take license to sin because you need not fear the death penalty of the law anymore? If yes, how might remembering the price Christ paid for your liberty help? If no, please move to the front of the class.

Read Galatians 5:13.

Our freedom from the penalty of the law does not give us liberty to sin, only liberty to live outside of the fear of its eternal wrath. Knowing this, we are to live our lives with an acknowledgment of the debt that was paid in order to secure such a freedom, while we strive to meet God's standard. We do so not out of slavery to the law, but from an indebted gratitude for the mercy He bestowed on us. We are to realize the magnitude of the penalty taken from us and understand the ultimate act of mercy that was required to remove that penalty.

We are still judged, but now we're "tried" by a judgment tempered by mercy. God's attitude toward sin is unchanged and unrelenting, but his attitude toward sinners saved by grace is abundantly merciful. Understanding where we stand in relation to that mercy should make us sensitive to sharing it with others. For he who seeks mercy must show mercy.

Read James 2:13 and Matthew 18:21-35.

Although this parable specifically addresses forgiveness, it speaks of God's heart of mercy and His intolerance toward unforgiveness. The cross paints the clearest picture of mercy triumphing over judgment. God's mercy teaches us to be merciful.

How does James 2:13 say the one who shows no mercy will be judged?_____

The highest price was paid in order to make a way for us to live righteously. At the heart of righteous living is loving others and living mercifully with them. When we choose not to, we are judged accordingly. We will not lose our salvation, but we will reap consequences in this life and this passage tells us they will be merciless.

Read James 2:12 again.

The verbs "act" and "do" are preceded by the adverb "so," or *houtós,* to stress their importance and put emphasis on their fulfillment in the present tense. If your teenager is acting like a two year-old, you may need to remind them that they are no longer a toddler and follow it with, "**So**, act your age!" James has done just that. He has reminded his readers that partiality is a serious sin, in that it violates the royal law. He has further illustrated the law that all Christians were once condemned by. Because we were all once condemned by the law and only the work of Christ could change that status, James teaches that no one should think of themselves more highly than another, for nothing they did secured their own salvation. When we humbly remember this, mercy should triumph and partiality should be a thing of the past.

Granted, today may have seemed a bit "off the beaten trail." But, it is important to our ongoing faith to be reminded of the absolute hopelessness from which we were saved. After a while, we Christians tend to take our salvation for granted; we often gloss over the severity of what

Freedom from the penalty of the law does not give us liberty to sin; but we can live without the fear of the law's eternal wrath.

If we want to receive mercy, we must extend mercy to others.

houtós – an adverb that means "in this manner"

we've been saved from and in doing so, we belittle what had to be done in order to avoid our punishment. Wayne Watson recognized this reality in his own life when he penned the lyrics to his song, "Say it All Again." While watching his church's Easter program, Watson found himself completely unmoved by the all-too-familiar salvation story. It had totally become "been there, done that" in his heart and mind. Convicted by how casually he was taking the gospel message of hope, he wrote these words, "If I've heard it once, must've heard it a thousand times. But, familiar truths get dusty in a cold, sarcastic mind. So say it all again, same old story, same old lines. It will warm my frozen heart, so say it over one more time." Today, if you find the old familiar truths have gotten dusty within a cold, sarcastic mind or they no longer move a frozen heart, would you take some time to humbly come before your heavenly Father and simply thank Him for saving your life? Thank Him "one more time." Thank Him for His perfect law, which showed you your desperate need for a Savior and for His willingness to give His Son to be that Savior, even though it cost Christ everything. Ask Him to give you a heart full of the same mercy that He was willing to show you and to remind you of that mercy in the moments when you need to show it, and not only during your time of prayer. Thank Him for the cross that shows us that although we walk in a fallen world that wears us down, not only did mercy triumph over judgment on Calvary, but it will continue to do so until the day of completion, when all sin will pass away and we will bask in His perfection and glory. Oh what a glorious day that will be!

Occasionally we need to be reminded of what we've been saved from.

Day Four – Faith in Action

As we begin today, let's review something we learned from Chapter 1. In Week 2, we said that James 1:22 could be the theme verse for the entire book of James. Write it below:

_____

If James could have chosen a modern-day logo and motto for his book, they likely would have been a "swoosh" and "Just Do It." Throughout the entire book, he demands action that demonstrates faith. It's almost like he's touched on it before, been hinting around about it ever since, and just can't seem to hold it in any longer. In this next section, he fully lays out his frustration concerning dormant faith. These verses likely made the original readers squirm a little in their comfortable seats. If we're honest, it should do the same for us. For it was a call to action, and that call rings just as loudly today as it did 2000 years ago.

James provided a call to action 2000 years ago that still rings loudly today.

Read James 2:14.

Hold on just a minute! Ephesians 2:8-9 tell us that we are saved by faith alone and that works of righteousness have no bearing on our salvation. In the books of Romans and Galatians, Paul argues emphatically that salvation is through faith in Jesus Christ alone. The entire Old Testament pointed to salvation through faith in the coming Messiah and the entire New Testament confirms it. What in the world could James mean here? Men, if you learn nothing else from this study, we want you to go away from it with this very firm truth that was first stated on Day One: Scripture **never** contradicts itself. Scripture **always** interprets Scripture and **context is king**. If there is a passage of Scripture that seems confusing while standing on its own, other Scripture will explain and support it. When it comes to interpreting anything within Scripture, its context must be considered.

By calling them brethren throughout, James acknowledged the fact that the recipients claimed to have an understanding of a saving knowledge of Christ. Yet because of their actions, or lack thereof, he's calling their faith into question. James isn't writing these words in order to shed doubt on the fact that true faith can save a man; he's calling the recipients out concerning the sincerity of what they are calling "faith!"

Sometimes the littlest words in a sentence are the most important; they can go unnoticed, and yet hold two valuable notions together, as glue does between two objects.

Scripture never contradicts itself. Scripture always interprets Scripture and context is king.

In the final portion of James 2:14, what does James ask his readers?

_____

The word "that" is vital to the meaning of this passage. Within the structure of this verse in the original Greek, the word "that" is implied with "faith," yet unfortunately, some (though very few) translations have left it out.[16] When "that" is left out, the question reads, "Can faith

---

16   Moo, TNTC, *James*, p. 114

save him?" which gives the impression that true faith is not enough to save. This was not James' intention at all. He does, though, intend to question the professed faith that produces no works, a faith that is a matter of speech but results in no action. By next giving a tangible example, James illustrates his point.

Read James 2:15-17.

Following on the heels of James' teaching concerning partiality against the poor, he uses a word picture with similar imagery. Although there is practical application to be found in the illustration, he is not intending it to be a lesson in kindness toward the needy. Instead, it is a visual image of the point he is trying to make concerning the type of faith he is concerned about.

Good intentions without followup actions are inadequate and worthless.

How useful was the good advice given to the brother in need?_____

It was good advice. It sounded great and it spoke of what was necessary for the one in need. But, the advice by itself was useless and inadequate because there was no follow-up action that proved the sincerity of the advisor. This insincerity is at the heart of James' concern. It illustrates the insincere faith that is not followed by life-changing action. In verse 17, James says that this faith, by itself, is dead.

When you see the words "dead faith," what impression does it give you?

_____

When the Greek word for dead, *nekros*, is used in this context, it means "useless, inactive, inert." This type of faith is unproductive and ineffective. But, what exactly does that mean? Thankfully, the next few verses shed a little more light on the meaning.

Read James 2:18-20.

Verse 18 is an example of a diatribe often used in New Testament letters where the author needs to make a point by inserting an imaginary objector into the "conversation." This objector is made to appear as if he is arguing with James so that James can, in turn, respond with a rebuttal.

nekros – useless, inactive, inert

What does this objector seem to be arguing?

_____

Obviously, James saw a need for inserting this objector's opinion. He must have gotten wind that this was the kind of argument being given within the churches in order to defend their lack of "faith follow through." This objector inserts his opinion by stating that, "Some have faith, whereas some do works, and that's just fine." James responds to this with a resounding, "No way!"

Within verse 19, we see the kind of "faith" that causes James concern.

What did James acknowledge that they believed? _____

Deuteronomy 6:4 says, "Hear, O Israel! The Lord is our God, the Lord is one!"

This passage of Scripture is known as the *Shema* and is a part of the Jewish confession of his faith. This is their way of proclaiming their monotheism, acknowledging that there is one, and only one, God. James tells us in verse 19 that the demons share this same academic understanding of a monotheistic God. The demons don't struggle with choosing which religion they think is accurate. They've seen our God, they know He's real, and they tremble. But, this intellectual assent has not brought them salvation. James simply illustrates here that an academic acknowledgement of who our Lord is does not produce a saving faith.

The demons have seen our God, they know He is real, and they tremble.

James is obviously concerned with the fact that his readers claim to have faith in God, but are apparently giving no evidence of this in their lives. Again, we know that he has consistently called the recipients of his letter "brethren," but as in every church, there were likely those who were living their faith and those who had merely made a verbal profession of faith without any obvious commitment.

Verse 20 begins with a poignant question. What is it?

_____

kenos – means empty

James is challenging the foolish ones among them, asking if they are willing to recognize that something is wrong in their lives. The word used for "foolish" here is *kenos*, meaning "empty." He is asking those who are claiming to have an understanding of something to recognize that they don't; that their understanding has been truly empty! This can be so hard, especially when we've been confidently advertising that we know. He's asking some of these church members to humble themselves enough to admit that their insincere faith is, indeed, insincere.

What word does he use to describe this faith at the end of verse 20? _____

argos – inactive, idle, lazy, thoughtless, unprofitable, injurious

This word comes from the Greek word *argos*, meaning "inactive, idle, lazy, thoughtless, unprofitable, injurious." How profound. A useless faith is obviously inactive, but it is also injurious. Studying this reminded me that in our city, there is a "gaming establishment" called The Argosy Casino – how ironic. It proclaims action and excitement, but in reality, people sit idly and thoughtlessly, they are unprofitable, and the vast majority of them become financially injured.

Likewise, how could a false faith that proclaims much, but does little, or even nothing, be injurious?

_____

Others may base their decision to accept or deny Christ on the works they see (or don't see) us do.

In its inactivity, an insincere faith causes injury not only to the person who possesses it, but to the rest of the Kingdom of God as well. In their own lives, people holding onto a false faith have fooled themselves into thinking that a mere confession of who God is, a confession equal to that of a demon, is all that is required for salvation. This is, indeed, unprofitable and injurious to them in the eternal sense; as such a profession does not save. As for the rest of the Kingdom, those who call themselves Christians, yet live a life that says otherwise, do great detriment to those around them. As the world looks on, we are judged by our actions, not only by our words. We injure others who may base their decisions concerning their acceptance or denial of the cross of Christ on the works that they see us do (or not do).

Our salvation is secure for eternity from the moment of our sincere acceptance of Christ as Savior and Lord.

In yesterday's lesson, we saw James call the churches to action. In the same way that we may tell our kids, "Act your age," he is telling his readers, "Act your faith." As we read these verses, we need to ask ourselves the same questions James was challenging the first century church to ask themselves. "If you say you're a Christian, are you acting like it?" "If you aren't acting like it, why do you say you're a Christian?" We've stated it before in this study and we'll certainly state it again: Our salvation is secure for eternity from the moment of our **sincere** acceptance of Jesus Christ as our Lord and Savior. That is not up for debate. Yet James poses the question – "Is your faith **sincere**?" Was it merely a verbal assent to the reality that there is a God or was it a proclamation of faith in a Savior worthy of active obedience?

There is a great praise song, "The Power of the Cross," with the following chorus:

Paul focuses on the root of salvation, while James focuses on its fruit.

> *The power of the cross is moving in my life,*
> *'cause the power of Your blood has saved me.*
> *The power of the cross still draws me to Your side,*
> *'cause the power of Your love has changed me.*
> *Oh, let my life be lost in the power of the cross.*

James wants to know if the power of the cross is actively moving in these church members' lives. Was their commitment to the Savior sincere enough that they allowed the power of His love to **change** them? Was their faith authentic if it wasn't manifesting itself in action? No, James is not disagreeing with Paul concerning salvation through faith alone, but he is asserting that a faith that doesn't consistently act, may not have been sincere in the first place. Paul focuses on the **root** of salvation, whereas James focuses on the **fruit** of salvation.

dikaioó – to declare righteous, or to show to be righteous

Read James 2:21-24.

James supports his position with the example of Abraham. When does he say that

Abraham was justified? _____

God declares us righteous in His sight, while we show ourselves to be righteous to others by our deeds.

We discussed yesterday that we are justified, declared righteous, or "not guilty," as in a court of law, at the moment of our salvation. Paul teaches that, and James supports it, yet James speaks of justification differently within this passage. There are two meanings for the Greek word used for "justification" in Scripture. *Dikaioó* can mean "to declare righteous," as we've seen, or "to show to be righteous" as we will see today.

Read Genesis 15:6.

This is where Abraham was first declared righteous, or justified, solely due to his faith and trust in God. No action occurred at this moment; he was proclaimed righteous in the sight of God because of the deep-seated faith he had that was going to change his life.

James 2:21 tells us that Abraham was justified when he offered up Isaac many years later (Gen. 22). It was at this time that he was justified in the sense that he "showed himself to be righteous," in the sight of man. The first event had an emphasis on God's perspective of Abraham; the second, on man's perspective of him.

This is the passage referenced on Day One that Martin Luther got hung up on, arguing that Paul and James were in disagreement. However, a close study of the text shows that they are not. "Paul wants to make clear that one 'gets into' God's kingdom only by faith; James insists that God requires works from those who are 'in.'"[17]

According to James 2:22, fill in the blanks: *You see that faith was* _____

_____, *and as a result of the works,* _____.

teleioó – to complete, accomplish, make perfect

By using Abraham, James gives an example of a faith that is not useless but is working in tandem with obedient actions. As two inseparable entities, faith and works were operating together in order to achieve a goal of spiritual maturity in Abraham's life. We've already studied a form of the Greek word, *teleioó,* used here for "perfected." It was the word first described on page 8 that spoke of implied perfection toward a given end; a maturity in order to fulfill a task. It speaks of something accomplished; a completion. Abraham's faith and works completed each other, and because of his works, there was no doubt of the sincerity of his faith.

Our actions match our passions. Do your actions demonstrate you're passionate about your faith?

James spent a great deal of time in Chapter Two reprimanding the recipients of this letter. Apparently, their actions were not matching their profession of faith and for that, he called into question the sincerity of their faith. Some of us need to ask ourselves if we would fall into the category that some of the original readers no doubt fell in to. Have we made a **sincere** profession of faith, or have we simply made an academic acknowledgement of God? If you are certain about the sincerity of your profession of faith, would the world recognize you as a Christian based on the fruit they see through your actions? Abraham demonstrated his faith to the world through his actions and not through a private, unspoken, undemonstrated faith. Our actions always match our passions. What do your actions say you're passionate about? Do your actions say you're passionate about your faith? The world is watching; what do they see in you?

---

17   Ibid., p. 114

Day Five – A Life of Surrender

Surrender. Even the mere mention of it may make us recoil. As men, we don't like the implications of giving up and giving in. It sounds and feels much too close to defeat. Yet, there can be no genuine Christlikeness without surrender.

Yesterday we saw that a faith that doesn't demonstrate itself consistently is useless; faith is not to be a one-time declaration, but an ongoing lifestyle. If it is sincere, it should change our actions, our focus, our choices, our very life. James used two illustrations of a working faith. The first was Abraham, who demonstrated his faith when he offered Isaac as a sacrifice to the Lord, even when the outcome seemed hopeless.

If our faith is sincere, it will affect every aspect of our life.

Read James 2:20-24.

The example of Abraham shows us that we are justified by the type of faith that can't help but demonstrate itself in complementary works. It's not about the value of the work, but the value of the faith that produces the work. At the risk of being redundant, let's reiterate that we are saved by faith and faith alone. When verse 24 says that man is not justified by faith alone, it is speaking of an insincere faith that has done nothing to change the life of the one who claims to have it. No work of our own can replace or add to what Christ did on the cross in order to get us "more saved." The emphasis on Abraham's "work" of offering Isaac demonstrates that his faith was sincere and that his trust in the God of his salvation was complete.

Would you say that your faith is consistently demonstrated by your actions? Would others agree? _____

Read James 2:25.

Rahab is often treated as an "afterthought" in this passage; however, God must have chosen her for a reason.

Most commentaries have much to say on James 2:14-26. They go to great lengths to prove that James and Paul did not contradict each other; they spend ample time elaborating on Abraham's justification and the amazing faith that he showed through his obedient action. When they come to verse 25, their message boils down to, "...and Rahab did a good job, too." Yet, it must be significant that out of all the figures God could have chosen to inspire James to use as an example alongside Abraham, He chose Rahab.

Why do you think God selected Rahab? Note your initial thoughts here.

_____

Read Joshua 2:1-21; 6:1-5, 16-17, 20-25.

The context of our passage in James focuses on something similar in the lives of Abraham and Rahab. But, let's first take a moment to focus on their dissimilarities. Abraham was, and is, an icon in the Bible. Particularly in the Jewish faith, he is held in extremely high regard. We as Christians like to ask, "What would Jesus do?" Children growing up in the Jewish faith may have worn the little bracelets that said "WWAD" - "What would Abraham Do?"

as they tried to follow his example. Abraham was willing to leave everything behind to follow God, he was willing to trust that God was going to do the impossible and give him a son in his old age, and he was willing to sacrifice that son. The list goes on. Although we do have examples of his imperfection, he is held in such high regard that his standard seems almost unattainable. If we're honest with ourselves, when asked whether we would be willing to go to the extent that he did in preparing to sacrifice Isaac, most of us would have to admit that we might draw the line there. Abraham was a model of working faith and no doubt deserves to be regarded with high esteem. But, as with many iconic figures, we tend to dismiss the possibility within ourselves of ever being capable of matching such a standard. It is therefore quite comforting that when God and James decided to give us examples of faith in action, they chose two people on such far ends of the human moral spectrum that we can all find ourselves somewhere in between.

How was Rahab referred to in the passage in Joshua? Rahab the _____

It is hard to imagine two more dissimilar people than Abraham and Rahab. But did they have something in common?

Whereas Abraham was the poster child for everything good to the Jews, Rahab was the questionable harlot. It is interesting that James chose to use her as an example of extreme faith following his chastisement of the churches for showing partiality within their fellowship. Certainly, Rahab would have been looked down upon and cast aside because of her sinful lifestyle. But, once again, God establishes the fact that He can, and will, be glorified by anyone who has faith enough to entrust their life to His hands.

Unlike Abraham, whose example might have seemed unattainable, Rahab was the underdog. We can picture Jewish children sitting eagerly as they listened to her story told again, cheering for the unlikely hero in a story where grace and mercy provided an underserved second chance. If God could use a prostitute, maybe he could use them as well!

Rahab shows us that God can, and will, be glorified by any willing vessel who entrusts their life to His hands.

Have you ever felt too ashamed, too guilty, too "anything" to be used by God? _____

How does the example of Rahab encourage you? _____

_____

When held to the example of Abraham's near-sacrifice of Isaac, it may be easy to throw up our hands and conclude that we will never measure up to such a faith. But Rahab, who seemed ordinary, or even hopeless, can help us to see that a life-changing faith can be realized by anyone willing to fully trust in God.

What did Rahab do in the story of Joshua and the battle of Jericho?

_____

God knew that Rahab's heart was available and ready to help; so He created an opportunity for her to act.

Thank God, He doesn't typecast in this story called life! He will, and does, use anyone who will sincerely recognize Him for who He is. In all of Jericho, the spies could have chosen anywhere to go, but God led them to "Rahab the harlot" "for God knew where they had a friend, though they did not."[18] He knew her heart was available and ready to help, so He created the opportunity for her to be used.

We live in a fast-paced society that thrives on activity and stress. When God asks, are you

---

18   Henry, *Commentary in One...*, p. 212

JAMES - LIVING A LIFE OF FAITH

too busy to take the time to answer with a "yes?" Are you too busy to even hear Him ask? Be very honest with yourself and God in this moment. Are you fully available for God's use today? If not, what stands in the way?

_____

_____

According to Joshua 2:3, who sent word to Rahab demanding the spies?_____

Are you available for God's use today as Rahab was?

Rahab was bold and daring in her faith, so much so that she was committing treason. Please note that this was quite possibly a new faith for Rahab. We don't know exactly when she chose to surrender her life to this God of the Israelites, but she certainly hadn't been raised in the teaching of the law as the Israelites were. She had only heard about the greatness of their God. Joshua 2:10 tells us that the inhabitants of Jericho had heard of the Israelite's deliverance from Egypt across the Red Sea and other ways that their God had provided for them in victory. Despite having no visual proof for herself, she had chosen to put faith in this God that she had only heard of. Verse nine records her telling the spies, "*I **know** that the Lord has given you the land...*" (emphasis added). Rahab's faith acted out of confidence in a God her eyes had never seen tangible evidence of. There is great irony here, as the Israelites had been wandering in the wilderness for 40 years because those who **had seen** God's miraculous provisions had doubted, and were denied entrance to the Promised Land.

Must God continuously "prove Himself" to you before you will trust and obey Him?

Rahab's faith acted in confidence in a God she had not seen.

Why or why not? _____

In a very real sense, Rahab had the threatening hands of death around her throat no matter what she chose. If she betrayed her king and country, she risked death at their hands. If she betrayed God, she would surely die with the rest of the city. Rahab recognized the God who stood above all manmade laws and chose to obey Him rather than men. Her faith in this crucial moment demonstrated more than academic knowledge of God.

Rahab's faith was demonstrated through her choices.

By this act, Rahab's faith was demonstrated through her choices. She knew why the spies were there and she knew that helping them might cost her life, but she recognized that this God was the One who was worth both living and dying for. If she lived, it would now be for His glory. If she died, it would be for the same. Her choice demonstrated confidence in God's nature, character, and reliability; her action made this apparent. Her choice was to obey; she simply could do no other. Pretty amazing faith from a "questionable prostitute." Surely, we can choose to live the same way; but do we?

What do your own choices demonstrate about our faith? - Your choices of time use? - Your choices in crisis? - Your everyday choices?

_____

Rahab's choice gave evidence that she had total reliance on the One who was able to provide. Our desired knee-jerk reaction is to become one that says, "I may not know what God is doing in this situation, but I know His character and I will trust Him. And I choose to act on that trust." Those actions affirm our sincere faith.

We've discovered that Rahab was an unlikely hero, and we are grateful that God gave us those examples in Scripture to give us hope when we feel hopeless. How appreciative we should be that He was willing to put her name beside Abraham's in order to give us another example of true faith. As awesome and relatable an example as Rahab is, we're still left wondering why James chose her out of all of the other faithful figures available. As Angie tried to answer that question she was repeatedly drawn back to one particular verse. Let's now focus on some similarities between Rahab, Abraham, and Christ that tie their stories together in a way that only God could orchestrate.

While James never tells us why he selected Abraham and Rahab as his examples of sincere, saving faith, there seems to be a common theme in their courageous acts that may connect them.

Read Joshua 2:14a, which follows Rahab's request for provision and deliverance:

> So the men said to her, "Our life for yours..."

In both Abraham and Rahab's examples, lives were being offered in obedience to God, and in both, deliverance from death was made available as a result of a demonstrated faith.

Many times our obedience to God must precede our understanding of His ways.

Abraham was willing to trade Isaac's life for obedience to God, having faith that one way or another God would work it out for good and continue to keep His promises. God had promised that Abraham would have descendants with numbers like the sands of the sea and the stars of the sky (Gen 15). To sacrifice Isaac was to threaten that promise, yet Abraham had seen God's miracles before and trusted that He would provide again.

God was willing to provide the blood of a ram to trade for Isaac's life when Abraham had shown great faith; the blood of one stood in place of another.

Rahab was willing to trade her own life for obedience to God, having faith that one way or another God would work it out for good and continue to be the God she'd heard of and placed her trust in.

Read Exodus 11:1,4-6 and 12:21-24

What similarities do you see between the Passover described in Exodus and the story of Rahab? _____

_____

In the story of Jericho, God instructed Rahab to display a scarlet cord in her window and remain within her house. In an act of great obedience that demonstrated her faith in God's adequate provision, she followed His specific instructions, and as a result, He protected her and all those gathered in her home just as He had promised. With striking similarity, God provided the same protection to all those gathered inside the Israelite homes displaying blood on their doorposts when the death angel passed by in Egypt. The scarlet-colored blood on the doorposts in Egypt provided immediate protection and showed their faith in a future provision of salvation.

Abraham and Rahab both offered lives in obedience to God; deliverance was made available due to demonstrated faith.

Abraham and Rahab both had faith that God would provide a way of escape; their actions demonstrated this faith in God's provision.

In both their cases, God had given specific instructions for Abraham and Rahab to follow; He gave them choices to make. If they followed His plans in obedient, surrendered faith, He offered a means of deliverance. **Because of their faith that acted based on their trust in God's reliable character, God provided a life-saving way of escape.** This willingness to trade one's life for faith in God is what symbolizes the deep faith God and James were trying to describe earlier in James 2, a faith that realizes the debt paid on our behalf, the life traded for our own. Today, God continues to offer a means of deliverance - His Son. What was true with Abraham and Rahab is true today; a sincere, obedient faith that acts is still required. On the cross, Christ was willing to say, "My life for yours." There was no provision for His own escape. He was, and is, God's only provision for our escape; He is our ram, our scarlet cord, the blood on our doorpost, our spotless Lamb.

On the cross, Christ said, "My life for yours." In response, are we willing to surrender our lives for His?

Does that really mean anything to us anymore? Rahab acted in faith because of the small amount she'd heard concerning the God of Israel. We have every miracle and promise in the Bible and the very clear gospel, which Rahab had no clue about. We haven't just heard a rumor of this great God, we have thousands of years of evidence of His worthiness of our service. Are we willing to trade our lives for His, to give our lives for service to Him? Are we willing to trade our life in for a life that shows faith through our every action, decision, choice, and priority? When we tell God that we "give Him our lives," what do we mean? You may sometimes sing the same praise song we do, "Lord, I give you my life, I give you my soul. I live for you alone." Really? Can we sing that in sincerity with a straight face? Or have those words become so cliché that we've forgotten their meaning? Is He truly the primary, passionate focus of our lives or just the focus of our extra time – should we happen to actually come up with any? Can we truly say we'd give up our lives for Him if we can't give up our time to spend in His Word, at His feet in prayer, or loving His people? If He doesn't win first place gentlemen, we lose.

We've asked if our faith is sincere. Now let's ask how deep it is. Is it deep enough to commit to Him our time, priorities, and passions, trusting Him to do more in, and with, our lives than we could have done holding onto them for ourselves?

It can be tempting to say that this type of faith can't be expected of just anyone, and certainly not too quickly. But, Rahab shows us differently on both fronts. She was likely an infant in her faith, and yet a giant in her obedience. It's humbling and challenging to consider her example of risking her life for the God she had only heard of. We also cannot argue that she was simply a woman of such high character that this sort of action came easily for her. No, we know that her past character was questionable, but what an awesome example of God's grace that is ready to clean the slate and use any who are willing. A tarnished life was cleaned and restored in order to be used mightily…"amazing grace, how sweet the sound" indeed. In fact, her life shows us that the greatness of sin has no bearing on the great impact God can still have on a surrendered life. Mercy is always available to the repentant, and that mercy is shown through the life of the forgiven as they walk forward in faith.

Rahab shows us that even "babes in Christ" can demonstrate tremendous faith and obedience.

Thank Him now for the mercy He has shown you, as well. Abraham and Rahab were each willing to risk great personal loss as they surrendered to God in faith. Ask Him what He'd like you to risk in order to follow Him in a sincere, surrendered faith. Your life is now His – He bought you at a great price. Go ahead and surrender it to Him guys – it's okay. In fact, the life surrendered to Him is the only one worth living!

WEEK FOUR: A CONTROLLED AND GENTLE FAITH

Day One – The Teaching Life

We've all heard the saying, "Put your money where your mouth is." James has spent a great deal of time emphasizing the necessity of "putting your action where your faith is." He has given a few practical examples of ways to do this, such as walking faithfully through trials and dealing with one another without partiality. He is now going to give instruction concerning an area of the Christian walk where we all need improvement – the use of our tongue. There is nothing that reveals the intent of the heart more clearly than the tongue.

James warned about teaching God's Word due to the greater judgment involved.

Read James 3:1.

What is the warning given in verse one? _____

What is the reason given for the warning? _____

First, it is important to point out that James is not discouraging his brothers and sisters in Christ from speaking boldly concerning the Word of God, for we are all called to go into the world in order to make disciples (Matthew 28:19). He is, rather, warning them about seeking a position teaching the Word within the church because of the greater judgment they will face.

didaskalos – instructor, a teacher, a master

We're going to employ our "context is king" rule for interpreting Scripture at this point and focus on the historical context of the passage. The Greek word, *didaskalos*, means "instructor, a teacher, a master." It is necessary for us to remember that this first century church was still influenced by the way they had previously conducted their religion as Jews in the past. Rabbis had been their teachers and were held in extremely high regard; *rhabbi*, in fact, means "my master, my teacher." The teacher who had taken the place of the rabbi was now respected highly, as were the apostles and prophets (1 Cor. 12:28). These teachers were responsible for relaying Christian doctrine, and this position came with much prestige, especially in areas marked by illiteracy. Teachers held great responsibility in their hands, as they were sometimes the only means by which the Word was conveyed and were considered the "be all and end all" of its interpretation. For this reason, James gives a strict warning about volunteering for this position.

rhabbi – my master, my teacher

What were some of the temptations that these teachers could have found themselves up against?

_____

_____

Read Matthew 23:8.

Jesus instructed His disciples not to allow anyone to call them Rabbi, for they only had one Master and were not to seek that glory for themselves. This is the distinction James is seeking to convey. While he does not want those who are spiritually-gifted in teaching (Rom. 12:7) to shirk their responsibility to answer the call to teach, he is warning them of the dangers of pride in that position. Even the meaning of rabbi, my master, implies greatness; it wouldn't take much for that title to go to one's head.

Now please read the verses preceding Jesus' warning: Matthew 23:4-7.

A teacher may be tempted to take credit away from God.

The Pharisees and scribes battled pride. Their position of authority and respect gave them a sense of piety that they could easily lord over the heads of the people. They would certainly be tempted to revel in their high places of honor at functions, would take pleasure in the unquestioning service of their followers, and would probably take great pride in any apparent advancement of their students. Instead of giving God glory and credit for what He has accomplished in someone else's life, a teacher is susceptible to falling into the temptation of taking that credit away from God. The statement, "He learned everything he knows from me," is an example of this sort of pride. The glory should belong to neither the teacher nor the student, but to God alone.

The teacher of God's Word is accountable for their influence on others – good and bad.

As the teacher's knowledge of the Word would be highly respected, they would, no doubt, be tempted to take pride in their level of insight. As their self-confidence grew, they may have taken liberties with their "right of insight," falling into the danger of twisting Scripture for their own purposes. Instead of admitting they may not have known an answer to a deep theological question, making something up would have been an option that would feed their pride and protect their ego. If they desired more subordination from those "beneath" them, translating Scripture in such a way that would demand this would be a simple way to make it happen. In this way, false teachers were capable of not only twisting minor details, but also the entire Christian religion for those who would blindly follow.

The fallen teacher gives his students cause to doubt God's Word.

Because of this extreme responsibility, the teacher of God's Word is under a stricter judgment. They are accountable for their influence on others, their ability to both nurture and harm. All of the temptations listed above for those teaching in the early church apply to those teaching in this day and age. Humble teachers will bless others and receive blessing from God; those who teach with pride and with selfish motives will have to answer to God for their actions. Knowing this is true, I try to follow the advice of one of my favorite Bible teachers, Chuck Swindoll, who daily asks himself, "What's your motive, Swindoll?" As I dare to teach, I need to ask myself the same question – "What's your motive, Vitt?"

Read Acts 15:24.

What had these false teachers done by what they had said?

_____

Confusion leads to chaos and Satan loves nothing more than causing chaos in a local body of believers. He also delights in inviting judgment on those who teach. If he is able to publicly destroy a teacher of God's Word, he can more easily get his hands on the students as well. The fallen teacher gives them cause to doubt.

For example, by pressing the topic of circumcision in the early church, false teachers troubled the minds of their followers, which led to confusion. The task of rightly dividing the Word of God should make every teacher live his or her life with a great deal of fear and trembling at the responsibility. By carelessly throwing out their own interpretations and mandates, these false teachers harmed the very students who trusted them, making their duty as teachers entirely counter-productive. Teachers of God's Word cannot base their lessons or leadership on their own speculation, opinions, or agendas. The ripple effect within the Kingdom of God following this sort of action is huge. The attitude behind teaching is of the utmost importance. God needs teachers to be tools in His hands; He doesn't need for them to think they are holding the tools that should be shaping others. Teachers are to be shaped by God and in turn, teach what God has shown them and allow God to shape others through the Holy Spirit. Teachers bear an awesome responsibility for nurturing people in the faith; this is to be done with great love and care. There is no room for selfishness and pride. As reminded in Acts 24:16, the teacher does well to always maintain a blameless conscience before both God and men.

Teachers cannot use their position to teach their own speculation, opinions, or agendas.

Read James 3:2.

As stated earlier, we **all** stumble, we are **all** susceptible to sin, especially sins associated with the tongue. The teacher has just been singled out as a specific example of one who bears great responsibility, and now his warning is narrowed down by specifying the agents by which he can do the most damage – words. The teacher of Scripture is a constant public example and his teaching has the ability to affect many. This holds him to a higher standard. The teacher's words can be used for great good or great devastation, and he possesses the possibility for causing either daily. The negative "loose tongue" of a teacher gives the impression to his followers that they can follow his example of careless speaking. The negative impact of such speech can lead to great destruction.

James 3:2 makes a transition from the "teacher" to "all," but the word "for" at the beginning of the verse implies that he is still referring back to the previous thought. Therefore, the message of this verse applies to the teacher as well as everyone else. Before we jump away from the topic of teachers, though, it is important to point out that this verse does not imply a "get out of jail free" card for those who do not hold positions as teachers. Before anyone says, "Phew, I don't have the gift of teaching, I'm glad none of this lesson applies to me," let's think about the broader application.

The tongue can be used for great good or great destruction.

Yes, James was specifically speaking to those who might fall into the temptation of pride associated with the prestige that came with the role of teaching within the church at that time. But, we can apply the truths to our everyday lives in a very practical manner as well. Unless you live in a complete bubble, your words and actions are teaching someone, somewhere. No matter how old you are, someone younger is always watching – and learning.

I am the youngest of three sons. For many years as a boy, I couldn't wait to grow up to be just like my older brothers, Chris and Joe. While they likely never realized it themselves, I was always studying their lives, looking for ways I could be just as cool as they were. Because Chris played golf and basketball, so did I. Because Joe lifted weights and sang in multiple choirs, so did I. I even chose my first college to simply be on the same campus as they were on. But, the thing that comes to mind most clearly about the uncanny influence they had on me has to do with the purchase of my first (and only) motorcycle - a Yamaha 400 Special. What a sweet ride. Only problem was, I was 13 years old at the time, and it would be 9 months before I could even ride it with a permit to and from school "by the most direct route." Did I mention that the high school was literally less than one block from my house? But, you see, I HAD to have a motorcycle, simply because my big brother had one. I was watching and I was learning what I thought a man was supposed to be from their example.

The point is this - someone is always looking up to us, and most times, we may have no idea that they are. Our lives, through spoken words as well as unspoken actions, are sending messages, and whether we like to admit it or not, we are always teaching. We hold a great responsibility to live a life pleasing to the Lord, so that "students" looking on will be pointed to Him and not turned away from the faith. Those younger in their faith are looking to those who are more seasoned. Others may be looking to your example in both good times and bad. Children watch other kids' parents to see how they relate. Teenagers look up to college kids, children to the teens. The list could continue indefinitely, but the universal truth is that our lives teach. The prevailing questions are, "What am I teaching – and to whom?"

The universal truth is that our lives teach!

Perhaps the most practical example of this may be the parent-child relationship. How many of us, as adults, have caught ourselves sounding just like one of our parents (and usually at a time when we wish we hadn't)? Even without trying, we, as children, learned their mannerisms and subtle characteristics through our time observing them. Likewise, our own children study us. What messages are we conveying to them? What characteristics of our own do we hope they do or do not pick up?

You may not be your child's schoolteacher, but your life is certainly teaching them by example. What are some positive characteristics that you hope they pick up on?

_____

_____

What are some negative areas you pray that they don't?

_____

_____

Your life is teaching your children by example; what are they learning?

Are you willing to make the necessary changes to teach them something different?

That question is not intended to make anyone feel guilty. In fact, we all know that none of us lead perfect lives and we all have room for improvement. Yet, it is important for us to consider that type of question and answer honestly, for when we gloss over these topics without thoroughly examining ourselves, we can be tempted to ignore any potential problems that may need addressing. As I examine my own life, I asked myself a series of questions. We will end with them today; I challenge you to honestly answer them yourselves. The questions have an emphasis on our influence over our children, but they go beyond our parental persuasion. As you reflect on these questions, don't only consider the answer for the way you influence your children, but for the others who are observing your life from day to day as well: coworkers, friends, family, acquaintances, fellow church members, strangers at the store…

-Am I living a life of faith that clearly shows my children that God is #1 in my life, or that He is a side note?

-Does my schedule tell my kids that church is optional? Do they see that everything else in life is optional, but time set apart for service to God is not?

-Do my kids consistently see God in and through my life, or do they feel justified in their own sin because I do "it," too?

-Is "Christian" my "stage name" on Sunday or the true description of my life in its entirety; does "Sunday Dave" match "Monday thru Saturday Dave?"

-Am I teaching my kids to be honest in their dealings?

- Would my children be right to call me a hypocrite?

-Do I want them to respond to hard situations in life the same way I do?

-Do they see forgiveness and peace in me or conflict and strife?

-Have I taught them humility by admitting when I am wrong, or pride by defending what I shouldn't?

-Am I teaching them the fruit of the Spirit by my actions and not just my words? Do they recognize in me: love, joy, peace, patience, kindness, goodness, faithfulness, gentleness, and self-control?

-This one really haunts me - Would my children be able to accurately describe Christ to their friends by simply describing their dad?

Read Hebrews 5:12.

Are we taking time to learn and grow in the Word?

Jesus warned about pride in one's status as teacher, but also commissioned everyone to go into all the world. James warns about the high standard set for those who attempt to teach the Word, but Hebrews chastises those who stay "baby Christians" when they should be learning enough to teach others. Obviously, there is a healthy balance to be found. Are we taking the time to learn and grow in the Word so that we are prepared to give an answer for our faith (1 Pet. 3:15)? Are we teaching others through our actions of faithfulness, or are we settled into a busy life that leaves that job to others whom we deem "official teachers?"

Ask the Lord to open your eyes to areas He needs to change in order to make you a better teacher to those who are watching and listening. Ask Him to reveal areas where growth is needed and then commit to making those changes. Change can be hard, even frightening, but with God's help, all things are possible. Even if in one moment we fail, we can begin fresh with the next and He is there with new mercy to start again. Ask Him to speak to you now. Be still and listen, and note any direction He gives below.

We need God's help to make changes in order to be a better teacher to those who are watching and listening. Will you ask Him for it?

_____

_____

_____

Day Two – Taming the Tongue

Yesterday, I wrote about the influence my brothers had on me as a younger man. One of those brothers was a serious bodybuilder and went on to win the Mr. Kansas title while we were in college. During those years, I was one of his primary spotters. We were both in great shape at that time – he was just a generally bigger shape than I was! By the time the Mr. Kansas competition came around, you could literally see every muscle in his body because each was so well-defined. Quads and calves, pecs and trapezoid, abs and deltoids – they all popped out on command. Yet, as massive and powerful as each muscle was, none of them contained the strength of the muscle we each try to subdue within the cage of our mouth on a daily basis. Ounce for ounce, the tongue is the strongest muscle in our bodies. No wonder it can do such damage, and no wonder controlling it is one of the most challenging tasks known to man.

If we can control our tongue, we can control our entire body.

The teacher has been warned in James 3:1. His primary tool for teaching is his tongue and James clarifies in verse two that with the tongue, we **all** stumble. We know from the context of our study, that James has been talking about what it is to have sincere faith. He is now preparing to elaborate on practical, everyday ways to demonstrate it.

Read James 3:2-5a.

Apparently, the tongue is at the pinnacle of our efforts at self-control, for if we can learn to control it, we can control our entire being.

This should sound familiar as James is continuing to build his case for our need to control our tongues one brick at a time. Let's reread James 1:26.

If anyone thinks himself to be _____*, and yet does not* _____

_____*, but deceives* _____*, this man's*

_____ *is* _____.

Sincere faith is marked by active obedience.

We studied this passage on Week Two, Day Five. On that day, we discussed that this man's "religion" is his worship and that worship is an "outpouring of selflessness in obedience to God in order to honor Him simply because He is worthy of honor." Our active faith is a life of worship. We have seen the word "perfect" appear multiple times already in our study. Each time, it has referred to a fulfillment or completion, a maturity in order to fulfill a task. Again, we find *téleios* (perfect) in James 3:2. As our understanding of what James has meant about a sincere faith has grown, we can apply *téleios* better. Sincere faith is demonstrated by active obedience and active obedience is genuine worship. As stated above, genuine worship consistently puts God ahead of ourselves. Sacrificing self for God in a consistent manner leads to maturity and wisdom, which makes us *téleios* – full grown, complete, and thoroughly disciplined. James 3:2 tells us that a thoroughly-disciplined Christian possesses a bridled tongue. We all stumble in many ways, but the effort to control the tongue is a worthy cause, for it affects our entire lives, not just one part.

To support his emphasis on the power of the tongue, James gives two word pictures: a horse's bit and a ship's rudder. We will look at two main points concerning these illustrations; namely, the impact each has on determining the direction of something else and the relatively small size of each in comparison to the "beast" it directs.

The bit for the horse, and the rudder of the ship, are both used to guide a "beast" in whatever direction it is to go. Likewise, the tongue defines the direction we allow ourselves to turn, which can impact how others perceive us and affect how we are received. How we are received directly affects whether we can or cannot be used by God. Someone who turns others away due to their uncontrolled speech cannot be an effective tool in God's hands. Instead, our words should be seasoned with salt that creates a thirst for God in others (Col. 4:6).

Our speech can determine the direction of our lives.

Do you think the way you speak allows God to use you effectively?_____

God placed our hands and feet in the open to be used freely for His work, yet He placed our tongues in an enclosed spot where we can readily bite them. The bit and rudder are best used when diligently working toward their positive purpose and in their proper, concealed place. When hanging in the barn, out in the open, the bit does the horse no good. In fact, it rusts. When it is in use, it determines the direction of the horse, but only when attached to reins that are held by a skilled rider. In James' illustrations, we are the horse, we are the ship, and the tongue (bit and rudder) may control our lives positively or negatively. Both have potential to lead their beast into safety or disaster; both the horse and ship can be used for great good or great destruction. The questions are: Who is holding the reins? Who is at the helm? Are you or is God? A horse cannot effectively hold its own reins; a ship cannot steer itself. Similarly, we cannot control our tongue on our own; it is a God-sized task.

Controlling the tongue is a God-sized task.

Verse 5 compares the tiny tongue to the body it controls. By stating that the tongue "boasts of great things," it would be easy to assume that it is speaking of prideful boasts that a person can make using their tongue. Keeping with the context of the examples, though, we see that James is still speaking metaphorically about the tongue. As the small bit can boast of the power it has over the horse, the tongue boasts of the control it has on the direction of our lives, and that direction can be either positive or negative.

What are some positive ways our words can be used?

_____

Never underestimate the power of the spoken word.

What are some negative ways our words can be used?

_____

Never underestimate the power of the spoken word. James is about to delve deeply into the negative impact it can have. However, let's first take a moment to appreciate its potential for good. Communication is vital to our human existence. If we all walked around in complete silence, we would all be suspiciously wondering what everyone else was thinking! God gave us our tongues to speak; He just wants us to keep them in check.

Read Proverbs 16:24 and Ephesians 4:29.

Make no mistake about it, the words you convey to others can be life-saving and "bone-healing." We live in a world that is judgmental and brutal; a kind, encouraging word in a cold, cruel world is an amazing gift from God. Never take for granted the value of a kind word; it's like medicine for the soul. As you walk through your day, if you think of something kind about those you encounter, tell them. Harsh words can crush a spirit, silence is nearly impossible to interpret, but a kind word is seldom misunderstood. Never assume those around you have had their fill of kind words and encouragement; we don't believe there is such a thing.

Harsh words can crush a spirit, and silence is impossible to interpret, but a kind word is seldom misunderstood.

Think of someone right now who you could extend an encouraging word to and make it a point to do so today. Making an effort to share encouraging words on a daily basis will not only bless others, but will bring blessing to you as well.

Read Colossians 3:17.

Absolutely everything, all of our deeds, and all of our words, are to bring God glory. We were created for this very reason – to worship God and bring Him glory. It must disappoint Him greatly when we use the most powerful tool He gave us in ways that do anything other than that. We have the potential to bring others to Christ with our spoken words. Like a warhorse and a battleship, we have the opportunity to fight against Satan in the battle he continues to wage against God and His people (Eph. 6). Our tongues, equipped with the Sword of the Gospel are our greatest weapons. As we walk through our days, we need to keep in mind that we are indeed in the midst of a battle and must constantly ask ourselves which army the weapon of our tongue is fighting for. Remember, the tongue guides us in the direction we will go. We must be on the alert not to allow it to guide us into the enemy camp.

All of our deeds and all of our words are to bring glory to God.

Read James 3:5-8.

James has gone from two examples of small things that have big impact (either positive or detrimental), to a very negative illustration of a tiny thing that can cause vast destruction.

What does James compare our tongues to in verse 6? _____

One fit of rage can unleash words that should never have been spoken, but will never be forgotten.

It only takes one spark to set ablaze a magnificent forest of trees that took hundreds of years to grow. One false rumor can destroy the testimony of another person in a matter of days or destroy a vibrant church before they even know what hit them. One caustic remark can crush the spirit of someone whom God has been working to build up for use in His Kingdom, causing them to doubt the progress He's made in them. One fit of rage can unleash words that never should have been spoken, but will never be forgotten. Although each fire eventually dies out, the damage is often catastrophic. Researchers say that we typically remember only 10% of what we read, between 20 and 50% of what we hear (so read this book out loud), but 80% of what we personally experience. Experts tell us that the best way to increase what we recall is through repetition. Men, those around us will NOT forget the destructive words we carelessly use because they experience them so personally, and even if they don't want to, they repeat them in the theater of their minds frequently.

Yet, it's amazing (and foolish) that we use our tongues so carelessly when they hold such potential for great danger. We've all seen TV shows where ticking bombs are handled with the most calculated care possible due to their potential to destroy lives. Our tongues should be handled no differently, for their power can do the same. We ought to constantly consider our tongues as undiffused bombs, capable of devastation, and carefully count the potential cost before each thing we say. A diffused bomb poses no threat of danger. Likewise, biting our tongue will diffuse destruction, whereas igniting it when we shouldn't will harm not only others, but ourselves.

Give an example of something you wish you could go back and "unsay."

_____

_____

Most of us learn the need for biting the tongue the hard way.

Most of us have many of those examples, and many of us have learned the need for biting our tongue the hard way. We know this is true because we find consistently firm instructions about it in Scripture. "Nothing seems to trip a believer more than a dangling tongue."[19] Wouldn't it be embarrassing if your tongue hung out so far that you could literally trip on it? If we did, we'd do whatever possible to keep it hidden; to prevent it from bringing us embarrassment and humiliation. Of course, we don't have a tongue that literally reaches the ground; however, because our speech can trip up our entire lives, we should take great care to control all we say so as to avoid our own humiliation.

Why, then, if we realize the dangers of our words, is it so hard to control our speech? Our tongues are the outlet for our hearts, and our hearts demand to be heard. We were born with a nature that believes we have a fundamental right to be heard. When babies want to eat, they make themselves heard. When toddlers don't get their way, they make themselves heard. No one has to teach us this skill; it's innate. As we grow older, we may no longer scream when we're hungry or fight for our right to the toys in the nursery, but we do still consider it our "right" to be heard. "I have the right to express my opinion." "My thoughts need to be heard." "I need to give them a piece of my mind!" "I *have* to defend myself!" "If no one can get this right, I'm going to tell them how it should be done." "That person is out of line, and if no one else is going to tell them, I will!" Or maybe worst of all, "I just can't hold this in, I *have* to tell *someone*!" Oh, the dangerous "spark" that lies within those sentences and so many more like them.

Our tongues are the outlets for our hearts, which long to be heard.

In C.S. Lewis', *The Horse and His Boy*, one of the children tries to speak with Aslan, the Lion, concerning the business of someone else. Aslan's reply was simply, "I am telling you your story, not hers. I tell no one any story but his own." "It's not your story" are four words that are repeated on a regular basis around the Smith home when someone tries to nose their way into a situation that does not involve them. May we challenge you to remember these words and apply them when you are tempted to interject your opinion into a story that is not your own? Our "two cents" that we think is worth a million dollars, may land us and others in great debt if they're spent where they don't belong. Most of the time, it is best to

It is best to concern ourselves only with our story.

19   Walvoord and Zuck, *BKC NT*, p. 827

simply concern ourselves only with **our** story. Aslan can handle everyone else's story – He doesn't need our help.

The range of sins that can be committed with our words is so vast that there is no way we can cover them in a short study. From the harm they can cause when used in a rage, to the devastation they can bring to an innocent party slandered, to every hurt in between, their potential is incalculable. The next few verses tell us why.

Read James 3:6 again.

The full range of sin can use the tongue for its outlet.

The tongue is the very world of iniquity. In other words, the full range of sin can use the tongue for its outlet. The tongue opens up the entire can of sinful worms. It is the outlet for bitterness, envy, and pride. Without it, a person might harbor sinful feelings, but they won't drag others into it if they remain silent.

Read Matthew 15:11, 18-19. What makes a man unclean?

_____

What comes from our tongue makes us unclean and reveals what is unclean within our hearts. The next portion of James 3:6 supports this. "*The tongue is set among our members,*" or "is the part of our body," that defiles our whole person. The word used here for defile is *spiloó,* which means "stain." We've already been told in James 1:27 that pure and undefiled religion (worship) is "*to keep oneself unstained by the world.*" James has been painting an entire picture of someone with sincere faith who is willing to act on it and mature in it in order to live a life of worship that is pleasing to the Lord. The unrestrained tongue can "spiritually stain" the entire person, causing detriment in the progress toward spiritual maturity. In contrast, the practice of holding one's tongue builds a reliance on God and an endurance in our faith. Perhaps today's entire lesson can be distilled to this: The whole body can be drawn into sin by the tongue, whereas the whole body can be rescued from sin by the control of the same.

spiloó – stain

Not only does verse 6 say that the tongue can negatively stain our entire lives, but it goes on to say that it furthermore sets the course of our lives. Simply stated, our tongues determine our course, which directly relates back to the illustration of the horse and the ship. Even more frightening is the fact that this life's rudder, with its destructive potential, comes directly from hell.

geenna – a reference to Gehenna and the Hinnon Valley

The word used for hell in this verse is *geenna,* meaning Gehenna. Gehenna referred to the Hinnom Valley south of Jerusalem where, in the Old Testament, the Jews had sacrificed their children to Molech (Jer. 7:31). In New Testament times, this valley had become the dumping site for putrid refuse that was burned with constant fire. Because of the hideous association with this valley, Jesus often used it as a word picture to describe the ever-burning fires of hell.

What's your reaction to the fact that your negative words are set on fire by hell?

_____

Angie and I each grew up in areas where a barrel could be used for burning our paper trash.

That smell brings back fond childhood memories to this day and the smell of a bonfire can't be beat, either. However, Gehenna referred to a valley that emitted only a nauseating stench; there were definitely no s'mores being roasted over this fire! Our core being is made known through our tongues, and all those who hear our words "smell" whether what is inside is good or rotten. When you walk into a house where dinner is being prepared, you're likely to have one of two possible reactions. 1) "Mmm, what's cooking?" or 2) "Ugh, what's burning?" When others hear the message of your heart expressed through your tongue, will they be pleased with what's cooking, or will they be turned away by what's burning? What do you smell like today?

What does Proverbs 16:27 say a worthless man's words are like? _____

Our words can assassinate another person.

Remember Gehenna as the source of lies, rage, complaining, cursing, boasting, gossip, slander, etc., the next time you feel that there are words "burning within you" that just have to come out. The source of that "burning" is hell, plain and simple. When we are reminded that the Valley of Hinnom had been a place of child sacrifice, we may wonder how could they do such a thing and still call themselves "children of God?" But, our words can so easily assassinate the character of another person. We hold life-giving and life-taking power in our mouths (Pro. 18:21).

I remember my dad teaching me to use a rifle. Wisely, I was not given an AK-47 to fire rapidly in any direction I wanted. I was handed a single-shot 0.22 and told to stop, take careful aim, steady myself, and then gently squeeze the trigger. Before we speak, we need to stop and think, because our tongues are like rifles and our words are the bullets. Before we "pull the trigger," we should literally ask ourselves, "What do I want this situation to look like five years from now? Will these words turn this into a day I will regret?" If we think our words might harm, we should choose to hold them realizing the potential long-term ramifications. We need to do everything possible not to haphazardly run ahead with our words. A fool rushes in with many words, but wisdom is found in the bitten tongue.

A fool rushes in with many words, but the wise hold their tongue.

James 3:7-8 simply elaborates on the difficulty of taming a tongue that is fueled by hell. The end of verse eight says the tongue is full of deadly poison, giving the picture of a venomous snake ready with his deadly strike (Rom. 3:13; Ps. 140:3). In the same sentence, the tongue is called a restless evil. This is why it is so difficult to tame; it is restless, constantly tempted by the fire within that is fueled by our sin nature. No wonder taming the tongue is a God-sized task. We say we just *can't* hold in our rage, we just *have* to let out our frustrations, we just *need* to express our opinion, it's *impossible* not to, we just can't... It's true, *we* can't, but we serve a God who can. Our God is the God of the impossible. As Angie's husband has said, "It only stands to reason that if He created the Red Sea and all the natural laws that keep it in place, He can also part the same sea." No one can tame the tongue, but the God of the impossible can give us the strength to hold it and use it for His good. Will we let Him?

We serve a God who can do the impossible; including helping us hold our tongue.

Men, as we close today, are there people in your life you have wounded with either a well-aimed or a stray bullet? If so, there is no better time than now to seek them out, ask their forgiveness and apply some bone-healing words.

Day Three – What Goes in is What Comes Out

The letter James wrote contains running themes. He never completely dropped an idea, but, like a turning wheel, each element keeps coming back up, allowing him to elaborate on it and deepen the level of understanding with each pass. One thing we can be certain of by this point is that he is thoroughly annoyed with double-mindedness. In Chapter One, James calls out the double-minded man, labeling him unstable and wavering. Such a man is not to expect anything from the Lord because he asks God for wisdom, yet refuses to let go of his own agenda. In Chapter Two, double-mindedness returns in the form of one who claims to have faith but shows no evidence of it. Now, in Chapter Three, the tongue, itself, is portrayed as double-minded and rebuked for speaking one way toward the Lord and another way toward man.

James contains running themes that keep coming back up.

Read James 3:9-12.

What does verse nine accuse the tongue of doing?

_____

What does the end of verse nine point out about the people we "curse?"

_____

kataraomai – to curse, doom, wish evil upon

To the devout Jew, blessing God was seen as the highest form of speech, whereas cursing was the lowest. To curse, *kataraomai,* someone in the ancient world was "to desire that they be cut off from God and experience eternal punishment,"[20] literally, to damn them. To wish such a thing on man, God's highest creation who was made in His image, is deplorable. Yet, cursing does not have to be this extreme. Soon, James will confront his readers concerning conflict, and his current comment about cursing could have been in reference to slanders and disputes. We do not have to wish a negative eternity on someone to make their earthly life miserable with our words. Either way, James emphatically tells us that we cannot both bless God and curse man. In fact, the language he uses in verse 10 is the strongest possible in the Greek. Our modern translations of verse 10 lose the impact, but when you read the words *"these things ought not to be this way,"* picture a very frustrated pastor, pointing his finger at a congregation full of backbiting gossips and shouting, "This is just WRONG! So, KNOCK IT OFF RIGHT NOW!"

The character of our heart is revealed by our words.

James is apparently very fed up with inconsistency in the church. He is calling for consistent faith, consistent action, consistent obedience, and consistent speech. The double-minded person may be able to fool their fellow Christians in the other areas that James addressed, but the tongue will always give them away. The character of the heart is shown through our words. As stated before, verse 9 doesn't have to strictly apply to the most extreme form of cursing. Christians can bless God in one moment and curse man in another in very subtle ways. Consider this completely random and hypothetical situation. Let's say that I spent the week preparing a top-notch Bible study lesson on the need to control the tongue, and on Sunday morning I walked into my classroom and wowed the class members with yet

---

20   Moo p. 133

another brilliant presentation of God's Word (you recognize sarcasm by this time I hope). Feeling rather satisfied with myself and being totally exhausted from being such a useful tool in God's hands, all I want to do when I get home is chill out on the couch and watch the final round of the Masters. A master teacher wanting to watch some master golfers – perfectly understandable, isn't it guys? Suddenly, one of my children walks into the room and has "the nerve" to stand between me and the 18th green at Augusta National. Are you kidding me? With a grunt, I mute the TV and shout, "Hello? What are you doing? Can't you see I'm busy?" While I did not specifically "curse" at them, I clearly sent a message that I wished they weren't around, and my careless words caused harm rather than blessing. Unfortunately, we do that sort of thing frequently. We teach our children to play nice and yet we turn around and gossip about a friend. We stick a Christian emblem on the back of our car and yell at someone when they cut us off in traffic. We talk so patiently to the stranger on the phone, and yell at our spouse as soon as we hang up. My friends, "these things ought not to be this way!"

Describe areas in your life where you may feel susceptible to this bad habit.

_____

_____

When our hearts and minds are set on God and His Word, our speech will honor God and edify others.

The heart is "telling." If our speech consistently brings honor to God and builds others up, it demonstrates that our hearts and minds are set on God and His Word. If, however, we are consistently found talking out of both sides of our mouths, our tongues have revealed the true "double" state of our hearts.

Read Psalm 119:11.

"I have hidden Your Word in my heart that _____."(NIV)

tsaphan – to treasure up

Yes, the tongue seems to be the unstoppable villain, but we said last time that with God's help we can be victorious. Thankfully, we are clearly given the silver bullet for conquering it in this passage.

Read James 3:11-12.

James uses rhetorical questions to support his point that two opposite things cannot possibly come from a single source. Since our heart is the source of what comes from our tongue, whatever comes out of our mouth reveals the heart's true nature. As mentioned in Day Four of Week Two, Jeremiah 15:16 says that Jeremiah **ate** the Word of God and it became **the** joy and delight of his heart. Nobody is suggesting that we eat our Bibles, but we are to metaphorically devour the Word because it provides life-giving nourishment beyond what any food has to offer. We are to breathe in His Word as if it were our very breath. The Hebrew word for "hidden" in Psalm 119:11 is *tsaphan*, meaning to "treasure up." We are to store up and treasure God's Word as if it were our most valuable possession. We are not only to treasure it in the sense of holding it dearly due to its great value; we are to consider it our treasure because it is our supply for life. His Word is to be the supply for our own provision and for feeding others. As we feed on it, we will in turn be able to feed others. As we inhale and exhale it, it will freshen our breath as **His** words flow from **our** mouths. It is Listerine for the soul, and most of us need to gargle with it more! ☺ If the Word, hidden in our heart, is the source from which we speak, we will not be double-minded in our speech and we will keep from sinning with our tongue.

Our breath will always be sweet if His words flow from our mouths.

Read Matthew 6:21. Are you spending enough time in the Word of God that it is the treasury from which you draw all of your speech? _____

Dusty Bibles lead to dirty lives.

Whatever a sponge absorbs, is what will ooze out of it when squeezed. Likewise, what goes into your heart is what comes out of your mouth. If you are taking in the Word, the Word will come out. But, in this world, the Word is not a popular thing to take in. We may spend countless hours absorbing numerous other things in the name of entertainment, while God's Word typically collects dust on the shelf and maybe gets opened once a week. According to the most recent Neilson report, the average American home has nearly 3 TV sets and only 2.5 people, with the average viewer watching over 5 hours of TV/day, 151 hours/month. According to George Barna, the average American home also has the same number of Bibles – 3. However, less than half of the people claim to have even read it at all in any given week, and among those who do, the average amount of time spent in God's Word was 52 minutes. Thirty-five hours of TV vs. 52 minutes of God's Word – is it really any wonder that we struggle controlling our words, when we continue to pollute the stream flowing through our hearts with contaminated water? It's bound to taint us.

With what are you filling your heart and mind?

What do you spend the majority of your free time doing?

_____

Because we freely toss words around constantly, we may forget that they are revealing our heart to others at all times. We may be showing things we never intended others to see. Our hearts tell all, just like our kids in Sunday School who tell every one of our family secrets during prayer request time! So, be careful little tongue what you say!

What does your tongue say about your own heart?

_____

Do you primarily seek to hear or to be heard?

Does your tongue say that your heart is selfish, quick-tempered, prideful, or greedy? We don't have to sound blatantly sinful for our tongues to get us into trouble. Do we dominate every conversation, giving the impression that we are the only one in the room who matters; or do we allow others to speak as well? Do we interrupt, giving the impression that what others have to say isn't important? Are we condescending? Do we always make sure we build ourselves up in public, sometimes at the cost of tearing others down? Do we twist the truth just enough to give a good impression, to get ourselves out of trouble, or to have the most impressive story? Are we critical concerning things that truly aren't important? Do we vent our own frustrations freely, not realizing that we may be weighing others down too much? Are we a constant source of grumbling and negativity, making others weary? Do we make inappropriate jokes? Are racist comments tolerated in our conversations? Do we voice our immediate reactions, or do we consider the long-term potential for damage?

"Challenge your tongue" by questioning your words before you speak.

Nobody can pass the test presented in that list every time. The tongue constantly challenges us. Therefore, we need to "challenge our tongue" by consistently asking several questions before we speak: Are the words necessary? Are they going to build someone else up, or could they potentially tear them down? Are they going to honor God, or are they going to show that your heart isn't as fully His as you would like to think? If all of our words are to be God-glorifying, then each of these questions needs to be answered correctly. If they cannot be, we need to learn to bite our tongues. When we choose not to bite them, we need to check our hearts to see if a correction needs to be made before we speak.

Read 1 Corinthians 13:1.

If my words are not seasoned with love, what are they as good as?_____

I'm convinced Paul wrote this verse after attending a nephew's elementary band concert! God bless all the band instructors who listen to students who are just picking up those instruments for the first time! The clarinets will squeak from time to time, and the French Horns might make noises that sound like a moose in heat. But, is there anything as irritating as that mistimed clanging cymbal? Shivers run up my spine just thinking about it. Yet, with patience, perseverance, and practice, those instruments in the same hands can one day produce beautiful music. The same is true of our words; until we learn to use them for their intended purpose, they will simply be a loud, clanging nuisance. By asking ourselves if our words are necessary before we say them, we are doing constant quality control, ensuring that our tongues are speaking words that are consistent with the purpose for which God created them and not just making racket at inopportune times.

Are your words sweet music to others or clanging gongs?

Read Colossian 3:23.

Whatever you do, do it with all your heart as if it were for the _____.

If we would remember that everything we say and do to others is equal to saying or doing it to the Lord, we might tend to weigh our speech and actions more carefully beforehand. Where do we want our relationship with the Lord to be? The way we use our words with others will directly correlate with how we help or hinder our relationship with Him. We cannot move forward and backward in a relationship at the same time, and the way we use our words affects the direction of that movement.

Let's be honest. Would we use our words as carelessly as we do if we were speaking directly to the Lord? Words can, and do, hurt more than sticks and stones, and their bruises last far longer. If you climb a tower and tear open a feather pillow outside on a windy day, the probability of re-gathering all of the feathers in order to put them back inside the pillow and restore it is zero. Our words are no different. The damage is done once they've left our mouths, and we've potentially loaded more baggage onto someone's back than they were ever intended to bear. If we wouldn't do such a thing directly to the Lord, we need to think harder before doing it to those who were created in His image.

Would we use our words so carelessly if speaking directly to Christ?

Instead, we are to bless the Lord and bless others as well. If we are inhaling the Word of God, our exhaled breath will be life-giving. God wants us to infuse life into others through encouraging words. There are those who are feeling suffocated by life, and we may be the source of fresh air that God uses to help them begin inhaling again. You know what it has meant to you when such an encourager has crossed your path; will you choose today to become a source of fresh air for all you meet?

Who can you encourage with your words today?

Describe a time when someone encouraged you with words. _____

_____

Thank God for those encouraging words and ask Him to give you the opportunity to extend encouragement to someone else today.

Day Four – The Power in "Prautes"

"Prautes?" Kinda makes you wonder doesn't it? Trust me; you'll want to read all the way to the end! As he did with the topic of the tongue, James has touched on wisdom a few times and now comes back to elaborate on it. As we're going to study today, there are two types of wisdom with two diabolically-different sources – God and the world. We will see, as we complete Chapter Three today and tomorrow, that James jumps back and forth between the two types of wisdom as he writes.

There are two very different types of wisdom – godly and worldly.

Within the context, we see that James went into detail showing that our speech reveals our heart and that good and bad cannot both come from a single source (James 3:11-12). We find in the following verses, that the true nature of the source is revealed in both word and deed.

Read James 3:13.

What is the first question James asks after his emphasis on the tongue?

_____

It takes wisdom, understanding and discipline to manage our speech.

Following his teaching on the condition of the heart, James seems to throw this question out as a challenge. He asks who **claims** to be wise, and promptly follows it with a challenge that says, "Okay; then prove it." Much like his argument concerning a true demonstration of faith, James is now looking for tangible proof of proclaimed wisdom. It takes **wisdom** to bite the tongue and it takes wisdom to use it carefully when we choose to speak. It takes **understanding** to *realize* the need to both bite it and use it carefully. It takes great **discipline** to act on wisdom and understanding, as one seeks to produce the good works James is describing.

According to James 3:13, how does one show that he has wisdom and understanding?

_____

In Scripture, gentleness and meekness never imply weakness, but a willingness to submit to God's authority.

True wisdom and understanding are always associated with certain qualities. Notice it doesn't say, "Let him show his wisdom through grand speeches, through teaching the hardest concepts, through elaborate prayers, or through having the most education, etc." No, he is to show, or demonstrate, his wisdom and understanding through good behavior. But, this behavior isn't fueled by lofty knowledge; the genuine source of this wise behavior is of all things, gentleness.

Oftentimes, gentleness gets a bad rap. We may think of gentle people as weak pushovers; those who can't, or won't, stand up for themselves. Yet, in Scripture, gentleness and meekness never imply weakness. Instead, the two qualities describe a strength of character that intentionally refuses to utilize the power available to them and chooses to place oneself under God's authority.

Read Matthew 11:29. How did Jesus describe Himself? _____

Fill in the blank: *"Take my yoke upon you and _____ from Me."*

In this verse, Jesus was telling the people that His burden was lighter than the burden of their sin and that His yoke would provide them peace and rest. While that is completely true, it appears that Jesus was seeking to emphasize something more that often gets over-looked – and we believe that something is found in the middle of the verse. It is there that He said, ***"Learn from Me, for I am gentle and humble of heart."*** (emphasis added) Why is it significant that we learn from His gentleness and humility in the context of this verse? Hold that thought; we'll come back to it! ☺

Read James 3:14-16.

James has told them to show wisdom through gentleness, but then he elaborates on what gentle wisdom is **not** before he expounds on what it **is**. Verse 14 is another verse where the subject and predicate are switched. It may make it easier to understand if we flip the sentence and read it this way:

> *"Do not be arrogant and lie against the truth if you have bitter jealousy and selfish ambition in your heart."*

The word **arrogant** in this verse is *katakauchaomai,* which means "to exult over, to boast against." It expresses the thought of "over-exalting one thing at the expense of another which results in wrong conclusions;" it downgrades truth "by boasting with a sense of false superiority."[21] In this context, it exalts one's self-proclaimed wisdom over God's truth.

katakauchaomai – to exult over, to boast against; over-exalting one thing at the expense of another

The word for **jealousy** here is *zelos,* which means "to have warmth of feeling for or against; to be zealous or jealous." It is actually a neutral word that must be translated by using the surrounding context. Its root, *ze,* "literally means 'hot enough to boil.' It is metaphorically used of 'burning anger, love, zeal.'"[22] It is an ardent passion for or against something. In James 3, it could be both, as it is a passion for one's selfish desires, as well as a passion against the truth it boasts over.

zelos – to to be zealous or jealous; burning anger, love, zeal

The word used for **selfish ambition** in verse 14 is *eritheia,* which means "rivalry, self-seeking." It "places self-interest ahead of what the Lord declares right, or what is good for others."[23] Recall from James 1:14-16, that the process of sin begins with lust, which is akin to selfish ambition. So, the sin in a person's heart drives him to boast of his own wisdom, which lies against God's truth.

eritheia – rivalry, self-seeking

By putting these words together, we can see that the wisdom fueled by a heart of zealous and selfish ambition exalts self, misrepresents the truth of God, and does not reflect His true wisdom. James has spoken about the heart as the source for words, expounding on the fact that impure words cannot come from a pure heart. In that same vein, he is now stating that gentle wisdom cannot come from a heart full of selfish ambition. Therefore, the one whose heart is selfish and impure needs to stop himself before presenting his opinion

Gentle wisdom cannot come from a heart full of selfishness.

---

21   Gary Hill, Helpsbible.com, http://strongsnumbers.com/greek/2620.htm
22   Gary Hill, Helpsbible.com, http://strongsnumbers.com/greek/2205.htm
23   Gary Hill, Helpsbible.com, http://strongsnumbers.com/greek/2052.htm

as being wisdom from God. We are not to boast against (lie against) the truth when our wisdom is tainted by our sin.

What sin might you be holding on to in your life that taints your wisdom, and therefore misrepresents God and lies against His truth?

_____

_____

Intellectual wisdom is based on human experience, education, or opinion.

James 3:15 begins with the words "this wisdom" which begs the question, "What wisdom?" Here, James is describing intellectual wisdom; wisdom that a person claims to have based on their life experience, education, or opinions. But, it does not reflect God's truth, which all things must be measured against, and so it is not the gentle wisdom God wants for us. We see this sort of wisdom all the time; our world is inundated with it. Talk show hosts and hostesses who are great humanitarians sway the masses with their "wise" words, yet they do so at the expense of the absolute truths in God's Word. Writers of books, magazines, journals, and blogs freely "bless" us with their wisdom of the ages, but so many of them don't use God's truth as the standard for their opinions. Their words of wisdom may sound good, logical, and appealing, but Satan works in crafty ways, and we must **know** the Word of God in order to recognize faulty wisdom when we encounter it.

What alternate sources of wisdom, as referred to above, have you seen sway those around you? Have you been swayed by them as well? If so, how? _____

_____

Unfortunately, we can hear this sort of wisdom in our Christian circles as well. "Zeal for the Lord lies all too closely to a selfishly motivated, harsh and violent fanaticism."[24] In other words, we can be so fanatical about our Christian misbeliefs and traditions that we fail to weigh them against the truth of God's Word. Or we can be tempted to twist the meaning of Scripture in order to support our dogmatic opinions. Some, seeking to appear lofty in their Christian knowledge, will say any number of things to demean others in order to lift themselves up. These are just some of the ways we misrepresent God (lie against the truth) that may drive others away from Him while we claim to speak in the name of His wisdom.

If our motives and understanding are not supported completely by God's truth and the gentleness of wisdom, they are earthly and evil.

This zeal is not from the Lord and it does not display wisdom in gentleness. Because of this, James says, "Don't boast in it, don't push it onto others, and don't say it's of the Lord!" It's really his very polite way of saying, "If what you're saying does not agree completely with the truth of God's Word, keep your trap shut!"

We must check our motives and our understanding. If they are not entirely supported by truth and the gentleness of wisdom, then they are earthly, natural, and demonic. Such wisdom creates disorder, and promotes every evil thing (v. 15-16). It is for these reasons that we are judged strictly concerning what we say and what we teach. If we claim His name as a Christian, we represent God; therefore, we must be ever so cautious.

---

24   Moo, *TNTC, James,* p. 137

Based on the wisdom you share with others, would those around you see a family resemblance to your heavenly Father in you? Why or why not? _____

_____

Now, let's get back to Matthew 11:29, where Jesus said, *"Learn from me, for I am gentle and humble of heart."* We will learn more tomorrow about the gentleness of wisdom, but today we will lay the foundation for the difference between gentle wisdom and the worldly wisdom we've just discussed.

The Greek word for gentleness, in James 3:13, is *prautés*, meaning "mildness, gentleness, meekness, humility." In Matthew 11:29, the word for gentle, *praus*, means "meekness, mildness, gentleness." Both of these words share the root word, *pra*, which is difficult to translate – there is no English equivalent word. It means more than meek. It expresses a gentle strength, a power that displays itself through restraint.

In non-biblical Greek literature, the word *prautés* was commonly used to describe a horse that has been broken. Such a horse is capable of extreme power and has the ability to use his strength to intimidate those around or to cause them harm. He is fully capable of showing off his potential, but because he has been broken, he has learned a new strength of character and obedience. He has nothing to prove and is now motivated to accommodate his rider in selflessness rather than selfishness. While his physical strength has not been compromised, his character is strengthened greatly through self-discipline and submission to his rider. On the other hand, a wild stallion that wants to establish himself as the strongest in a herd, exhibits his strength with the desire to intimidate and pays no attention to the damage he may cause to anything in his path. He cares for nothing outside of himself and his position within the group.

Jesus was the epitome of *prautés*. He was God incarnate, yet He bridled His omnipotent strength because He had nothing to prove, only a mission to accomplish. Mockers could say what they wanted to Him; He felt no need to vindicate Himself or stroke His own ego. If anyone has ever had the right to flaunt their wisdom, or throw their weight around, it was Jesus while He was on this earth. But, He didn't. Instead, He told us to learn *prautés* from Him, and IF we would, we would find rest for our souls. <u>Gentle</u>men, if there's one thing others need to see modeled better in us, it's a strength that is humble, restrained, and gentle.

How might learning strength under restraint bring rest to our souls? _____

_____

Read Matthew 11:28-30.

In verse 28, Jesus speaks to those who are burdened and heavy-laden. This burden is understood to be the weight of sin in a person's life. He's saying, "Come to me, all of you who are so burdened with the weight of your sin that you long to escape its grasp."

In James 3:14-16, we explored the grasp of sin on one's heart. Sin's hold taints our opinions, fooling us into thinking our opinions are wise when they may be entirely foolish. Sin promotes perpetual evil in our lives, which leads to chaos. Sin may seem harmless or even fun

prautés – mildness, gentleness, meekness, humility
pra – a gentle strength; power displayed through restraint

Jesus was the epitome of prautés.

Sin taints our opinions, promotes evil, and leads to chaos not wisdom.

for a while, but ask anyone who has let it go too far, and they will tell you what a burden it can become. Once it snowballs into something out of control, the chaos and confusion are consuming, suffocating one's heart while it desperately tries to gasp for air. As verse 16 says, where selfish ambition exists, there is disorder and every evil thing. Wisdom cannot manifest itself amidst such confusion.

As you know, all sin is not outwardly obvious. Many sins simply have to do with our selfish mindsets. We can become consumed with thoughts of what would please us, what angers us, what affects us, etc., all of those thoughts are driven by selfish ambition. When consumed with "self," our opinions are tainted and our egos cannot seem to find a way to swallow our pride. Because of this, we are constantly tormented, or at the least, frustrated and unsettled with life.

Only prautés, modeled and taught by Jesus, will bring real rest.

Jesus invited us to take off the yoke of sin, the selfish ambition that brings constant inner struggle. When we do, we can learn *prautés* – an ego under control, power under restraint – which will bring us the rest we long for. Christians have the opportunity to live a life of peace even in the midst of storms (as we saw in James 1). We know we are on God's winning team, and we know that He holds us in His hands. Therefore, <u>we don't have to spend our lives striving to prove ourselves</u>. We, like the powerful but trained horse, can know our full potential, yet walk in peace while we submit to God. We can choose to be like the gentle horse - a massive force to be reckoned with. He walks peacefully and when he runs, it's under powerful self-control. The other alternative is to resemble the wild stallion. He's skittish, jumpy, dangerous, aggressive, and never at peace. Jesus invites us to learn His Word, learn His ways, and live His peace. In that peace, our minds will grow calm and the inner torment will quiet. When we're quiet, when we resist selfish ambition, we will be able to grow in true wisdom - the wisdom of gentleness.

Do you struggle with a constant battle of the mind? Do you want peace but feel you are always fighting for, or with, something? How's your mind?

The gentleness of wisdom does not seek its own glory or recognition.

James 3:13 says our wisdom will be evident through our good behavior and deeds in gentleness. Remember, what we have to say means little if not matched with what we have to show. The one who spouts great knowledge of the Bible and yet bulldozes over people in his path, is not showing gentle wisdom. The one who gives eloquent answers and recites elaborate prayers, yet makes others feel small and inferior is not exhibiting the gentleness of wisdom. Wisdom does not seek its own glory or recognition. If what we project toward others is not loving, graceful and mercy-filled, we are misrepresenting our God. Our job is to display His true character in order to draw others in. When our motives seek to draw others to **us**, or to vindicate ourselves, it is **our** sinful character we are displaying and we are therefore not showing them the true character of God.

Have you heard people say that they don't want to be a Christian because all Christians are hypocrites? Even those who live a righteous and upstanding Christian walk need to be ever so careful not to give off an air of piety, but of gentleness and an ego under control. We are the only impression of God that some will ever see.

If you were the only Christian a person ever knew, would they see the true character of God? Why or why not? _____

_____

We may be the only view of God some people will ever see.

When I was a new Christian, I couldn't wait to tell others about my new-found Savior and faith. Unfortunately, I lacked gentle wisdom when doing so; but, don't fear, I made up for it with zeal! What a deadly combination. As an "educated scientist," I was going to evangelize the world with logic, reason, and good old-fashioned debate. In short, I was going to outsmart the fools who just didn't "get it." Would you believe that most of the time my knowledge of the facts about God just did not draw others to Him? Go figure. A presentation of the gospel that is condescending and reeks of a "know-it-all" or "holier-than-thou" air will not produce the results God is after. However, those same facts presented with the gentleness of wisdom will convey God's love when mere data cannot. Although it was likely one of his anonymous speech writers, Theodore Roosevelt is credited with having said, "Nobody cares how much you know until they know how much you care." We couldn't agree more; nothing opens the ears of another more than wisdom's gentleness. Whereas pride may only want to win an academic argument, *prautés* wants to win the heart and soul of another.

The presence or absence of wisdom's gentleness determines if others will hear our words.

What wisdom are you conveying through your life? Is it from above or earthly? Whatever consumes your heart and mind, will form your opinions and become your source of wisdom. What is your wisdom based on at this point in your life? Is it true wisdom, intellectual knowledge, or tainted opinion? Are your opinions based on God's Word or anything else? What are you consumed with that boasts outwardly? Are you riddled with sin, gasping for air and relief? If so, Jesus says, "Learn from Me..." Is your heart "sold out" for the Lord but still carrying an air of pride? To you, Jesus says, "Learn from Me..." Jesus had everything to prove, but sought to prove nothing aside from what His Father had sent Him to do and say. Even in this, He says, "Learn from Me..."

Are your opinions based on your feelings or on the Word of God?

Tomorrow we will look at the specific aspects of what makes wisdom gentle, but for today, pray that the Lord will teach you and that He will help you to be open to learn from Him and Him alone. Ask Him to show you the peace that comes from not barreling forward with opinions and self-proclaimed wisdom, but to be like the tamed horse, full of potential power, yet peaceful and under control. Whose control is your mind under today? Ask Him to clear your mind of every misconceived notion, and replace them with His truth. Ask Him to help you learn His gentleness and humility. Journal as He leads below.

If Jesus were in the room next to you and He said, "Come, learn from me..." could you tell Him no?

_____

_____

_____

_____

_____

Day Five – The Gentleness of Wisdom

Yesterday we learned that true, godly wisdom cannot come from a heart or mind tainted with selfish ambition. Instead, it must come from the pure source of a godly mindset. We saw that the mind cluttered with sin is too chaotic and tormented to be still enough to absorb the true gentleness of wisdom.

Before we dive into the practical aspects of how to live out gentle wisdom, let's look at a few verses that prove our need to have a peaceful mind in order to clearly process true wisdom.

Read Isaiah 26:3. What will be provided for the one whose mind is steadfast in his trust of the Lord? _____

Read Psalm 119:165. Great _____ have they who love God's law, and nothing can make them stumble.

Read John 14:27. Our minds need not be troubled, anxious, and confused with sin, as Jesus offers us _____.

Read Philippians 4:5-9.

The mind cluttered with sin is too chaotic to absorb the gentleness of wisdom.

These verses are an amazing summary of so many things that James has said. Verse 5 tells us that our gentle spirit needs to be obvious to all. In other words, the peace that God gives us should show through our actions which demonstrate our faith to the world. Verse 6 reminds us of the way James has instructed us not to panic in our trials. Instead, we can go to the Father with our concerns, not allowing our spirits to become anxious and troubled, because we trust that He is near.

Our gentle spirit needs to be obvious to all.

What does verse 7 say that the peace of God will do for our hearts? _____

Our hearts that are so easily troubled in a fallen world, and our minds that are so easily swayed by selfish ambition, are guarded by the peace of God for those of us who **choose** to consistently set our hearts and minds on Him. Verse 8 follows that line of reasoning with an exhortation to focus our mind and dwell on only that which is pure and of the Lord.

God desperately wants us to demonstrate His love to a dying world.

According to verse 9, how is God referred to? _____

He is our God of peace; Jesus is the Prince of Peace. The fact is, God desires for us to know peace. But, not simply because He wants us to enjoy a life of peacefulness, free of stress. He never promises such a thing; in fact, He promises that this life will be filled with trials. He needs us to have peace in our hearts and minds to process the wisdom He wants us to have without having it corrupted by the confusion of sin. If our minds are set on Him, and not cluttered with sin and strife, we can effectively show His character through our actions. He desperately needs for us to do so in order to demonstrate His love to a dying world. However, when our minds are torn and confused with our own selfish ambitions, we not only confuse ourselves, but we can also confuse others as they seek to find God in our actions.

Read James 3:17-18. The wisdom from above is pure, peaceable, gentle, reasonable, full of mercy and good fruits, unwavering, and without hypocrisy. We'll look at each in turn.

The wisdom from above is first _____.

After describing worldly wisdom that is contaminated by sin, James begins his description of godly wisdom by noting that first and foremost, it is pure. It is free from the confusion of sin, free from any selfish motives, incapable of promoting anything evil. The Greek word used for pure here is *hagnos*, meaning "free from ceremonial defilement; holy, sacred." It speaks of a purity inside and out, to the center of one's being. It has no guilt, nor anything condemnable mixed within it.

First, and foremost, godly wisdom is pure.

Right off the bat, we can all see that none of us will be able to attain that sort of wisdom on our own. Our minds **must** continuously be set on Him in order to hear Him speak His wisdom to us so that we might, in turn, live it out, sharing it with others.

Are your heart and mind places of purity where God's wisdom can be received? _____ If not, what changes do you need to make? _____

After purity, wisdom is then _____.

hagnos – free from ceremonial defilement; holy, sacred

Peace runs throughout our passage on the gentleness of true wisdom. Not only does God need our hearts to be a place of peace in order to properly process wisdom, but once we receive this wisdom, its outpouring should promote peace. It promotes peaceful relationships with others and with God. When guided by peaceable wisdom, we will not be quick to judge, argue, or belittle others.

Peaceable wisdom seeks to remove animosity. Its goal is to produce healing and understanding in order to convey the truth and love of God. A person with a pure and peace-filled heart never pursues an agenda of his own, but seeks to promote only the truth that directly reflects the Word of God.

Godly wisdom promotes peace and removes animosity.

Peaceable wisdom is interwoven with the next two descriptions.

Following peaceable, wisdom is _____ and _____.

The following truth is one that can literally change our lives when we come to understand it and allow it to become a filter for all our thoughts and opinions.

"Why is wisdom *peaceable*? Because it is also *gentle* and *open to reason*. To be *gentle (epie-ikés)* is to be kind, willing to yield, unwilling to 'exact strict claims.' The person who is *open to reason (eupeithes)* is one, literally, who is 'easily persuaded' – not in the sense of a weak, credulous gullibility, but in the sense of a willing deference to others when unalterable theological or moral principles are **not** involved."[25] (emphasis added)

Wisdom is peaceable because it is gentle and open to reason.

Yesterday, we covered the way that impure wisdom lies against the truth and misrepresents God. When we hear comments like that, our natural tendency is to assume it is talking about "serious" sin. But, sin manifests itself in even the tiniest ways that can cloud our judgment. Let's set aside the "serious" sins for a while and consider some "minor" situations where tainted wisdom might cause ripples of conflict.

Above, we saw that the word gentle, in James 3:17, speaks of being kind, willing to yield, unwilling "to exact strict claims." This is different than the word for gentleness that we

---

25   Moo, *TNTC, James*, p. 140.

studied yesterday (*prautés)*, although they work hand in hand. *Epieikés* refers to being equitable and staying true to the "**spirit** of the law" by relaxing overly strict standards that seek to fulfill the "**letter** of the law."

Christians can exact strict claims on one another without realizing that we aren't acting in gentleness. Depending on our culture, we often grow into certain traditions that we come to hold as dogmatic truths. Because we expect others to adhere to our same "Christian beliefs," we tend to become judgmental when they may not adhere to them as well. As an example, think about the unwritten "dress code" at your church. Likely, there are those in your congregation who firmly believe God wears a suit and tie in heaven, while others picture Him sitting on the beach in a Hawaiian print shirt and flip flops! Unfortunately, the two camps may occasionally do battle over something that Scripture is silent on. The pastors may actually feel pressured to change outfits between services to appease each camp. This example may seem trivial and silly, but it is an example of the way traditions can easily be considered "right" and any infraction of them may be considered "wrong."

epieikés – equitable and true to the spirit of the law

What are some "Christian" expectations you can think of that are based on human traditions or opinion, but don't have their basis in Scripture?

_____

_____

Many of the expectations we place on other Christians are not based on Scripture.

To finish this illustration, we need to look back at the quotation above that describes the person who is not only gentle but also open to reason. According to James 3:17, the description of the person who is open to reason is also one who is easily-persuaded. Without reading the rest of the definition, this would seem to fly in the face of all Christian belief! Aren't we supposed to be firm in our belief of our God, Savior, and Scripture? Yes, we absolutely are. The rest of the definition explains that we are not to be weak, gullible, or naïve, but willing to consider the opinions of others "**when unalterable theological or moral principles are <u>not</u> involved**." Simply stated, if Scripture doesn't say that men shouldn't wear Hawaiian shirts into the church building, and there are no other scriptural implications that it is a sin, we need to be open to the possibility that it may not be a sin at all. In weighing our traditional opinions on the scale of Scripture, we may find that many of our "hang ups" aren't things God cares to put much emphasis on at all. It is important for us to realize that we need to extend the freedom Christ died for to our brothers and sisters.

When unalterable theological or moral principles are NOT involved, extend freedom.

The tricky part about this is identifying these areas in our own lives. How do we identify areas of personal opinion when we've been raised believing they are absolute truth? <u>The key is staying open to reason</u>. As others cross our paths who don't exactly share our opinions, we need to ask ourselves if Scripture supports our disagreement with them or if this is a time when we get to practice this "willing deference" to others. In gentleness and grace, choosing to allow them to exercise their freedom in Christ may just knock their socks off. Give it a try – but make sure your church allows bare feet first!

It is very important to remember that the Holy Spirit works uniquely in each of our lives. There will be areas in each of our lives that we feel convicted about, even though they are not unalterable theological or moral principles (something that Scripture is emphatically for or against). Romans 14 tells us, that if we are convicted about something and continue on with it anyway, we are sinning. Within the same chapter, it is stated that a fellow Christian can participate in the same action and not be sinning. It is wrong for the convicted Christian to progress against his conviction, but it is also wrong for him to expect all other Christians to fall in line with his convictions. Again, this is ONLY speaking of things that are **not** clearly stated in Scripture. This is not permission to commit murder if you don't feel convicted about it! Scripture is emphatic concerning right and wrong, but there are areas where a willing deference to each other is emphatically necessary as well.

Back to beach wear for a moment. Let's say that one man consistently comes to church wearing shorts and flip flops, while another may always wear suits. It is important for neither of them to be offended by the other, no matter where their own conviction lies. If the one who consistently wears suits feels that he would be disrespecting God, and therefore sinning by wearing shorts to church, then **for him** it would be sin and he needs to hold to his conviction. But, because Scripture doesn't address this topic directly, it would show the gentleness of wisdom if he were open to reason, accepting that the other man in shorts may not share his conviction. The man in shorts, as well, would need to be respectful of his fellow suit-wearing Christian and not condemn him for his convictions, nor try to press his own liberty onto him.

The Holy Spirit works uniquely in each of our lives.

The list of examples could go on and on. Those who feel that the only way to truly worship in song is through praise music need to be gentle and open to reason with those who feel adamantly about hymns, and vice versa. A person who feels that they would be sinning by going into a restaurant that serves alcohol must adhere to that conviction, and yet respect the liberty of the one who is able to dine at Applebee's without conviction. The bottom line is that there must be pure wisdom to begin with, and after that, there must be a willingness to be gentle and open to reason. The purity of wisdom will recognize actual sin as clearly-defined in Scripture and stay away from it; while the gentleness of wisdom will provide for the situations where conviction and liberty are involved.

Being open to reason requires accepting one another's convictions and liberties.

What are some areas in your own life where you may have expectations of others that may be based on your own traditional opinions or convictions and not necessarily dogmatic scriptural truth? Are you willing to learn to be gentle and open to reason in an effort to show the gentleness of wisdom?

_____

_____

Read Proverbs 16:21

People are attracted to a loving God when they see His love through our gentleness.

You have likely heard the phrase, "You catch more flies with honey than with vinegar." If our traditions and opinions are making others feel uncomfortable because they don't share them yet feel we expect them to, we aren't exhibiting the love of God and are guilty of acting like Pharisees. We are to hold to our convictions, but also be filled with gracious love toward others that reflects God's grace and mercy as well as His righteousness. We aren't going to attract people to a loving God if they can't see His love through our gentleness and willingness to be reasonable.

Pure wisdom will help you discern right from wrong as you obey the conviction of the Holy

Spirit and search the Scripture for truth. As you do, your kind words, or gentleness of speech, will promote God's love to those around you much more than harsh dogma. The grace of God should soften us; which will show up in our interactions with others.

What are the next two descriptions of wisdom in James 3:17? _____

Hand in hand with being made more gentle, wisdom shows itself in our lives through mercy. James has already described mercy in 2:8-13 as impartial love for all without exclusion. Mercy extends love to others even when judgment may be deserved. Only the gentleness of wisdom can show this sort of kindness, for it is so much easier to ridicule when it is deserved than to show mercy in the moment.

*adiakritos –
unambiguous,
without uncertainty,
undivided,
whole-hearted*

Good fruits and mercy are closely tied together in this verse, implying that acts of mercy bring forth good fruit. This good fruit is harvested in the lives of those giving the blessing as well as those receiving the blessing.

Finally, what are the last two descriptions given for wisdom? _____ and _____

Adiakritos means "unambiguous, without uncertainty, undivided, whole-hearted." In true James fashion, he had to throw in that true wisdom is not double-minded! It is unwavering, steadfast, and sure. It is set upon Scripture and does not waffle in opinion.

Closely-related, godly wisdom knows no hypocrisy; it is sincere. *Hypokrisis* was a word used to describe an actor playing two parts in a production, switching his mask quickly to give different impressions of himself to the audience at different times. Wisdom from above is genuine, tried, and true. You will not find a truly wise person of God speaking one way to some and quite another elsewhere. Those who hold godly wisdom do not wear any masks. They are sincere at home, at work, and at play; there is no shifting of their character.

*hypokrisis – used
to describe an actor
playing two roles*

We have all been tempted to be one person in certain groups or situations, and a completely different person in others. What situations are most difficult for you to maintain your Christian character? _____

_____

*Are there aspects of
godly wisdom you
need to work on? Are
you in need of a good
brain washing, too?*

James sandwiches his description of the gentleness of wisdom between bookend descriptions of peace. No doubt, true wisdom can only be harvested when grown in the soil of peace. Whereas those who boast of flawed wisdom promote "disorder and every evil thing," those who seek and know God's righteousness, pursue lives of peace and produce peace as an out-flowing of their wise and merciful conduct.

That was admittedly a lot to learn in one day. Let's review quickly: Godly wisdom is pure, peaceable, gentle, reasonable, full of mercy and good fruits, unwavering, and without hypocrisy. After thoroughly examining the practical side of the true gentleness of wisdom, which of these attributes are you able to recognize in your own life? Which areas might you need to work on? Sometimes what we need is a good brain washing! We think of being brainwashed in a negative sense. But, when our own faulty thinking is cluttering our minds, keeping us from realizing the peace we require in order to understand true wisdom, we need God to wash our minds clean and speak His wisdom to us so that we might understand Him more. Does your mind need washing, too? Are you willing today to ask Him to still your mind, so that you can hear His voice past all the distracting noise?

WEEK FIVE: A PEACEFUL AND HUMBLE FAITH

Day One – Conflicting Interests

Sunsets over the beach. Golf courses at dusk. My grandpa's porch swing. The sounds of the 70s. Conflict. Yes, these are indeed a few of my favorite things! Well – almost. Conflict. As much as we may try to avoid it, it seems to show up everywhere, including our study today.

Read James 4:1-2b.

When James wrote his original letter to the churches, it had no chapter breaks and no divisions between verses. It was one continuous letter that flowed from one thought to the next. Therefore, James likely did not intend for there to be a break in thought between his discourse concerning using the tongue with peaceable wisdom and the next section on conflict. Conflict cannot be fed without the tongue, bitter envy or selfish ambition, and it will not be fueled by the gentleness of wisdom. Therefore, these two chapters blend together seamlessly.

James poses a question for his readers and immediately answers it in the form of another question. What did he identify as the source of their quarrels? _____

In the same way that he doesn't allow us to blame our temptations on anyone but ourselves (1:14), James makes us take responsibility for our disputes and quarrels as well. Certainly, Satan and his demons promote spiritual warfare that can lead to all kinds of conflict, but we cannot escape the burden of personal responsibility. Conflict causes all sorts of disorder, and James 3:16 told us that disorder and every evil thing originates with jealousy and selfish ambition. However, we choose whether or not those characteristics rule us enough to cause conflict.

In the second question, James identifies the source of quarrels and conflict as our pleasures. The Greek word for pleasure in this verse is *hédoné*, meaning "pleasure, lust, strong desire." It is the same root from which we get "hedonistic" and speaks of that which is enjoyable to the natural senses. We need to note that these pleasures do not necessarily have to start out as inherently bad. In fact, there are many things in this world that God intended to bring us pleasure, but when we allow our focus to get out of balance, even those good things can turn into a selfish desire. Or, if life doesn't readily afford them to us, we may allow our pursuit of them to frustrate us and our focus may become unhealthy. We've just learned that sin causes confusion in our minds. When anything we find pleasure in consumes us to the point that we cannot find contentment without it, disorder in our mind is promoted. A confused mind can consequently create disorder with others in the form of conflict.

Conflict cannot be fed without the tongue, bitter envy, or selfish ambition.

hédoné – pleasure, lust, strong desire

Imagine this illustration (it shouldn't be too hard for most of us)! A parent and toddler are at the store and pass the toy department. When a particular toy catches the child's eye, the youngster thinks he must have it NOW – because **this** toy will make him so happy. There really isn't anything wrong with the toy or with them enjoying the thought of having it. The problem comes when Dad says no, and the child decides they literally CANNOT live another day without THAT toy! Suddenly, what was a healthy desire for a good thing has turned into irrational behavior and the conflict between parent and child begins. A healthy desire quickly turned into selfishness, which altered rational thinking and led to irrational actions in a matter of moments. Unfortunately, we are not entirely above this as adults.

A healthy desire can quickly turn into selfishness.

Read James 4:2a, b.

"You _____ and do not have; so you commit _____.

You are _____ and cannot obtain; so you _____."

The beginning of both of these statements identify the underlying issues, and the ending of each show our human tendencies. As much as it may hurt our pride to be compared to a toddler, the fact of the matter is, when we want what we can't have, we can act like spoiled little brats. It would be easy for us to jump to the conclusion that we are "in the clear" on the first indictment because we've probably never committed murder, but a closer look into Scripture may tell us differently.

Read Matthew 5:21-22 and 1 John 3:15.

With what do these verses equate hatred? _____

James is saying that those of us who lust and become envious for what we cannot obtain, go so far as to hate those who have what we cannot, which leads to quarrels and strife. Let's remember our historical context for a moment. These were persecuted Jewish Christians who were struggling tremendously. They may have believed that the things they wanted (peace, freedom from persecution, etc.) were justified, but their desires consumed them to the point of actually hating others; it was causing enough dissension within the church that James caught wind of it. I'm certain that tensions were running high within the churches at this time, and it is at such times that conflict is anxiously waiting at the door.

Do not make decisions in the heat of conflict.

It is much easier to lash out at others when your tensions are running high. How have you seen this truth in your life? _____

_____

When tensions are running high and conflict ensues, we run the risk of doing things we never intended to do. We may also say things we ordinarily wouldn't say, possibly things we don't even mean. As mentioned last week, we all have things we wish we could "unsay" and undo in our pasts. It is so important not to make decisions in the heat of conflict. When we do, our words and attitudes can become murderous. **We need to proactively and specifically <u>try</u> NOT to hurt each other**.

In Angie's household, there are certain excuses concerning conflict that aren't even allowed, because everyone in the house already knows the response they will hear from her. Anytime hurtful words or actions rear their ugly heads in her home, followed by excuses such as, "I didn't mean to hurt you," or "I wasn't trying to make you feel bad," her response quickly follows, "But did you try **not** to?"

If we are going to allow God to be seen through us, then we need to start in the privacy of our homes with those who see us at our worst. We have to make a determined effort to see them with His eyes of grace, touch with His hand of mercy, and love with His unconditional love. If we are willing to swallow our pride, we can often stop conflict before it begins. If conflicts do occur, we must have the self-control to stop and ask ourselves in the midst of them if our words and actions are truly necessary, or if they are simply adding fuel to the fire.

For others to see God in us, we must see with His eyes of grace, touch with His hand of mercy, and love with His unconditional love.

Have you ever been in an argument with someone and thought, "They're so far off-base and out of touch with reality here that their thinking is completely whacked."

Men, are you willing to consider the possibility that, at times, it might be you whose "perspection" is clouded with sin and pride, rather than the conflict being anyone else's fault? (See page 16 for a reminder of what "perspection" is.) _____

Let's face it, conflict is downright hard, and any time multiple people get together, there's bound to be some. What we each need to focus on is our own responsibility in each situation.

Read Romans 12:18 and Hebrews 12:14.

In both of these verses, the emphasis is put on "you" for keeping peace. We cannot be responsible for how others are going to react in conflict, but we are entirely responsible for our own attitudes and reactions. No one else can **make** us respond with unreasonable emotion; we choose to. We've already suggested that considering the way we want a situation to look like five years from now can help us avoid saying or doing things now that we'll later regret. Similarly, it is helpful to weigh the gravity of a situation before acting on it. For instance, if the subject of the conflict is not going to matter in the least 20 years from now, it may just be best to let it go. We all have endured days in our past that resulted in regret because of something we said. Unfortunately, those days didn't begin with a warning that told us, "Danger Will Robinson. Danger! This is going to be a day you will regret forever." But, having learned from past regrets, we can wake up each day and say, "On this day, I will guard my speech and actions if conflict should arise, for although I cannot retract what I've already done, today I can prevent any future damage I may still do."

We are each responsible for keeping the peace, and for our actions during conflict.

Proverbs 19:11 says that wisdom gives us patience, and it is to our glory to overlook an offense. Think back over the last several conflicts you have encountered. How could choosing to overlook an offense have been a wiser choice?

_____

_____

Let's briefly look at a few examples of conflict given in Scripture. Not all conflict looks alike, but there are consistent lessons we can learn from each.

For our first example, we will be looking at the lives of King Saul and David. King Saul was envious of David, and it consumed his very being. From their first encounter until their last, David did nothing to provoke Saul, and yet Saul's envy led to one of Scripture's most famous conflicts. God had laid His hand on David's life, and although David knew that one day he would become king, he did not pursue that position and he did not covet what Saul had. In fact, he humbly submitted to Saul as king and chose not to take his life on multiple occasions. Yet, David's popularity grew steadily and as a result, Saul's hate for him also grew. Saul possessed the crown, and yet he was insanely (literally) jealous of what David had that he did not; namely, success in battle and the respect and admiration of the people. Just as James pointed out, envy fueled the conflict.

This particular conflict was chosen because we often hear that "it takes two to tango," meaning that in every conflict there are two sides, and both must be somewhat at fault. Although, this is usually true, there can be cases where one person is living smack dab in the middle of God's will and conflict still finds its way to him. This was the case for David with Saul. There are times when Satan paints a bull's eye on an innocent person who is living for the Lord and does what he can to take him or her down by means of conflict and strife. Jesus, Himself, was a perfect example of this. Conflict surrounded Him on every side, but it was due to the bitter jealousy of others, not as a result of any wrongdoing on His part.

We can learn from the examples of both Saul and David. On one hand, Saul was so overcome with envy and jealousy that he refused to let go of the hate that consumed him. He likely felt justified in his anger because he felt that his crown was threatened. Due to his clouded thinking, Saul likely would have told you that the conflict was David's fault. But, by refusing to let go of his jealousy, Saul lived the rest of his years in an extremely tormented state. His hatred for David became an obsession in his life, which caused him to lose all focus and rationale. As a result, he could no longer hear God nor be effectively used by Him.

David's life, on the other hand, was obviously affected by Saul's hatred and frequent murder attempts. But the consistent, God-honoring choices he made kept him blameless in the matter and available to be used greatly by the Lord. Although he could have easily justified retaliation, as he knew that God intended for him to eventually be king, David allowed God to handle the matter and he **never** allowed a revengeful spirit to overcome him when dealing with Saul. From David's example, we can learn that although we may not start the conflict, and we might not be able to stop it, we can do everything in our power not to contribute to it.

Some battles simply aren't worth fighting. It is to your glory to overlook an offense.

It is possible to be in the center of God's will and in the center of conflict due to no fault of one's own.

We may have no choice in whether a conflict starts or stops, but we can do everything possible not to contribute to it.

Are your reactions to conflict more like Saul's or David's? Do you think your opinions, feelings, and positions must be vindicated immediately by your own efforts, or do you allow God to work things out in His way and in His time? Explain.

_____

_____

Our second and third examples of conflict will likely resemble what we face more regularly. Our next example is Joseph and his brothers. In this situation, there was absolute guilt, fueled by jealousy and anger, on the part of the brothers, while there was quite possibly unintentional fault on the part of Joseph. Much has been taught about Joseph's lack of discretion in "bragging" about his dreams to his brothers who did not want to hear that they would one day bow down to him. We can't know for sure what the intent of Joseph's heart was. Perhaps he was bragging; perhaps he was just amazed at the visions God was giving him. Either way, he did contribute to the conflict because, due to immaturity, he apparently hadn't learned the value of biting his tongue when tensions began to run high.

In many conflicts, both parties share in at least part of the responsibility.

We again see from the brothers' example, that when we allow envy and jealousy to overtake us, we become consumed to the point of extremely irrational behavior. None of them were probably the type to murder a family member, and yet James tells us that our lusts and jealousies can drive us to murderous extremes, whether emotionally or physically.

Joseph gives us a look at the person who comes out on the other side of the conflict, having grown in wisdom through experience. He did show immaturity in his words, which promoted conflict. But, he grew in wisdom through his experiences and later learned not to bolt ahead with his emotions, even when he knew he was in the right. Through his experience with trials, conflicts, and hardships, Joseph **changed** for the good.

Like Joseph, we can change, for God can change our hearts.

Because change is always possible, we cannot hide behind the excuse that we are simply confrontational people saying, "That's just the way I am." Like Joseph, we too **can** change, for God **can** change our hearts. Psalm 51:10 says, *"Create in me a clean heart, O God, and renew a right spirit within me"* (ESV). We know what our natural human tendencies are in the midst of conflict. But, we need to ask God to help us break the spirit of anger that fuels conflict and give us a renewed spirit that He can use as an instrument of peace. It's not enough to ask God to help in the heat of the moment, although it is welcomed then, too! Even during the calm seasons, we need to ask God for an "attitude transplant" like the one Joseph had. It grew him up, it built his faith, and it prepared him for every trial and conflict ahead.

What begins in hatred can end in love if one party is willing to put love and forgiveness ahead of their need to be right.

After reaching "superstar" status in the kingdom, Joseph could have done extreme harm to his brothers when they suddenly appeared in his presence, had he harbored bitterness toward them all those years. But, the way he handled the past affected the way he chose to deal with his present circumstances, which entirely altered the course of their future. What had begun in hate, ended in love and miraculous healing, because one man was willing to put love and forgiveness for others ahead of his need for vindication. A restored relationship was more important to him than getting his side of the story settled once and for all.

Are you looking for miraculous healing in a situation you're facing? If so, how much love and forgiveness are you willing to extend to another in the form of controlling your own response to conflict? Will you trust God and allow Him to take care of the rest?

_____

_____

Jacob and Esau were both motivated by envy over what the other had.

The final example of conflict we'll examine is between Jacob and Esau. In this case, both brothers shared equally in the blame. Jacob was envious of Esau's birthright and blessing, and perhaps the favoritism of their father. Esau was envious of the birthright and blessing after Jacob "repossessed" both of them, and he may have resented the favoritism Jacob was shown by their mother. These two give us a classic example of purely selfish conflict. Both were motivated by their envy for the pleasure of life they were certain they couldn't live without. Both wanted what the other had; both were driven to hate, and one even threatened murder. Incidentally – they were both flat out wrong, too.

The need to be "right" can be as much of a source of conflict as anything tangible.

This set of dysfunctional twins clearly shows us that lives can be entirely altered and ruined by an obsession for what we "must" have, and James tells us that this is the source of our quarrels. It would be tempting to say, "But, I don't obsess over wanting any "thing." My conflicts usually involve times when someone wrongs me and I want it made right." Make no mistake, the need to be proven right or innocent can have just as much to do with "fulfilling our pleasures" as anything tangible. Feeling the satisfaction that justice for our own purpose has been served is a way of feeding our pride and selfish pleasure as well.

Where is your true pleasure found? Is it found when your own thoughts and opinions are finally heard and vindicated, or when God's heart is seen through you?

_____

To be used by God, we must let go of our need to fight and hold on to His promise to take care of us His way.

When you constantly strive to be heard, do you really ever find peace, or do you find it is a never-ending process, much like a hamster on a wheel? Explain.

_____

In your effort to make your opinions and feelings heard in the midst of conflict, do you consider the damage you are contributing to the situation, or do you bolt ahead without considering the cost? Explain.

_____

Read Romans 12:19

Conflict is consuming, and it can be a tool of the enemy to steal our concentration. To focus on God the way He intends, He needs our full focus all day, every day. When we are consumed with conflict, we may mull it over in our heads over and over again. We replay conversations, script new ones, prepare defenses for future battles, etc. If we desire to be used effectively by God, if we want to move forward in His will and allow Him to show us the best He has for us, we must LET GO of our need to fight and HOLD ON to His promise to take care of it all in His own time, in His own way. We can take a holy "chill pill" knowing that vengeance is His. Remember, choosing to let someone "off your hook" does not mean they are off God's hook. Trust Him – He can handle it!

Peace, and the wisdom it produces, cannot coexist with a spirit that produces conflict.

In his constant argument against the double-mind, James again points out two things that simply cannot coincide. Peace, and the wisdom it produces, cannot live in tandem with a spirit that produces conflict. We must pray for a renewed spirit that can see and think with the eyes and heart of God in order to put our own selfishness aside.

What are you willing to do to diffuse conflict in your life? Remember, you may not have started it, and you might not be able to stop it, but you can do everything in your power not to contribute to it.

Day Two – A Greater Grace

You may have noticed yesterday, that although we read James 4:1-2, we didn't cover the final sentence in verse 2. Although that sentence does refer back to the previous thought, it more readily ties in with the sentences that follow. Therefore, this is where we will pick up our reading today.

Read James 4:2.

We can create turmoil by wanting what we don't have, and by taking matters into our own hands.

In essence, James is saying, "You're fighting with each other because you're unsettled. You're unsettled because you want what you don't have. You don't have, because you don't ASK!"

Have you ever walked in on an argument between your children that could have been avoided had they just consulted you first? Their fight stemmed not only from what they wanted, but by their desire to take the matter into their own hands. Had they asked you, the answer may have been a quick yes or no and there would have been no need for them to argue among themselves.

All too often we do that with God. We get so wrapped up in our worlds, so frustrated with the way we want things to go, or maybe with the way we want others to act, that we forget God's place in the equation. At this point, James shifts the emphasis away from the conflict between people and refocuses his attention on each individual's failure to acknowledge God in every situation.

Our Heavenly Father wants to give us good and perfect gifts. He is just waiting for us to ask.

Read Matthew 7:7-11.

There are things that God is just waiting for us to ask Him for, things that He longs to give us as a loving Father. Just as an earthly father desires to give good things to his children, our heavenly Father wants to give us perfect gifts so much more. But, oftentimes, He waits for us to ask. James says, *"You do not have because you do not ask!"* We are to live in an ongoing, healthy relationship with God where we are in constant communication with Him. When that is not a priority in our life, and we fail to come to Him for our needs, as well as our heart's desires, we may be missing out on incredible things that He is just waiting for us to ask for.

Yet, there are a couple of disclaimers. Read James 4:3.

You ask and do not receive, because you ask with _____,

so that you may _____.

Selfish desires show up in wrong motives when we pray.

James isn't promoting prosperity theology here. This isn't his way of saying they can "name it and claim it." We know this because immediately after he tells them that they have not because they ask not, he says, "When you do ask, you don't receive because you're asking with the wrong motives!" Again, he takes them right back to the source of their quarrels – their selfish desires, which he now says can show up even in their prayers. The individuals are not in right relationship with God, which is made evident by their apparent self-focused, rather than God-focused, prayers. Because this stirs up sinful frustration within the individual, it can also stir up conflict within the church body.

Since this causes so much personal, as well as corporate, disruption, it is imperative for us to seek to maintain a healthy focus on the things that God would choose for our lives rather than what we would choose based on our own sinful natures. If we strive to be spiritually-minded, our desires will line up with what God desires for our lives, and our motives in our requests will be pure.

Read 1 John 3:21-22.

What condition is given for approaching God with confidence?

_____

Our hearts must be right when we take our requests to God.

Our hearts must be right when we take our requests to God. We can confidently place our requests before Him only when we are living our lives seeking to keep His commandments as His servants.

Read 1 John 3:24. The one who keeps His commandments _____ in Him.

The NASB uses the word "abides" in this verse. Other translations use the words "lives, fellowships, remains, dwells, and continues." All of these translations accurately portray the essence of the verse. The Greek word for abide is *menó*, meaning to remain, stay, wait for, await. Those living a life worthy of coming with confidence to the throne of God are those who are living out His commandments **because** they live their lives "remaining in Him." God is not a "go to" God where we simply bring Him our Christmas wish lists when we have desires of our own. It is only when we are consistently remaining in Him, abiding in Him, fellowshipping with Him, and waiting on Him, that we are able to come to Him in confidence.

menó – to remain, stay, wait for, await

It is hard for me to think about the word abide without the closely-related word, "abode," coming to mind. Abode – the place I reside, my dwelling place; the place I choose to call home. A place of comfort, security, and tremendous familiarity. I can go anywhere in my abode, even in complete darkness, because I am that familiar with every corner, nook, and cranny. Likewise, when we are abiding in our heavenly Father, we are so closely knit with Him that we see Him, hear Him, and recognize Him in everything around us; even if it's completely dark at times. When we allow ourselves to become this close to Him, it is our heart's most sincere desire to please Him and follow His commandments. Anyone who truly knows the Father and knows the security of abiding with Him, wants to do everything in their power to serve Him in any way. This is the child of God who can come to the Father with confidence in their requests.

To abide in Christ is to walk so closely with Him that we recognize Him in everything around us.

How do you approach the Father in prayer? As a demanding child making selfish requests of "Santa," or in quiet confidence because you have been abiding in Him? How can you abide in Him more this week?

_____

_____

Abiding in the Father, and having constant fellowship with Him is only part of what is required for receiving what we ask for in prayer.

1 John 5:14 says – "*This is the confidence which we have before Him, that, if we ask anything according to His will, He hears us.*"

According to this verse, how must we ask God if we want Him to hear our request?

_____

We are to pray according to God's will. Our requests cannot be filled with selfish motives; they must align with the heart and mind of God.

We must ask according to God's will if we want to be heard.

How do you know if what you are praying for is in God's will or not? What do you think it means to pray according to His will?

_____

_____

When you are submitted to His will, you can find peace in His answer, whatever it is.

When we are abiding in God and He is abiding in us, we will know immediately that there are some things that we should not even entertain the thought of requesting in prayer, because it is simply out of line with what He wants for us. Truth be told, when we are not abiding in Him and are not trying to align our thinking with His own, we are entirely capable of doing this. But, there are obviously times when our prayers can be pure in their intentions, yet we are not sure what God's final will is in a given matter. It is at these times that we can approach Him in the confidence of a clear conscience, knowing that our requests and heart's desires are pure. At this point, we must submit ourselves to His will and find peace in whatever His answer is. Praying according to His will doesn't mean we will always know the exact thing to pray for, but with an honest heart, we will pray for His will to be done (Matt. 6:10).

According to James 4:3, it is evident that, at times, we do not receive what we request of God because our requests are simply to satisfy our sinful pleasures. What are some examples of requests you previously made that you can now see were more for your pleasure and not aligned with His will?

James equates praying with selfish motives to spiritual adultery.

_____

_____

Read James 4:4.

James begins his next thought with, "You adulteresses!" You may wonder, "Why the harsh language?" He is reprimanding the person who prays to God, claiming to be His servant, and yet prays with selfish motives, which shows that he is actually a servant of self and the world and not of God. He "wants to have his cake and eat it too" and God says, "No deal."

What does verse 4 call friendship with the world? _____

What does it call the man who wishes to be a friend of the world? _____

It is so easy to read these verses and dismiss ourselves from them, thinking that we aren't friends with the world if we aren't committing those "big, serious" sins. But, the verses directly before these statements simply focused on the selfish intentions of the mind and heart in prayer. If our mindset and "heartset" are self-seeking and not God-filled and grace-filled from abiding in God, then we are living in hostility toward God and making ourselves His enemy.

Once again, we see James tracing the origin of the problem back to our old enemy, "double-mindedness." We cannot live for ourselves and live for the Lord at the same time. Oftentimes, the Old Testament referred to those who were unfaithful to God as adulterers. Time and time again they turned away from God and worshiped false idols, committing spiritual adultery. We are the bride of Christ, and we will see in the next verse, that He takes that very seriously.

We cannot live for ourselves and live for God at the same time.

Read James 4:5.

James is clearly frustrated with the recipients of this letter. He has just called them adulterers and he begins the current verse by asking a pointed, rhetorical question. He is quite literally saying, "Do you think God is just wasting His breath when He says that He is jealous for you?" God is rightfully jealous for the love of His bride. He paid an unthinkable price in order to call us His own; we owe Him a lifetime of gratitude, and He expects it.

Occasionally, during our Sunday morning worship service, we sing the song "You Are My King." Consider these words *"Amazing love, how can it be, that You, my King, would die for me..."* The thought of our King stepping down from His throne in order to take the death penalty for me, a guilty subject who knelt before Him, is tough to comprehend. But, He did and how great a debt we owe – amazing love, how can it be? Our King died in order to rise again and take us as His bride. In return, He deserves our endless love and faithful service.

God is rightfully jealous for the love of His bride.

Read Zechariah 8:2. While this verse obviously speaks of God's chosen people, Israel, it reveals to us His jealous nature for His people. We, the church, are His bride and His jealousy extends to us.

"With great wrath I am jealous for her..." It's a great love story, but it's also very serious business. He paid the price, He's offered us joy beyond imagination for all eternity, and He's offered us His peace in this life. But, we are not to take those gifts and live our lives selfishly. We are to live understanding the debt of life we owe and realize that His jealousy comes mixed with wrath when we turn away from Him and don't make Him the priority of our lives.

Our King deserves our endless love and faithful service.

Are you living faithfully with Christ? Of what other "loves" might He be jealous?

_____

_____

Read James 4:6.

Let's review. Our self-seeking hearts are made evident even in our prayers, and our friendship with the world is hostility toward God. He has every right to be angry and jealous of our spiritual unfaithfulness, but thankfully, it doesn't end there.

Fill in the blank according to verse 6. *"But, He gives us a greater _____."*

Although God is serious in His jealousy, although He is the righteous Judge whose standard is perfection – **He gives us a greater grace.** This is such a short sentence; it can get glossed over so easily. We have a debt that we cannot pay. Christ had to die for it. Although our lives are still owed to the One who is worthy, when we fail to live our lives perfectly, His grace is sufficient to meet the standard of His own jealousy. He is Jealous God, He is Righteous Judge, but He is also Grace, and Mercy, and Love.

I've mentioned that I (Dave) have a daughter with a neurologic condition that has made life "challenging," shall we say. When she was younger, she would throw such violent tantrums that I often had to physically restrain her. At times, as heart-breaking as it was, I was forced to confine her to her room and hold the door shut while her fury stormed on the other side. Far too frequently, she would grab whatever she could find and gouge holes in the walls or the back of the door. At times, while under restraint, it was not uncommon for her to scream all kinds of hateful things at me and use her only weapon available – her head – sometimes to head-butt me, other times to literally spit in my face. Once her fury receded (and it always did), I would hold her, cry with her, and always, always, always reassure her of my love and forgiveness. Sometimes, I would tell her how much I loved her as I literally filled in the holes in the wall, or as I put Band-Aids on the wounds she had made with her fingernails. Over and over this scene would be played out – the one wounded and offended extending love, grace, and forgiveness to the one who had wronged.

That is the way God is toward us when He must be firm with us, yet in His love, chooses to follow discipline with grace. He looks at us through righteous eyes that expect our very best, and He will discipline us accordingly when we fail to live for Him. But, He follows it with grace and love that doesn't give up on us even when we "spit in His face." He gives us a greater grace.

What are some areas in your life where you frequently stumble and fall for which God has to repeatedly give you His greater grace?

_____

_____

He is Jealous God, He Righteous Judge, but He is also Grace, Mercy, and Love!

To whom does the end of verse six say He gives this grace? _____

It is the one who humbles himself before the Lord, allowing God to have His will in his life rather than seeking his own satisfaction, that will receive infinite grace when he stumbles. God opposes the proud and doesn't hear their selfish prayers as they have declared themselves His enemies. But, to the humble – those who are willing to pray, "Not my will but yours," living his life in gratitude for the price paid for him – to such as these, He gives grace beyond reason.

What "holes in the wall" would God need to address as He firmly, yet graciously asks you for **all** of your faithfulness to Him?

_____

Those who humble themselves before the Lord will receive infinite grace when they stumble.

Day Three – Joy Comes in the "Mourning"

Yesterday, we left off with *"GOD IS OPPOSED TO THE PROUD, BUT GIVES GRACE TO THE HUMBLE."* Our next verse in James brings us to a "therefore" moment. You'll remember from Week 2, Day 3 what question we need to ask when we encounter "therefore in Scripture. What was it?

_____

Read James 4:7a

This verse begins with *"Submit therefore to God."* Therefore refers back to what was previously stated and is followed by a command related to how to respond. So, what has James said? In a nutshell, he has stated, "We are a mess. We're self-absorbed, we have selfish motives that lead to conflict in our own lives and the lives of others, we're friends with the world and enemies of God. Even then, however, God will give grace to those who are **humble** – THEREFORE SUBMIT TO GOD!"

What does the word submission mean to you?

_____

First, submission is **not** abject humiliation and forced obedience. It is a willing deference to another, a rearranging of one's priorities for another, which results in obedience. In reference to God, it means to forego what we want and do all in an effort to please Him.

Who do you serve daily with even your smallest actions? Do you think about God's place in all you do, or is He an afterthought for whom you do **some** specific things, but not **all** things?

_____

"Submit to God" is such a broad statement because it entails surrendering every tiny facet of our lives to God! Where do we start? Thankfully, James lays out some simple guidelines to follow in order to live humbly in God-honoring submission.

Read James 4:7. What is the command following submission? _____

What is the promise that comes with that command? _____

In order to humble ourselves and rightly submit our lives to God, we must resist Satan and the things that Satan loves. Remember, Satan isn't actively behind every temptation to sin, but his fingerprints are all over every sinful act, and we must learn to resist attitudes and actions that would portray any likeness of him within us. The Greek word used for resist in this verse is awesome. *Anthistémi* means "to stand against, oppose, withstand, set against." It isn't a timid, feeble attempt to survive temptation and hope that Satan, or the temptation, will eventually just go away. This type of resistance doesn't play defense. No, it is a bold, offensive

There is grace for those who will humbly submit to God.

Submission is a willing deference to another, voluntarily placing one's priorities under another's.

anthistémi – to stand against, oppose, withstand, set against stand against sin, a direct opposition to Satan, a mind set against anything ungodly, and a will that chooses to withstand the attack of the enemy with firm resolve. Make no mistake, this tells us that the truly humble Christian is **strong**! To make such self-disciplined decisions day in and day out takes strength of character and fierce determination.

What happens when we resist the devil? _____

Read James 4:7-8.

In these verses we find a series of cause and effect statements. <u>If</u> we boldly stand against sin, <u>then</u> Satan will flee and temptation will subside. When we remove one thing, it makes room for another.

If we boldy stand against sin, Satan will flee and temptation will subside.

According to verse 8, when we remove sin, who has room to draw near? _____

If we put aside our sin, we are sacrificing the part of our thoughts, desires, and motives that make us double-minded. It is the single-minded person, who strongly resolves to live solely for the Lord that finds security in His nearness. Our sin pushes us away from God, yet when we resist, He is able to draw near.

We know we need to submit. But, how do we do that? We resist sin and draw near to God. How do we draw near to God? We realign our character to match His. How do we do that? We're glad you asked. ☺

Our sin pushes us away from God, yet when we resist, He draws near.

What command is given after we are told to draw near to God? _____

James gives us a quick list of commands that are intended for instruction in keeping our hearts aligned with God's. The first of these commands is to "*cleanse your hands.*" When we are saved by grace, we are washed clean by the blood of the Lamb. Sin doesn't change that eternal status, but we can certainly get our hands messy from time to time while living in this fallen world. Sometimes we just need a good hand washing.

Here James calls for a "**re-do.**" Our hands symbolize our outward actions, the things we **do**. We need to look at our lives, our actions, our external behavior, and decide whether or not they line up with God's standard. If they don't, we need to recognize sin for what it is, wash up, and get right.

If our hands (our outward actions) don't meet God's standard, we need to wash them.

Read Psalm 24:3-4.

According to verse 4, list the first two requirements for the one who can stand before the Lord (or in James' words – "*draw near to God*").

_____

According to James 4:8, after cleansing our hands, what are we commanded to do as we submit to God?

_____

Not only do we need to "re-do," we need to **re-think.** Both the psalmist and James agree that purifying our outward behavior is not enough; a purified heart is required of the one who wants to stand before, or draw near to, the Lord. The Pharisees prided themselves on their impeccable outward appearance, but Christ said they were rotten where it mattered most – in their hearts. We've already seen that our outward actions can't help but demonstrate our inward attitude; these verses merely support the fact that both have to be clean to be in right standing with God.

Read James 4:9.

Fill in the blanks: Be _____ and _____ and _____.

Well, isn't that just the icing on the cake? Why in the world would James tell us to be miserable and mourn and weep? Does he want us to be perpetually dismal, gloomy, and forlorn? Wasn't he the one asking us to consider our trials as joy at the beginning of the book?

A pure heart is also required of those who want to be drawn near to God.

What might James be implying when he gives such an instruction?

_____

James doesn't mean to say that the Christian life should be bleak and depressing. Rather, he is calling for the Christian to **repent**. Be miserable living in sin, mourn for the place it has brought you to, for the effect it is having on your life, and weep for the distance it has placed between you and God. Repentance is a complete turning away from something, a new path chosen that entirely forsakes the old.

As you think about this picture portrayed of misery, mourning, and weeping, you may think of past sins that consumed you – habits that were addicting, sinful characteristics that controlled your life. Perhaps you're tired of being ruled by things that are only dragging you down, and you hate who you have become at the hands of your own sin. If so, you may need to literally mourn the loss of what you could have been due to what you've become. You may simply need to repent and submit.

Read 2 Corinthians 7:8-11.

Paul felt somewhat badly for hurting the feelings of the church in Corinth for the previous letter he'd had to send calling them out on their sin. But, not badly enough to regret sending it or to regret its effects. He hurt for them as they needed to mourn their previous state, but he knew it was necessary and was grateful that his bold words of chastisement brought his desired result.

We are to be miserable living in sin, to mourn where sin has taken us, and to weep for the distance it has created between us and God.

What does verse 10 say their godly sorrow brought? _____

What does verse 11 say their godly sorrow produced? _____

_____

When there is true, godly sorrow over one's sin, it produces all sorts of positive reactions that become life-changing as a person moves forward. There is an eagerness to leave the old behind and move forward in freedom, a hatred of the sin that once chained them down, and a healthy fear of ever returning to that miserable state in life.

Verse 10: Godly sorrow produces repentance without _____.

Be miserable, mourn, and weep over your current state of sin, allow it to make you feel sick enough that you are ready to get well, but repent and move on in joy. Godly sorrow does not lead us to the pit of self-loathing. That is exactly where Satan wants you to find yourself, but God says, "Repent and move on." We need not keep any record of the past. God keeps no record, but Satan certainly wants us to. It's by this method that he tempts us to live in guilt and defeat. But, God wants us to only remember enough of our sin to have a healthy fear of ever returning to it. He doesn't want us to live under the weight of guilt, for that will only keep us from being useful for Him.

What healthy fears from the past have you developed that prevent future mistakes in specific areas of your life?

_____

What past regrets do you have that you need to let go of in order to move forward in the freedom of His forgiveness?

_____

Godly sorrow leads to a hatred of the sin that once chained us down, and a healthy fear of ever returning to it.

James 4:9 – *"Let your laughter be turned into _____ and your joy into _____."*

Again, James is not calling for a dismal existence. He's told us to "re-do," "re-think," "repent," and now he is commanding us to "**rearrange**." We must rearrange our lifestyle, our commitments, our priorities, and our convictions, to match those of the Lord's. What formerly brought us laughter, we must now mourn over; what we previously felt would bring us joy, needs to bring us gloom if we realize these things were sinful. It is good for us to mourn the sinful things that we formerly thought would bring us happiness, because it is then that we realize that our thinking was skewed and we can open our hearts to new, godly thinking. We are to mourn for the state of our sinful hearts, for **then** we are prepared to humble ourselves.

God says, "Repent and move on." We need keep no record of our past.

Read James 4:10.

It was when James humbled himself and realized that he'd been so wrong and that Jesus had been so right that God was able to effectively use him. Only when James realized that life wasn't about himself was God able to exalt him in his humility. It was necessary for him to realize that his selfishness had clouded his mind and that he wanted nothing more than to move forward with God.

We must rearrange our convictions to match those of the Lord's.

Notice how our position, relative to God, progresses through these verses. The beginning of the chapter showed us the mess that sin and selfish ambition gets us into. The following verses show us how to make room for God to draw near as we resist sin and realign our hearts. Assuming we have followed those instructions, we can find ourselves, according to verse 10, in the presence of God, drawn near. Through this process we have humbled ourselves to the point where it is now HE who can exalt us. As we exalt ourselves, we push God away and don't allow Him to exalt us in the amazing ways He'd like. But, when we die to self, oh the amazing things He has in store for us.

When we die to self, He can exalt us.

Who do you think can exalt you better – imperfect you – or the Creator of the universe? In what ways do you need to humble yourself, so that God can exalt you?

_____

_____

Admittedly, this is a hard process and His "exalting" won't be the same as what your own would have been. But, He may blow your mind with what you never expected or fathomed possible. We must, though, allow ourselves to become broken enough that we mourn who we are and what we've become in comparison to what He'd have us to be. What God has for us is joy beyond reason, joy that can be found in the midst of trials, joy that enables us to love unconditionally in the midst of hurt, joy that finds supernatural strength in our weakest earthly moments. But, this joy is a result of our humility, submission, and mourning. We often sing that "joy comes in the morning." May we submit to you that "joy comes in the **mourning**?"

Joy comes in the mourning over our brokenness.

Can you remember a time when God replaced your mourning with His joy?

_____

_____

Is there any sin you need to mourn now to allow Him to replace it with His joy? Remember, joy comes in the mourning.

Today is a good day to: "re-do" (wash your hands); "re-think" (purify your attitudes); "repent" and "rearrange" your priorities (submit).

_____

_____

Day Four – To Judge or Not To Judge

Even Christians have a tendency to eat our own with our words.

Gerbils, wolves, wolf spiders, polar bears, hippos, and Evangelicals. All species that have been known to eat their own. Before you argue too strongly, read on. Yesterday, we ended by looking at the way God exalts the humble man. Interestingly, in verse 11, James begins showing us ways that man exalts himself, actually going so far as to assume the role of God in the lives of others.

Read James 4:11-12.

Do not _____ against _____ _____, brethren.

By referring to his readers as "brethren," James reminds us that he is talking with Christians. How sad it is that he has to keep reminding fellow Christians about the dangers of their spoken words. But, the truth is, we have a tendency to "eat our own" with our words. It's ugly, and God needed James to address it. We have already discussed the source of our words, and the fact that they are powerful tools, but today we are going to get specific concerning a few ways those words can cause trouble.

katalaleó – 1. to speak evil of / slander; 2. to rail at; 3. to talk down

The Greek word used for speaking against another in James 4:11 is *katalaleó*. This word includes the concept of gossip, but it reaches much further in its meaning. It means "to speak evil of, slander, to rail at, to talk down."

Using the definition above, list several ways in which we can "speak against another."

_____

_____

By speaking against others, we place ourselves in a position of superiority over them.

Verse 11 says that the one who speaks against his brother, speaks against and judges the law. This makes him not a "doer of the law," but a judge of it. The law tells us not to speak against each other but to love our neighbor as ourselves. When we speak against our fellow Christians as their judge, we are placing ourselves in a position of superiority over them. By doing this, we are assuming that our opinion in a matter is correct and theirs is incorrect. Speaking against them, in the manner portrayed in verse 11, shows that we have disregarded the part of the law that tells us not to do such a thing. Instead, we judge them concerning some other parts of the law that we are certain they have broken and need to be made aware of.

We disrespect God's authority by taking His matters into our hands.

According to verse 12, whose responsibility is judgment? _____

Fill in the blank: "...*but _____ _____ _____ who judge your neighbor?*"

In other words, "Who do you think you are? Who died and made you the judge?" By exalting ourselves to the position of God in judging our brother, we are not only harming our brother, but we are entirely disrespecting God's law, and His authority in the situation. We disrespect God's law by disregarding a portion of it in order to promote our own opinions or preferences. We disrespect His authority by taking a matter out of His hands and placing it in our own. Either way, we are walking on dangerous ground. Let's first look at how being judgmental affects us personally, and then we will focus on how it affects others.

Read Matthew 7:1-5.

When working with children, especially siblings, it is painfully obvious that they are often quick to lay blame on kids around them. How often have parents said to their kids, "You worry about you; I'll worry about your brother or sister." Jesus is saying that very thing in these verses. How dare we use the time that should be spent on correcting **our** sins for pointing out what we deem to be the sins of others? When we break the law in order to point out our opinion of someone else's infraction of the law, we are nothing more than a guilty hypocrite.

By what standard does Matthew 7:2 tell us we will be judged?

_____

_____

The more grace we lavish on others, the more grace God will extend to us.

Long before Schwarzenegger was the Terminator, yours truly was "The Determinator." In my mind, I was blessed with the uncanny ability to determine everything I needed to know about a person upon first glance. If you asked, me, I could accurately size people up in an instant, judge and execute them justly on the spot. Unfortunately, the Determinator rarely saw the need to give grace; I was much more interested in handing out my brand of "justice." Then Matt 7:2 got a hold of me. I learned that the more judgment I dished out, the more severely I would be judged. I was in BIG trouble. Thankfully, I also learned that the more grace I was willing to give to others, the more grace God was willing to extend to me. As this truth soaked in, I found myself praying more for others, asking God to show them grace, knowing that I needed His grace just as badly, if not more. Seeing myself as guilty before a just God softened my heart, making it more pliable and ready for God to use in the lives of others.

When others think of you, do they fear your criticism, or know that you will treat them with grace?

_____

_____

When your family thinks of you, do they fear your criticism, or know that you will meet them with grace?

_____

_____

When we criticize others, we invite God to do the same to us.

We ask that second question because, sad as it is, we often over-criticize our families in ways that we would never consider doing to others outside of our home. It may be a universal truth, but James says it's universally wrong and should be stopped.

When we lead with criticism, we are inviting God to do the same to us. We are telling Him that this is the standard by which we would like Him to judge us. The thought of that should scare some sense into us! We should run from the harshness that invites equal harshness from the *"One who is able to save and destroy"* (James 4:12).

Now that we've seen how speaking against others adversely affects us, let's turn our focus to a few of the many ways it can destroy others. Remember, when we judge in this manner, we are exalting ourselves to the position of God. But, what does that really look like?

We said earlier that there were 3 parts of the definition of our Greek word *katalaleó*. The first one we will pay specific attention to is "to speak evil of, slander."

How is speaking evil of another, or slandering them "playing God" in their life?

_____

There is no such thing as harmless gossip. Gossip of any type can land others in a prison of hurt.

As guys, the word, "gossip" may not have immediately come to mind. But, gossip is not something that only women are prone to. It is a fierce enemy that wreaks havoc in the lives of the one being slandered, the one listening to the gossip, as well as the deliverer of the juicy bit of news. We've already seen that the deliverer is inviting judgment on himself. But, what of the other two?

What effects can gossip have on the victim who is the object of its focus?

_____

Read Genesis 39:6-19.

If he were standing here today, I wonder what Joseph would say to us about the damage one person's words can do in the life of another. Potiphar's wife certainly stepped into the role of God, taking into her own hands what would become of Joseph after she slandered him to others. She was miserable, and if she couldn't have her way, she was going to make him miserable, too. She threw out her words carelessly because it mattered little to her what would become of him, and as far as she knew, it wasn't going to cause any discomfort in her own life. But, what of Joseph? Her careless words landed him in prison for longer than two years when he'd done nothing wrong. Punished and imprisoned for having done nothing more than stand for his integrity, his entire world was changed due to what one person said and how others were forced to respond to it.

It would be easy to look at this extreme example and excuse ourselves from the application, thinking that we would never throw out careless lies about such a serious topic. But, gossip of any shape and size can land others in a prison of pain. Even if the message relayed is not intended to be false, when we speak against another, we are casting that person in a negative light. Based on our messages, they are trapped by the negative impression we've made of them. You may think, "I didn't try to cast them in a negative light." The question back to you – "But did you try **not** to?"

Can you see how gossip is a form of judgment and speaking against another? Is this a problem area in your life that you need to address? As you've read about speaking against another, has the Holy Spirit brought someone to mind – do you need to apologize?

_____

_____

Read Romans 14:4.

Who are you to judge another man's servant? For you dads, what happens inside of you when someone speaks against one of your children? I know my kids aren't perfect, but they're MY kids and I know them well and love them completely. When someone else thinks they know them better and speaks against them when they clearly have their facts wrong, I begin donning my Rambo gear 'cuz trouble's coming. Yes, there are negative things about them others could say that are true, but I have unconditional love and grace for them, because I am their daddy and I want others to understand the good in them even more than any bad habits or faults. God is like that with us. When others take the liberty to speak against us, thinking they know our hearts and motives, but not having our best interests in mind, God says, "Hey Buster, that's MY child you're talking about! You might want to think twice before you say any more!"

No matter how much insight we think we have into a situation, unless we are God, there is no way we have all the facts and we need to graciously bow out of the "conversation." It is not our place to assume the position of judge when so many extenuating circumstances surround every facet of life.

We simply can't know all the facts in all situations; therefore we should usually bow out.

Your authors simply refuse to grow old. We will always love cartoons and a line from one relates to this topic. In the movie, "How to Train Your Dragon," the Vikings had thought for hundreds of years that the dragons were mean, vicious beasts. But, after capturing one of them and nursing it back to health, the main character, Hiccup, says, "Everything we know about you guys is wrong." The irony of his statement is so telling. "Everything we **know**…" Rather, it should have been "everything we **thought** we knew…" We can be so assured that our opinion concerning others is right, but it can be so wrong. **We don't know what we don't know**. We have no idea how much more there is to learn about others and their situations; only God knows the heart of man. In other words, our "Determinators" are just plain wrong. So, let's allow Him to show us what we need to know about others instead of formulating our own opinions. In addition, we need to avoid leading others to form wrong opinions as well.

We don't know what we don't know. Only God knows the heart of man.

Do you form an opinion about every person or situation you hear about? Are you willing to begin saying, "I don't know all the facts, therefore I can/will stay out of it?" How might this attitude be beneficial to you and those around you?

_____

_____

Sharing gossip places the one we've told it to in a very awkward position.

Not only do we harm ourselves and the victims of gossip when we speak against others in this way, but we also cause hardship for the one we are speaking to. If we speak negatively with someone about another person, we have put something on their plate that God did not intend for them to have to deal with. Suddenly, we are forcing them to have to decide via second or third-hand information whether or not what we're saying is true and what they are going to do with it. In other words, when we tell "person A" something about "person B," "person A" has to decide whether to believe us or to give the other person the benefit of the doubt. They must further decide whether or not to tell anyone else, keep it to themselves, or act on what they've heard. Truly, this is playing God and we need to keep well away from it. Who are we to think we should have such influence in the lives of others?

Describe a time when you were placed in an awkward situation when someone shared information about another person that you didn't need to hear. How did you handle it? Would you do something different next time?

_____

_____

katalaleó – to rail at

The next part of the definition of *katalaleó* emphasized today is "to rail at." In a sense, we play God when we rail at someone, too. By doing so, we are acting as judge, jury, and executioner as we pass them their guilty verdict and serve them their penalty in the form of a verbal bludgeoning. Ever been completely lambasted by someone's words? It's not much fun, is it? Ever been the one doing the railing? The next time the temptation to do so comes your way, remember that you are inviting the same measure of judgment on yourself from the One who would look at you and say, "That's MY child you're judging!"

What are the implications of this sort of "speaking against" another? First, we are giving the other person the impression that they are not worthy of being treated with basic human respect. The way you speak to, or at, another person conveys to them the value you place in them. Do your words value or devalue those inside and outside of your home? Second, the message of our words can burden them with extra baggage. Do you really need others weighing you down with more baggage than you already carry by the hurtful impressions they scream into your lives? If we answer "no" to that question, is it fair for us to play God and do it to others? God has plans for His servants, and if we are weighing them down with hurt and baggage that they have trouble unloading, we've taken God's place and kept them from being able to do His will as freely as He'd like them to.

The way you speak to, or at, others conveys the value you place in them.

Words can easily form one's self-opinion. Recall a time when someone's words affected who you believed you could or couldn't be.

_____

_____

How might the way you talk to others be affecting what they believe they could or couldn't be?

katalaleó – to talk down

_____

_____

Closely-related is the last part of the definition for *katalaleó*. "To talk down" can injure as much as either of the other two meanings. To criticize and condescend can make a person feel small, useless, unworthy, and may give them the impression that they will never amount to anything. God tells us time and time again in His Word how much He values us, how amazing He finds us, and how much He loves us. It is interesting that He, who has the right to judge, goes to every length to build us up, while we, who have no right to judge, go to great lengths to tear each other down. Let us all remember what Paul wrote to the Ephesians, "*Do not let any unwholesome talk come out of your mouths, but only what is helpful for building others up according to their needs, that it may benefit those who listen*" (Eph. 4:29, NIV).

Next time you're tempted to criticize another, take a moment and ask if it's really necessary. In the long run, is the criticism of any eternal significance? Even if it is, is it really your place to give it? Instead of sending a condescending message, could a message of grace potentially work a miracle?

Have you ever been in the middle of an absolutely terrible day when someone decided to pick you apart about the most trivial thing? On a day like that, you may not even have the energy to respond with more than a defeated shrug and a head hung low. That person didn't know where you were in that moment, but their words cut and it was the last thing you needed. Friends, this life is hard, and we are all carrying hurts that perhaps no one else even realizes. Before speaking against anyone in any manner, remember that you can't possibly have all the facts; only God does. Your words may be cutting deep into a heart that you don't realize is already breaking. God says, "Don't do it. I will judge when I need to judge. You worry about you. I'll worry about everyone else." Think before you speak. When we exalt ourselves to the place of God, we tread on dangerous ground. It will be hard to see the fingerprints of God on those we've covered with our bruises. Make sure it's His impression being left on those He loves, not yours.

It is hard to see the fingerprints of God on those we've covered with bruises.

Day Five — Caution: Construction Ahead

Five years ago, could you have possibly fathomed where you are right now?

Is there anything more frustrating than waking up later than you intended, having to rush out the door without your coffee or breakfast, and drive like a maniac only to encounter the dreaded orange traffic cones and signs that read, "Road Work Ahead. Right two lanes closed. Please merge left"? We may think (or shout), "Lord, of all days, not today!" But, who has honestly ever said, "Fantastic! Today is a great day to sit in bumper-to-bumper traffic for an extra 30 minutes! I am so glad this is happening." Not on your life. We like "our lane" wide open for smooth sailing and we hate to yield to, and merge our plans with, a higher highway authority. Yesterday, we looked at the way man can exalt himself by "playing God" in the lives of others. Today, we will see how he can assume the role of God in his own life.

Read James 4:13.

To illustrate his point, James directs his attention to a man making his business plans. This man has his eyes set on a profit and has made a deliberate plan, with absolute confidence in its success. James isn't condemning the man for wanting to make a profit; rather, he is calling him out on his arrogance and self-reliance.

Read James 4:14.

Why is it foolish to plan with absolute confidence in oneself?

_____

We don't even know what tomorrow holds! Think of wherever it was you were in life five years ago. At that time, could you have possibly fathomed where you find yourself right now? Although you may be working the same job, have the same friends, and live in the same house, have circumstances and events altered your world during those five years in ways that were entirely out of your control? We know firsthand that life is filled with changes that we could not have imagined, and we would guess the same could be said for most of you as well.

It is foolish to believe that we know more about our future than the One who holds the future.

James says, "*…you do not know what your life will be like tomorrow.*" But, there is One who does. It is quite foolish for us to believe that we know more about our future than the One who holds the future in His hands.

Imagine encountering a group of children who are planning to ride their skateboards through your neighborhood after school. As an adult with a broader understanding of surrounding events, you know that this is not a good idea because road construction is scheduled to begin that very evening. You know that the condition of the road is going to be altered and not only will this interrupt their plans, it will also be dangerous for them to try to ride their boards in the midst of the construction. The intention behind their original plan isn't wrong; you just know more about the situation than they do.

God knows about every upcoming, unforeseen "construction project" that is going to alter our path. Our insistence on sticking unwaveringly to plans on the paths before us must look foolish to His all-knowing eyes.

What are some of the "plans" we make, and what is our motivation in making them?

_____

_____

Our stubbornness to stick to our plans must look foolish to God.

Like Angie, I grew up a very "plan-oriented" person. I had 1-year, 5-year, and 10-year plans. I even carried my annual goals in my wallet. I like organization and my ducks to be as God intended – in nice, neat rows! So giving this area of my life over to God hasn't been easy. Learning to find the balance between personal planning and structure and giving God the freedom to change my "structure" is just plain tough. Again, there is nothing wrong with being orderly; in fact, it helps simplify much of life. The issue is not with structure, but with an adamant, self-assured attitude that gives no consideration to God and leaves no room for Him to work in the midst of that structure.

In order to look at this practically, let's consider a popular Bible figure: Jacob.

Read Genesis 25:27-34.

Jacob manipulated situations by means of being a crafty planner, which left no room for God to work out the details in his life. In this case, his motive was his **selfishness**. He had a desire to have what his brother, Esau, had and he was willing to do whatever it took to get it for himself.

Planning and structure are not the problem. Leaving no room for God to work in, or change, that structure is.

In this particular example, Jacob's motives were self-seeking, not giving thought or care to the damage that his plan would inflict on his family. At times, we, too, can be selfish in this manner. We may have our eyes so fixed on an end goal, that we don't give any thought to how the ripple effects of our plan may adversely affect, or even burden, others. Like Jacob, the ones most likely to pay the price for our selfish plans may share our last name. We know that God is never in the midst of this sort of plan; He does not support the selfish desires of His spoiled children.

God does not support the selfish desires of His children.

Consider your most significant plans; what possible costs are they placing on others?

_____

_____

God knows every circumstance that is going to demolish the very ground we plan to walk on.

James 4:14 –

"You are just a _____ that appears for a _____ while and _____ away".

Reread that verse and think about it for a moment longer, letting its truth sink in deeply. Our lives are vapors; we are here today and gone tomorrow. How can we, mere mists, suppose we know more than our heavenly Father? Our God knows the bigger picture; He realizes every "construction crew" that is going to demolish the very ground we plan to walk on. He knows the "construction" that is going to take place in our lives and in the lives of others, and

He miraculously knows how every detail of that fits together from eternity past to eternity future. He's got the entire picture to organize, and when we have the audacity to think that our selfish desires should alter that master plan, we will learn through much heartache that they don't after all. You are a mist; He is the Maker – leave the planning to Him.

Read James 4:15.

We often do everything we can to secure our own blessings.

Realizing the brevity of our lives in the grand scheme should help us to maintain a God-directed perspective. When we come to this realization, we must alter our prayers to ask whatever we ask according to His will. James begins His "sample prayer" with such a broad focus that it covers all other things. *"If the Lord wills, we will LIVE..."* (emphasis added). Our very lives are in His hands; whether we are here or gone tomorrow is completely at the mercy of His sovereign will. With this truth always at the forefront of our minds, we should understand that our own plans, even the smallest ones, are futile, and everything we do should be done with God's permission.

True or False: I always seek God's will for the direction of my life. _____

True or False: I generally make my plans first, and then ask God to bless them. _____

What can you do to bring God into your planning process? _____

_____

We've seen one of Jacob's plans motivated by selfishness, let's continue with him and see what other motivating factors drove him in his ambitions.

Read Genesis 27:18-33.

Invite God into the planning process and accept His answers.

Attaining his brother's birthright wasn't enough, Jacob wanted more. He was looking out for his future and he was motivated by a desire for **smooth sailing.** Indeed, the con job Jacob pulled on his father was absolutely fueled by selfishness, but let's look at the specifics. By attaining the blessing of the first-born son, Jacob thought he was sealing the deal on a cushy retirement! He would be blessed with material wealth, his own extended family would eventually serve him, and God's hand of protection would be on him. This plan was to attain the mother-load of all blessings. We all long for security, so can you blame him? This was the guarantee that the 401K was steady and secure, his climb up the ladder of success was certain, and his worries would be behind him (or so he thought).

Let's be honest guys - we do this in our lives, too. We may not trick someone out of their own blessings, but we often do everything we can to secure our own. We make strategic investments, we settle ourselves in a nice house in an excellent neighborhood, we find a church that meets all of our "requirements," we choose our children's schools where they will have the best, etc. We are on a constant search for what will make us "happy," and the plans we make for our lives often revolve around that pursuit of smooth sailing. We may read that list and wonder what would be wrong with any of those goals. This is America after all, where we hold to the inalienable right to the "pursuit of happiness." There is nothing inherently wrong with this. The question is whether or not we invite God into the planning process and whether we will accept His answer or deny it if it doesn't match our plan.

How often do we plan so stringently that we don't allow God to disrupt us by sending in a "construction crew" to come and fix our potholes? God knows that disruptions in our lives can be the very things that make us closer to the creation He wants us to be. We may desire smooth sailing, but we must still submit our plans to Him and ask Him if they are His will. His answer may be something entirely different than what we had hoped for. I have found that traveling the rough and rocky road can bring us to the most beautiful places. Certainly, we will experience a greater variety of scenery during this trip called life than if we'd stuck solely to our perfectly-planned paths. Oftentimes, joy is found in the journey; even when detours are involved.

God can use the disruptions in our lives to make us into the creation He wants us to be.

One of the saddest parts of Jacob's story is that God always intended for Jacob to receive his father's blessing; Jacob never needed to manipulate the situation. His mother was given that promise when Jacob was still in the womb (Gen. 25:23). But, neither Jacob or Rebekah were patient enough to allow God to work out the details. When they thought that time was running out, they intervened and took matters into their own hands. Yes, Jacob received the blessing, but he suffered harsh consequences as well.

Are you willing to wait for God's timing or do you generally push forward with your own plans?

_____

Have you regretted plans you made without God's input? If so, how?

_____

Read Genesis 27:41-45.

Verse 44 says that Rebekah told Jacob to run away and stay with Laban for a few days until Esau cooled down, and Jacob did so. This plan was for his future **safety** and **security.** Notice the specifics of the plan. He was to stay with Laban for a "few days." Whether what is meant here implies a few literal days or even a few years, God proved that their plans were futile compared to His sovereign authority. They made a hasty decision without consulting God, and their details didn't work out anything like they intended, as a "few days" turned into 20 years.

God determines the success or failure of all plans.

Read Proverb 19:21

God determines the success or failure of all plans. Whether we like it or not, it's out of our hands.

When Jacob and Esau had this falling out, they were 77 years old; Jacob did not return home until he was 97. He was swindled by an uncle who was even more shrewd at manipulation than he was, and he was forced to forego his own plans for reasons he'd never expected. He was safe and secure with Laban, but he never fathomed how long the "construction crew" would be working on this particular road. His plan worked out in the end, but the details that he thought he had control of were completely out of his power.

Even when our intentions are as reasonable as safety and security, we must submit our requests to God and ask Him for **His** will to be done, not ours. But, Jacob took no time for such things at this point in his life.

In what ways have you tried to create safety and security (for yourself or others) through your own efforts, instead of relying on God?

_____

_____

Even when our intentions are reasonable, we must submit our requests to God.

During the 20 years that Jacob was forced to work for his uncle, he did grow in his relationship with the Lord. But, old habits die hard, and Jacob's knee-jerk reaction was still to plan quickly for himself without consulting with God. He continued to struggle with submission to God's will when it differed from his own. Our next passage finds him at age 97, traveling home carrying his old habit in his back pocket.

Read Genesis 32:3-12.

What did Jacob do in verses 7 – 8?

_____

What did he do in verses 9 – 12? _____

When Jacob heard that Esau was coming with four hundred men, he instantly assumed the worst and made a plan motivated by a need for **survival**. *After* he executed his plan, he prayed; after he got all of his ducks in a row, he went to God. Certainly there couldn't be anything wrong with seeking to assure one's survival, could there?

Look again at James 4:15: *"If the Lord wills, we will _____..."*

Our very lives are in His hands, and as hard of a pill as this may be to swallow, even our survival plans need to align with His will for us.

The time to pray is before we make our plans.

I remember several terrifying occasions as a teenager when my life depended on making split-second decisions. During those times, I shifted into "survival mode" and my thoughts weren't entirely rational. I made quick plans and decisions out of sheer panic. Jacob's plan to separate his huge entourage of servants as well as his family was strategically savvy. His plan, though, while apparently sound, was executed in panic.

Read Genesis 31:3.

God had just told him to return home, promising that He would be with him. The blessing that he'd received 20 years earlier included the provision that his brother would eventually serve him. But, Jacob didn't recall God's promises in the midst of panic; he resorted to his natural instinct and made a swift plan.

The next morning, he would find that his plan and panic had been for naught. Esau greeted him with kisses. We have the benefit of hindsight of their story in Scripture, but when we face our own urgent situations, it can be very difficult to not go into "quick fix" mode and do everything we can to survive an overwhelming hardship. We have many of our own promises from the Lord, but in moments of panic, they may not be what initially rises to the surface in our thinking.

We've all had crisis moments; times of fear and possible panic. When you find yourself in a fearful situation, do you respond like Jacob did and attempt to get your ducks in a row for God ahead of time? How might a situation have turned out better if you'd consulted God before making your plans?

_____

_____

Although it is difficult, we need to recall God's promises in the midst of our panic.

As stated earlier, planning is not bad. In fact, Scripture teaches the wisdom of planning before making commitments, etc. It is our motive and our inclusion of God, along with submission to His ultimate will, that make the difference. Paul gives us a good example of this in the following passages.

Read Acts 18:20-21, 1 Corinthians 4:19; 16:7.

Paul had a consistent pattern of praying for things that he was certain had godly motives, yet he humbly submitted to the fact that God might have other plans.

Read Romans 1:9-10.

Make it a consistent pattern to pray in all things; humbly submitting to God's plans.

Paul had tried repeatedly to visit Rome in order to bring them the gospel. Surely, intentions and motives can't be any more pure than that. Yet, God, for reasons unknown to Paul at the time, repeatedly stopped him from making it there.

One of the most wonderful facts found in the historical context of the book of Romans surrounds this very issue. Paul desperately wanted to make it to Rome to share the details of the gospel, but due to the fact that God did not allow it, he was forced to write it all down in a letter. This letter, which became the book of Romans, gives the most exhaustive explanation of God's righteousness revealed in the gospel found in any one book of the Bible. Because he wasn't able to establish a church in Rome, Paul wrote them a letter that gave them every detail he would have shared with them had he been able to come in person.

We have the book of Romans today because Paul did not get what he wanted years ago.

Paul's motives were pure and his intentions were great, but God had a bigger, better plan that involved a "construction crew" working in ways that Paul could not see. While the construction project was undoubtedly frustrating, what was being constructed contributed to the Kingdom far more than Paul could have imagined. For that, believers should be eternally grateful.

This is always the case. God knows best, absolutely. There is no getting around the fact that we can have the best of intentions, but if they do not work with God's will, the best intentions don't make the best plans.

With the benefit of hindsight, can you see the bigger blessing that came about because you specifically did NOT get what you hoped or prayed for? How? Remember, that blessing may have occurred in the life of another.

_____

_____

Christ prayed, "Father, not My will, but Yours be done." We cannot ask for more.

Read James 4:16-17.

In verse 16, James called out the planner who boasts in his arrogance. We, too, are called out by this passage for taking credit for our own success and placing absolute confidence in our plans. Even as our Savior prayed concerning His imminent death on the cross, He prayed, "Father, not My will, but Yours be done." We have no right to ask for more.

Verse 17 holds the reader accountable for all he has learned. He has been told that he is to submit to God's will in **all** things. Ignorance is no longer bliss after reading this passage, or the rest of James for that matter. To discount what has been taught, would now be sin.

We must allow God's Word to change our hearts, minds, and actions.

We are accountable for all we have learned thus far in our study of James as well. We must be what God wants us to be, do what God wants us to do, speak as God wants us to speak, and sense what God wants us to sense.[26] Not allowing what we have read in God's Word to change our hearts, minds, and actions, is sin.

We have completed four of the five chapters in James. Take a quick look back over the previous weeks; what have you learned to this point that you know you need to let change your heart, mind, and actions? Today is a great day to do the next right thing. Remember gentlemen, God's orange cones are reminders for us to slow down, yield to His authority and merge our plans with His. His construction project may be you – let the Master craftsman build!

_____

_____

_____

_____

------

26   Walvoord and Zuck, *BKC NT*, p. 832

WEEK SIX: A PRAYERFULLY PATIENT FAITH

Day One – The Lord of Sabaoth

Welcome to the beginning of our last week of study. It's gone quickly, hasn't it? We have consistently noted that the book of James was a letter written to Jewish Christians. This next portion of the letter, though, was a prophetic declaration concerning a particular, unsaved group.

James 5:1-6 is written about the unsaved, rich man.

Revisit James 2:1-7. Who was persecuting the Jewish Christians? _____

Earlier in James, we were able to see that references to the "rich man" in Scripture do not always have to be negative. In this case, though, the rich are definitely being called out for their misdeeds. To make sense of this passage, and what we're about to read in Chapter 5, it may help to remember that what is true today was true back then as well; namely, not everyone who sat in church was saved. It's not too hard to picture a hypothetical situation where the unsaved, rich oppressor has been shown his choice seat in the church, far from the poor man who was asked to sit on the floor. How the rich dude must have squirmed in his seat as this portion of the letter was read in front of the congregation concerning his own fate.

Read James 5:1-6.

We know this portion of James was not written to accuse rich Jewish believers for multiple reasons. For one, the absence of James' consistent reference to them as "brethren" is quite conspicuous. Even more so, the strict accusation with no accompanying message of grace or deliverance also marks a stark contrast regarding who this charge is against. This is not to say that the Jewish Christians did not benefit from its inclusion in the letter, as this segment will remind them not to envy the evil rich man, but to have faith that God will judge them in His time.

James 5:1 *"Come now, you rich, _____ and _____ for your miseries are coming."*

klaió – to weep; ololuzó – to howl – both describe the reaction of the wicked to coming judgment

Elsewhere in Scripture, the words weep (*klaió*) and howl (*ololuzó*) are both used to describe the reaction of the wicked to the coming of the Lord in the end times. "In fact, *ololuzó* is found only in the prophets in the Old Testament and always in the context of judgment."[27] James knew this and chose to use this word as its judgmental significance would quickly grasp his readers' attention and set the tone for the gravity of the message to follow.

Understanding the use of these words helps us accurately interpret the meaning of the rest of the passage. Based on these definitions, what "miseries" were coming their way?

_____

---

27   Moo, TNTC, *James*, p. 164

This passage is announcing the final, eternal judgment of the unrepentant, rich oppressor. As a reminder, neither James, nor any other biblical author, condemned wealth, but boldly rebuked an unhealthy love of, and misuse of, wealth.

James does not condemn wealth, just the love and misuse of it.

Verse 1 tells them that their miseries are "coming," but verses 2-3 use the present tense to describe the demise of their riches now. Even though James is warning them of the end times, the present tense depiction of material decay showed that those material items are truly worthless even in this present life. Since they hold no spiritual value, they have no eternal significance. These "treasures" were no good to them now, and would certainly be no good to them in the end, when wealth has no way of saving them from the fire.

By referring to both silver and gold as "rusted," James effectively points out the temporal nature of wealth by stating that even precious metals, though they cannot really rust, will come to ruin.

Material items hold no spiritual value; therefore, they have no eternal significance.

James 5:3 – "...their rust will be _____ and will consume your flesh like fire."

The material items they held onto for security would actually bear witness against them, pronouncing their final condemnation. The treasures, themselves, are not inherently evil, but the fact that they are all some people have to show when they meet the Lord, will seal their fate. Not only would the material items come to ruin, but the love of them would bring man to ruin as well.

In what temporal things have you tried to find security? How secure have you really been in them?

_____

_____

Not only will material items come to ruin, but the love of them can ruin us as well.

Reread the final sentence in verse 3. The first century churches looked for the return of Christ to occur during their lifetime. As a result, those who truly knew Christ should have been living with eternity in mind, holding loosely to the things of this world. However, the unbelievers in their midst, were storing up treasure in what they thought were their literal "last days." Foolishly, they were hoarding when the end was near, but what they were really storing up was their own coming judgment.

Read Matthew 6:19-24.

Matthew 6 tells us that whatever we treasure will eventually capture our hearts as well.

It would be easy to look at the first 3 verses in James 5 and wonder what is so wrong with saving money. After all, isn't saving being a good steward of what God has given us? Matthew 6 clearly tells us it is the devotion to money that makes it a danger. When money becomes consuming and what we truly serve, it takes the place of God in our lives and we tread on dangerous ground.

We will see in the following verses of James 5, that these rich oppressors were not just being savvy with their savings. They were hoarding, at a great cost to others, and ironically, to themselves as well.

Read James 5:4 and Deuteronomy 24:14-15.

According to Deut. 24, how often were the workers to be paid? _____

Why? _____

In that culture, a daily wage paid for daily bread for a laborer and his family. To withhold it was to potentially withhold life. Again, James uses the same imagery as he did in verse 3, stating that the unpaid wages literally cry out in accusation against the rich, cheating employer.

Read James 5:5. *"You have lived luxuriously _____ _____ _____..."*

Those who had hoarded their wealth at the expense of other people's lives were doing it in order to live in luxury during their stay on this earth. Their focus was that of instant gratification in this life without any concern for eternity. Even though the Lord had told them to be watching for His return, they were only watching out for a return on investment, instead of investing their lives in the Kingdom of God.

James condemns hoarding wealth in order to live in luxury here and now.

Are you living your life as if you could be in your last days? If you knew you only had a few months to live, what would you hold on to? What would you release?

_____

_____

What might you be hoarding? Are you holding onto something at the expense of others? What might it be costing them? Are you willing to loosen your grip just a little? Remember, two things cannot occupy the same space at once; what needs to go?

Two things cannot occupy the same space in your heart at one time.

_____

_____

Although this passage was written specifically about the hoarding of wealth by the unsaved rich man, we as Christians can find spiritual application within it. The rich kept to themselves what they were obligated to share for the benefit of the poor. What they had to share was life-giving, and hoarding it produced deadly results. Hoarding our faith is far more costly than any tangible wealth we might keep from others. We are to share the salvation we've been graciously given with the spiritually-poor. When we withhold our faith and do not share the Word daily, we are contributing to their death, just as the rich man who didn't give daily wages to the starving servant. By withholding the gospel, we are contributing to their eternal death, a demise far greater than mere physical death. Those unpaid "wages" cry out in accusation against us. What is our excuse? What are we allowing to stop us? In our selfishness, are we content with the "luxury" of our own spiritual security, not caring that we are living in a lost and dying world? Do we assume someone else will "pay" the spiritually-poor what they desperately need in order to live? Are we willing to watch them starve while we take care of our own needs and discount theirs?

By withholding our faith and the gospel, we are contributing to the spiritual death of others.

At the end of James 5:5, we see that, just like the fattened calf, the rich oppressor was doing nothing more than fattening up his own heart for the imminent day of slaughter. His last days were coming, and he was preparing his heart to that end.

Our last days are coming. To what end are you preparing your heart?

_____

_____

Read James 5:6.

Verse 6 gives further evidence that lets us know that this portion of the letter was directed toward the unbelieving listener, as it references the believer whom the rich man is oppressing. The Greek word for the condemning of the righteous man in this verse is *katadikazo*, a judicial word meaning "to pass sentence upon." Remember, these rich tyrants had drug poor believers to court and ruthlessly taken their property and possessions. We see in verse 6, that they had even gone so far as to murder some of them. They stepped in to play the role of God and judge in the righteous man's life. As the previous verses have shown us, they will reap what they have sown; their judgment will be severe.

katadikazo – to pass sentence upon

How did the righteous man respond to the persecution in 5:6? _____

The image of the poor, believing laborer not resisting his persecutor is tragic. But, the story does not end there.

We previously visited a verse in Romans that I would like to touch on again.

Read Romans 12:19.

Our revenge stirs up trouble and pain; God's vengeance is just, pure, and brings benefit to us.

Do not take vengeance for yourself; the Lord will take care of all things in His perfect time, in His perfect way. Your revenge will stir up trouble and cause you, as well as others, additional pain. God's vengeance will be just and pure and will work to the benefit of those who love Him.

Do you ever wonder if God is really listening when you ask Him to take care of a situation where you choose not to retaliate on your own? Fill in the blanks from James 5:4 below.

"The outcry of those who did the harvesting has _____

of the _____."

No matter how silent God may seem at times, He always hears our cries.

Rest assured, no matter how silent you may feel God is at times, the cry of His people **has reached His ears**. This portion of James was harshly prophesying against the unbelieving oppressor, but portions of it would have been encouraging to their victims. Many times, the persecuted Christians must have wondered if God was hearing their cries or if they'd been forgotten and left all alone. Had God abandoned them? Was He not returning after all? Did He even care to hear their cries? James assures them that, yes, He has.

We've all gone through "dark nights of the soul" – times when God seemed distant and uncaring. Describe such a time, and how God showed Himself faithful in the end.

_____

_____

The name of God used in this verse is the "Lord of Sabaoth." There are many names of God used in Scripture. Each points to a different attribute or characteristic of who He is, and the biblical authors appropriately used each name intentionally within the context of their surrounding verses. James chose this title, at this time, very carefully and deliberately. The Lord of Sabaoth means the Lord of hosts. It might not seem all that impressive until we realize that the "host" referred to includes His limitless, unseen, angelic armies fighting all around us. He is the God of armies. Not only does He have full control over earthly armies, but He has legion upon legion of physically-undetected, supernatural soldiers ready at His command.

In the book of Haggai, the Jews were being commanded to resume the rebuilding of their temple. They had built the foundation, but had ceased construction for a variety of reasons. When Haggai exhorted them to resume, they did so, but quickly became discouraged. As he urged them to persevere, he encouraged them by using the name "Lord of Sabaoth" 14 times within 38 sentences. As they said, "We can't go on," he reminded them that the Lord of armies beyond their wildest imagination had their backs. They needed to move forward; He promised to be their defense.

The Lord of Sabaoth means the Lord of all armies, both seen and unseen – the Lord of Hosts.

Read 1 Samuel 17:45 below.

> *Then David said to the Philistine, "You come to me with a sword, a spear, and a javelin, but I come to you in the name of the LORD of hosts, the God of the armies of Israel, whom you have taunted."*

You guessed it - the name David used here for God was "Lord of Sabaoth." This is a scene most of us readily recognize. Young David is preparing to fight giant Goliath and he comes in full confidence. Why would he have such confidence? David said in all boldness, "I come in the name of the God of armies, seen and unseen, and you have no chance of defeating what God wants to defend."

James intended to encourage his brethren at the end of verse 4. We may not have readily recognized the Lord of Sabaoth or Lord of Hosts before, but after today, when you see your God referred to in this way, it should bring you great peace and assurance.

That same Lord of hosts, who defended His people as they rebuilt their temple under opposition, the same Lord of Sabaoth, who brought victory to the Israelite armies again and again, hears our cries and will defend and avenge his righteous followers when they are wronged. In His time and in His way, He will make all things right. He is our ultimate protector against things seen and unseen at this present time and into eternity. "*If God is for us, who can be against us?*" (Rom. 8:31b, NIV). Do you need to be reminded of that today?

The same Lord of Sabaoth still hears His children's cries. He still defends and avenges His own. He makes all things right in His time and in His way.

What "impossible" situation do you need the Lord of armies to march into today? Lift your voice to Him knowing that your cries will reach His ears. Feel free to write your requests to Him.

_____

_____

_____

Day Two – Waiting...

In the previous verses, we saw that James had a direct, prophetic message concerning those who were oppressing the poor believers. At the same time, we saw that this message was intended to comfort those being persecuted, as it reminded them that the "God of all armies" (Lord of Sabaoth) would hear their cries and avenge them.

Read James 5:7-8.

James' message – be patient until Christ's return.

Beginning in verse 7, James makes a very clear shift, as he once again addresses his listeners as "brethren." The use of the word "therefore" in this verse signals the fact that what he is going to say is based off the previous passage. In light of the judgment that is certain to fall on their oppressors, James makes a request of his Christian audience.

"Therefore, be _____, brethren, until _____."

Don't seek revenge. Don't envy their wealth. Don't despise your own existence. Don't anything, except be patient until Christ returns. Did James really have to take us there? He's asked us to refine every area of our lives. But, patience until He returns or until we, ourselves, pass away? The thought alone can be so wearying.

We all ache while we wait for Christ to return and make all things right.

Let's look at another similar passage. Read Psalm 37:1-11.

Like James, the psalmist tells us not to concern ourselves with the evil man. We're not to envy him or let his luxuries steal our focus. Instead, we're told to refrain from anger and wrath toward him. We are to delight in the Lord, commit our ways to Him, and be still while we patiently wait to meet Him face-to-face. We are told to trust Him and hold on as both punishment and blessing will come to those it is due.

Think about an ongoing trial you're facing. What about it requires the most patience? Are you making it harder by comparing what you don't have to what someone else appears to have? How can taking delight in the Lord, and keeping your eyes upon eternity, and off of others, help you endure?

heós – until

_____

_____

Patience is flat-out hard, even when we have an absolute end in sight. Patience in waiting for the Lord to return and make all things right can seem unbearable at times. Repeatedly, different biblical authors cried out to God saying, "How long, O Lord?" as they suffered through this life. Just as they did, we ache for the day when pain of all types will be wiped away. But, as we ache, how are we to wait?

The word for "until" (*heós*) in verse 7 conveys a "pregnant or expectant" quality. As we wait for the Lord, we have an anxious expectancy, **knowing** the "due date" is coming, although we cannot pinpoint His arrival. We know that it is necessary for a baby to go through a full developing process while we await its delivery. In the same way, James describes a complete growing process that we must wait through before we are finally delivered into our new life in heaven. To illustrate this waiting process, James uses a picture of a common farmer.

The farmer anxiously waits through the full growing season for "the precious produce of the soil" to arrive. He waits through the early rains and the late rains. He waits as pestilence eats some of his crops, storms break and bend them over, and the sun scorches and burns areas that are too weak to withstand the heat. Yet, he waits, and in the end, life emerges complete, full, and worth the wait.

Likewise, we wait for our own lives to be brought to completion. We groan under the stress of our own pestilence, storms, and heat. Yet, while we wait, we are encouraged by the psalmist to be still, and by James to strengthen our hearts.

We need to be still and strengthen our hearts while we wait.

How can keeping your focus on the coming "harvest" help you weather the storms of life? Do you allow yourself to think about the promise of heaven, or do you think that's wasted time or just wishful thinking?

_____

_____

How do we find strength when the trials of life beat us down? The Greek word for strengthen in this passage is *stérizó*, meaning "to fix firmly, strengthen, establish, direct myself toward." This word gives the effect of being solidly planted and set fast. When inanimate objects age, they may become worn down, brittle, and frail. Their strength and endurance weakens. Living things, though, have the capacity to strengthen through hardship. A living tree, for example, is strengthened through pruning; a bone heals stronger after being broken. In the same way, if our hearts are firmly-rooted in Christ, and we are holding fast to the Word of God, we can be strengthened as the storms of life come. We can endure them with hope as our eyes are fixed on the coming of the Lord. Notice the end of the definition of *stérizó* – "direct myself toward." Just as a plant, firmly-rooted in the ground, follows the path of the sun as it daily passes overhead, we are to be firmly-rooted in the soil of our faith, and deliberately direct ourselves toward the Son while we await His return. As we are still deeply-rooted in our faith and eagerly awaiting the fullness of the life awaiting us when our Savior comes, our hearts will strengthen in both the good times and the bad. Our strength is only found in the source of life-giving Light that we must direct ourselves toward daily.

stérizó – to fix firmly, strengthen, establish, direct myself toward

Read Revelation 22:20.

In James 5:8, he tells us that the coming of the Lord is near. In Revelation, Christ, Himself, assures us that He is coming "soon." Yet, we often wait for "soon" with weary hearts, convinced that "soon" couldn't possibly come soon enough.

Soon. Christ said He was returning soon; yet, it's been more than 2000 years. Has this ever made you scratch your head in confusion? How would you explain His apparent "delay?"

_____

_____

The word for "soon" in Revelation 22 is *tachu*, meaning "quickly, speedily." It does not imply an immediate action, or even give allusion to something that will happen in a short time. Rather, it means that when an action does begin, it will be sudden and swift. Keeping this in mind, we need not become discouraged as if Christ has forgotten His promise. While we wait, we must stay firmly-established with a determined resolve to allow our faith to be strengthened, ready at every moment for His swift and sudden return.

Read James 5:9.

Oh, that troublesome tongue keeps returning! In trying times, it's so easy to grumble and complain. The word used for complain in this verse, *stenazó*, means "to groan, expressing grief, anger, or desire." Interestingly, it is a groaning due to pressure exerted forward, as in the pressure of childbirth. Depending on the context, it can refer to either an intensely pleasant or an anguishing pressure from what is coming on.[28] Again, as we expectantly await the coming of the Lord, we are both joyful at the promise, and burdened by our current "labor pains." During this sort of time, where there can be anxious unrest, we may tend to want to grumble.

When all is not as you wish it were, do you tend to grumble and complain? Or are you still and quiet as you wait patiently for God?

tachu – quickly, speedily

stenazó – to groan, express grief, anger, or desire

When the going gets rough and the road gets long, we often complain. When we complain, we frequently do it in a way that blames others for our sorrows or hurts them as we "unload." Again, James reminds us of the danger in doing so. Our Judge will not only judge us in the same manner that we judge others, but He is "waiting at the door."

Guys, our children know what they can and can't get away with saying to their sibling in front of us. How many times have you stood on the other side of a door, listening to what they don't realize you can hear? God is no different. He hears it all, sees it all, and even knows the intentions of our heart behind it all. He is waiting at the door. What does He find on the other side? As Dad, there have been times when I've heard enough and opened the door, making my intimidating presence known, only to be greeted by kids with bug eyes at having been caught. We don't know the day that Christ is coming, but we've been told that it will be swift when it happens. Do we want to be grumbling at one of His other children when He opens the door?

God hears all, sees all, and knows the heart behind every word and action.

If Jesus were standing on the other side of every door in your home, office, or school, how would you change the way you talk to others?

Read James 5:10-11.

28   Gary Hill, Helpsbible.com, http://concordances.org/greek/4727.htm

As another example of patient suffering, James refers to the prophets of the Old Testament. Many suffered excruciating lives as they proclaimed the message of God, only to be ignored, humiliated, and persecuted. Oftentimes, they must have felt they were just beating their heads against a wall, making no progress with the children of God who refused to listen. They also lived with constant hate from the outside world that despised their very existence. They had much to complain about, but although they voiced their woes to the Lord and cried out to Him in anguish, they did not abandon or give up on God. As a result of their endurance then, they are considered blessed today.

As a prime example of a man who went through much, and yet faithfully endured alongside the Lord, James reminds us of Job's story. Job endured the loss of his family, his personal health, and his possessions. If anyone did, Job had reason to complain. He did question; he did struggle. But, he did not turn his back on God.

We can question; we can struggle; but we must not turn our back on God.

In order to find application for our own lives, let's examine all Job had to endure. **In essence, Job wanted back what couldn't return and wanted to lose what he couldn't get rid of.** Death had ravaged his family and in this world, death is permanent. His grief and sorrow must have been all-consuming, as he suffered so much of it at one time. In rapid succession, he was told about the death of his 10 children, his livestock, and the loss of all his other possessions. Waves of grief must have overcome him again and again as reality continued to set in. The question "why" was at the forefront of his thoughts day and night. He was overcome with sorrow, and endurance seemed impossible, especially as he was forced to endure alone.

Whether we like to face it or not, death is an undeniable reality in this life. With death, comes grief. Describe a time you were forced to grieve the loss of someone, or something, you couldn't have back.

Permanent losses lead to great sorrow, making endurance seem impossible.

_____

_____

Although Job endured his inner turmoil alone, he wasn't physically alone. While they tried, those with him didn't help Job endure. In fact, they made his endurance more difficult. They were a great part of what he probably wished he could get rid of; but like a bad fungus, they just wouldn't go away. Although Satan took much from Job in his attack, he left him with what he knew would cause him greater pain. He was left with excruciating boils, a wife who discouraged him, and "friends" who forgot this wasn't "their story," and took the opportunity to share their hurtful opinions. The pain in his own body was something he couldn't escape. Chronic pain is enough to drive a person mad. Heaped on top of mourning the loss of the lives of all of his children, this additional, constant reminder of his new state of being must have been entirely defeating. If that wasn't enough, while doing everything he could not to turn his back on God, his wife told him to do just that. Then, his friends chose to share their "wisdom" to boot. At the peak of his suffering, Job's friends could hold their tongues no longer. To be perfectly honest, much of what they had to say was "wise" in general terms. Yet, they lacked the discernment to see that their "wisdom" did not apply to Job's situation. As they threw out advice based on their traditional understanding, they did not have the insight to realize that Job's trials were not intended for his discipline. They assumed, based

The right words, spoken at the wrong time, can be as devastating as the wrong words.

on their own beliefs, that there was a one-size-fits-all wisdom that Job must have been lacking, and their decision to "teach" it to him in the midst of his pain stung his very soul.

Think about a time when the advice from another person during your trials was hurtful, because they did not know what God was doing or have all the details.

_____

_____

Might you have hurt someone else in a similar way? How?

_____

_____

*hupomoné –
endurance,
steadfastness, patient
waiting for*

During this time, Job needed support, understanding, compassion, and love. However, we see none of that given to him, which added greatly to his trial, and yet he endured. Endurance in this passage is *hupomoné*, a compound word of *hupo* meaning "under" and *meno* meaning "endurance, steadfastness, patient waiting for." Whereas the patience referred to in verses 7 and 8 is a long-suffering patience with a loving attitude (*makrothumeó*), *hupomoné* refers to a patient, enduring attitude that denotes a strong, determined attitude with which we are to face hardship. In other words, Job "strengthened his heart" as we elaborated on in verse 8, even in the midst of the greatest struggles we can fathom. He was firmly-rooted and following the "Son" even when it seemed to make no sense at all.

*Like Job, we are
blessed because of the
reward awaiting us in
eternity.*

Look back to verse 11. What do we count those who endured? _____

I'm pretty certain Job wouldn't have told you that he felt blessed during this period of his life. But, remember what the beatitudes taught us on Day Five of Week One. Job was blessed because of the reward awaiting him in eternity after faithfully enduring this life that brought him such tremendous suffering. Even though he couldn't always readily see the reward, Job **always** had a reason to hope.

Verse 11. *"You have heard of the endurance of Job and have seen the _____ of the Lord's dealings..."*

*telos – an end,
purpose*

The word for outcome in this verse should be somewhat familiar to us as we have seen a form of it multiple times. *Telos* is used here, meaning "an end, purpose." It speaks of the consummation of an end goal, a closure with all its results.[29] The other forms of this word previously noted referred to a "perfect" result, a completion toward a given end, a peak of maturity (James 1:4). In the story of Job, we get to see *telos* in the outcome of the Lord's dealings with Job. As the story goes, Job's faithfulness held strong, and he was tangibly rewarded in the end. But, James shows us an even more beautiful outcome at the end of verse 11. The Lord's dealings with Job showed that He is full of compassion and He is merciful. Job let endurance have its perfect result, and despite his times of loss, questioning, and struggle God remained compassionate and merciful.

_____

29   Gary Hill, Helpsbible.com, http://concordances.org/greek/5056.htm

Job struggled, he hurt, he questioned, but his heart was steadfast in his unwavering faith, because he was deeply-rooted in truth. Living a life of faith takes both patience and endurance. We must have patience as God refines us on the journey of our Christian walk. We must endure as the trials of life knock us down, even as we seek to be refined. We must not lose heart as we eagerly await the Lord's coming, even when our hearts are crying, "How long, O Lord, how long?"

As we consider all we have learned in these five rich chapters of James, we now find ourselves accountable for all we know. We must keep our guard up; we must keep our hearts right. Our Lord is standing at the door and His return is near. Until that day, we are living through the early and late rains, the pestilence and the storms. How will He find us when He returns? Will we have endured well, giving Him opportunity to show His compassion and mercy? If we have not so far, are we willing to begin today? Let us endure together; He's coming back soon…and oh the eternal glory that will be ours when He does.

Despite our questioning and struggling, God remains compassionate and merciful.

> *Therefore we do not lose heart, but though our outer man is decaying, yet our inner man is being renewed day by day. For momentary, light affliction is producing for us an eternal weight of glory far beyond all comparison, while we look not at the things which are seen, but at the things which are not seen; for the things which are seen are temporal, but the things which are not seen are eternal. (2 Cor. 4:16-18)*

Day Three – Let Your Yes Be Yes

Yesterday, we focused on maintaining patience and endurance in the midst of suffering. In addition, we examined the danger of using our words to complain and grumble against one another in such times.

Read James 5:12.

In the New Testament, we are ordered not to swear at all.

Today, we will see that when we are going through hard times that we long to escape, times that tempt us to grumble, we may a have a tendency to run on at the mouth. One way we do this is by trying to ascribe God's name, ways, and support to our viewpoints and opinions. We think that if we can prove to others that God is on our side by assigning His name to our situation, we elevate ourselves and our point.

Read Matthew 5:33-37.

As you can tell, James was practically restating the words of Jesus in verse 12 of his letter. Verse 33 of Matthew 5 refers back to the original Levitical law concerning oaths. Leviticus 19:12 stated, *"You shall not swear falsely by My name, so as to profane the name of your God; I am the LORD."* Unlike the words of Jesus and James, this law only forbid the breaking of an oath made in God's name, for it would profane the name associated with it. In the New Testament, though, we find the order not to swear at all.

Although some have believed that this instruction prohibits Christians from taking **any** oaths, official oaths to authorities don't seem to be the issue. Rather, the concern seems to revolve around personal, voluntary oaths.

In your opinion, what danger could there be in making personal oaths?

_____

_____

A man's word should be enough, without having to swear by any other means.

The primary issue here seems to be associated with the value of one's word and the potential for bringing irreverence to God. A man's word should be enough, without having to swear by any other means. His goal should be to live in such a way that when he is questioned, his answer is readily accepted because he has always been proven reliable and trustworthy.

When someone says, "God as my witness," they are attempting to give credence to their particular claim. Though not always, at times this effort is fueled by pride. Pride is hard to swallow, and it certainly rears its head when we feel vulnerable. Let's look at a few ways that our pride may lead us to swear oaths while we're vulnerable.

"God as my witness, I **know** I'm right about this!" At times, we can be absolutely convinced that we are right on a subject, and to bolster our argument, we pin God's name to it. The truth is, no matter how sure we are of ourselves, or a situation, we have already discussed the fact that none of us possess the capability of knowing every detail surrounding any circumstance. There is always room for error whenever a human is involved. In swearing by God's name, we subject His infallible reputation to something that has the potential of proving fallible.

Can you remember a time when you felt **100% sure** about something, only to realize later that you were not **100% right**? How might remembering this possibility help you avoid swearing in the future?

_____

_____

On the flip side of that coin, there are times when our pride doesn't like to admit that we are wrong. We tread on dangerous ground when we swear by God as our Witness that something we fully know is wrong, is indeed right. It hurts our ego when we have to admit defeat or a lack of knowledge where we feel we should have it. It is at times like these when we may be tempted to swear something falsely simply to save face. Saving our face while defacing the Almighty God is no laughing matter. His reputation means everything to Him; it should mean everything to us as well.

Whether we swear by His name or not, by simply taking on His name as a Christian, we constantly put God's reputation on the line. Have you let your pride get in the way of admitting when you're wrong? How may this have affected the way others view God as a result?

_____

_____

"I swear I'll do it!" Not only do we swear by our accuracy at times, we also may have a tendency to swear by our ability. We often make commitments to carry out actions without weighing the possibility that we may not be able to fulfill the promise. With the best of intentions, we make promises that are at times beyond our ability to fulfill. Just as we are not able to know every detail of other's lives, we are also not able to know if our own circumstances will allow us to keep the commitments we swear to. In Luke 14, we find Jesus addressing the crowds about the cost of being His disciple. There, Jesus spoke of the wisdom of considering the personal cost before making personal commitments. "Who begins a building project," asks Christ, "without determining if he can afford to complete it?" Or, "What king goes into battle against another without first calculating if he has enough troops to win?" To start something, but not complete it, is not only foolish, it opens us up to the ridicule of others as well. In the end, it tarnishes our name and the name of God.

In the classic story, Romeo and Juliet, Friar John agreed to hand-deliver a note to Romeo explaining that his beloved, Juliet, was not dead, but had only faked her death in order to avoid marrying another man her parents had chosen for her. Despite his good intentions and promise to come through on time, Friar John was detained due to illness beyond his control and was sadly never able to deliver the note. As a result, Romeo arrived at Juliet's tomb, saw her sleeping and wrongly concluded she was dead. In response, he poisoned himself and died at her side. The fair Juliet later awoke only to find her man dead at her side and she then ended her life as well. Good intentions, promises made, oaths sworn – if not fulfilled, all are for naught. Instead, we would all do well to use the humble response one of Angie's daughters regularly used when she was little. Whenever asked to do a task, she would simply reply, "Mommy, I promise I'll try." While, as her parent, Angie would have preferred to have heard guarantees, in reality, it was much better for her daughter to avoid making an absolute commitment to do something in a future that she did not hold in her own hands. Her intentions were to follow through, and she usually did. But, in her caution, she kept herself from giving her word when extenuating circumstances could have prevented her from completely delivering. Friar John would likely approve of her simple promise to try.

In swearing by God's name, we put His reputation at risk.

God's reputation should mean everything to us.

We should not make commitments without considering if we can fulfill them first.

It is better to promise to try, than to promise to complete.

In the same way, when we promise to fulfill even the smallest commitment, we need to guard the reputation of our word as well as God's name, for as Christians we represent Him to the world.

Would you say that you are largely regarded by others as a "man of your word?" Do you carelessly make promises without considering the impact if you don't keep them?

_____

_____

We need to guard the reputation of our word as well as God's name.

If we're honest, there may also be times when we agree to something that we never have any real intention of following through on. Have you ever asked one of your kids to clean their room and have them respond with, "Okay," yet see no intention of follow-through? Surely, they just forgot! Truthfully, there are times when a quick "yes" is given to appease the one asking. It may be embarrassing to admit that we don't believe we can handle a task, or we may be embarrassed to admit we simply don't want to. We may not want to "face the music" of saying "no" and so we give the answer we believe someone wants to hear in order to escape the moment without subjecting ourselves to scrutiny, judgment, or further discussion on the topic.

There is nothing wrong with lacking an ability. However, saying you'll do something and not following through is wrong.

Admitting we cannot, or do not want to, fulfill a task can be humbling for a man. We might feel that we are admitting inadequacy, or revealing some incompetency, which hurts our pride. We can't stand the thought of looking like a failure to others, and in that fear, we may agree to do something while all along planning to conveniently "forget" or find a way to back out at a later time. The irony in this situation is that the latter (planning to not keep your word) is the only actual failure in this scenario. An honest admission of a lack of ability or lack of desire to fulfill a task is not sinful – lying, however, is. When we give our word and do not keep it, we shed doubt on the integrity of that word. After multiple incidents of such, our character can prove to be entirely unreliable.

In Matthew 21, Jesus told a parable about a man who had two sons. *"He came to the first and said, 'Son, go work today in the vineyard.' And he answered, 'I will not'; but afterward he regretted it and went. The man came to the second and said the same thing; and he answered, 'I will, sir'; but he did not go. Which of the two did the will of his father?" They said, "The first."* Making a promise and not following through is to be outside the Father's will.

As Christians, we always reflect the God we claim to serve.

Have you ever said that you will do something fully knowing you won't? Why? What would be the outcome of simply saying you can't, or won't, do something instead?

_____

_____

James tells us that our "yes" needs to mean "yes" and our "no" needs to mean "no." As Christians, we constantly represent the God we say we serve. When our "yes" is "no," it reflects poorly on Him and we misrepresent His character. When James tells us not to make oaths, he is telling us that we shouldn't need to. If our "yes" is always "yes," then people will come to rely on our word without any need for attaching an oath to it. "We should never need to use an oath to prove that 'this time I really mean it!' Instead we should always 'really mean it.'"[30]

---

30   Zane C. Hodges, *The Epistle of James*, p. 115

Practically speaking, when we get into the habit of not staying true to our word, we damage our name. Men, a good name – our good name – is to be valued above gold, silver, or any other wealth (Pro. 22:1). If we consistently fail to keep our word, others will come to the place where they know they cannot rely on us. We need to ask ourselves often where we stand on this. Based on how we live our lives and fulfill our commitments, what messages have we conveyed concerning the value of our word? Do our children know that when we commit to do something with or for them, that we will follow through? Do our spouses know that they can rely on us and the commitments we've made to them? Do our friends know that they can come to us with any need because they can rely on our character to be true and our follow- through to be dependable? Do our churches know that when we agree to fill a position, they need not worry about our level of commitment? Do they know that our "yes" means "yes" and that because we have given our word, we will give our utmost devotion to keeping it?

What are the ripple effects of having an unreliable reputation?

_____

_____

If our "yes" is always "yes," people will rely on our word without the need for an accompanying oath.

The ripple effects of unreliability are immense. When we give others our word, they place their hope and trust in us. When we don't keep our word, that hope is dashed. Proverbs 13:12 puts it this way, "**Hope deferred** *makes the heart sick, but desire fulfilled is a tree of life.*" (emphasis added) Are we trees of life to others, or are we making their hearts sick? Raising children who cannot trust us will greatly affect the way they raise their own children and relate to others (including their future spouses). A lack of dependability with a spouse, even in things that may seem trivial, wears down a relationship and has the ability to wreak havoc in a home. Friends who can't be found trustworthy, end up losing friendships. Churches suffer greatly when volunteers don't take God's work seriously, showing up only when they feel like it, not giving their commitment serious consideration because they consider church work "optional."

A good name is to be more desired than great wealth, favor is better than silver and gold (Proverbs 22:1).

The ripple effects of unreliability are vast.

The list of examples could go on indefinitely. But, the greatest detriment done in breaking our word is the harm done to God's name. God's "yes" is an absolute "yes." We need not worry about Him being fickle. His Word is true and without hypocrisy. The gift of salvation that He offers us is offered in absolute truth; His commitment to hold us securely once we have accepted Him until the day He brings us home, is unconditional. His "no" is also an emphatic "no." What God is against is irrefutable. The sins that He lines out in Scripture are not to be questioned or debated. He is unwavering. He is just. He is true. There are many people, though, who will never crack open a single book of the Bible to hear His truths directly from Him. Because of this, He relies on His people to represent His character. Just as we are able to fully rely on God's "yes" and "no," others should find that same characteristic in us, which should, in turn, draw them to the God whose character we exhibit.

God's "yes" is an absolute "yes." He is never fickle.

Your life may be the only glimpse of God others ever see. Based on your "yes's" and "no's," are they getting an accurate view of Him? If not, what needs to change? To whom have you made yourself accountable for the promises you make?

God relies on His people to represent His character.

_____

_____

Day Four – Restoration and Righteousness

In this final chapter of James, he has brought us full circle back to the place where we began in Chapter One. Two days ago, we revisited the topic of pain and suffering and the need to endure, as Job did, with patience as our eyes remain fixed on the Lord. Yesterday, we saw that during times of trial, when our patience may run thin, we need not rush into making oaths that cannot be kept. Today, we will see that "suffering in some form or other is sure to come, and the sovereign remedy for all suffering is prayer."[31]

Read James 5:13-18 paying special attention to each mention of the word prayer.

"Suffering in some form is sure to come; the sovereign remedy is prayer."

You may have noticed that the words "pray" or "prayer" are woven through every verse. As noted before, repetition in Scripture is never a coincidence. James clearly wants to end his letter with a bold emphasis on prayer.

Prayer involves lifting our voice to the Lord, silently or aloud, in order to communicate with Him. Verse 13 covers the fact that we need to do that in all situations and circumstances. When we are hurting, lift it to the Lord. When we are joyful, do the same. We often go to God with our hurts, but forget to lift a prayer of praise during good times. But, it is during those times of prayerful praise that we acknowledge all of the good He has provided in our lives. When we have done that, we can draw from those times of joyful communion with the Lord, during our future times of drought. Praise fills the well of the heart and provides refreshment to draw from in times of suffering.

Under what circumstances do you most frequently go to the Lord in prayer? Do you remember to go to Him with praise, or are most of your prayers a vocalizing of hurts and needs? How can you bring more balance to your prayer life?

_____

_____

We are to lift our voice to Him in all circumstances – painful and joyful.

The next two verses of James have caused endless debate over the years and were even the basis for the adoption of "Extreme Unction," or "Anointing of the Sick," into the Roman Catholic list of sacraments. The use of these verses to support Extreme Unction was based on the belief that they refer to physical healing. The New International Commentary of the New Testament states, "In the 16th century, at the Council of Trent, the so-called Sacrament of Extreme Unction received authoritative definition in the Roman Church, that Council declaring that this manmade Sacrament is 'implied by Mark, and commended and promulgated by James the apostle and brother of the Lord.' There never was a more glaring travesty of Scripture."[32] Translating these verses in such a manner is the basis for all debate concerning their meaning. Due to the original Greek language used and the context of the surrounding verses, it is our belief that this passage does not relate to physical healing. We'll explain more as we proceed.

---

31 Alexander Ross, *The New International Commentary on the New Testament, Commentary on the Epistles of James and John*, p. 97

32 Ibid. p. 99-100

Have you ever read these verses, prayed earnestly, and wondered why physical healing did not occur? What went through your mind as you watched a loved one succumb to illness?

_____

_____

So far in Chapter 5, James has covered oppression by the unsaved rich and how to respond to that sort of suffering. He also addressed the fact that some of his Christian readers might be participating in actions and conversations (as a response to this suffering) that may cause them to fall under God's judgment. James even warns them that the Judge is standing right at the door. To best understand verses 14-16, we need to place them in line with the context of the previous verses, as well as the ones yet to come. We will also look at the Greek to more closely evaluate the passage.

asthenei – to be weak

Fill in the blank according to James 5:14. *"Is anyone among you _____?"*

The Greek word for sick in this passage is *asthenei,* which literally means "to be weak." "There is no reason to consider 'sick' as referring exclusively to physical illness. Though it is used in the Gospels for physical maladies, it is generally used in Acts and the Epistles to refer to a weak faith or a weak conscience."[33] The Greek word, *kamnonta,* used for the "sick person" in verse 15, supports this understanding as it literally translates "to be weary." By understanding this as well as the chapter context, we realize that James was referring to those who had become morally and spiritually weak and weary due to their sufferings. Their "sickness" is of a spiritual nature, and it is they who should call on the help of the leadership of the church.

kamnonta – to be weary

Why call on others in the church? Read 1 Thessalonians 5:14.

We as Christians are commanded to "help the weak." The word for weak in this verse is the same word we find in James 5:14. Those who are struggling in their faith, because this life is bearing down on them, need the prayers and encouragement of fellow believers. When a believer comes to the point where he realizes that overcoming the sin that has entrapped him is more than he can handle alone, it is beneficial for him to come to his fellow believers for prayer, support, encouragement, and accountability. Of course, even a private, repentant heart is heard by God, but isolation from others makes walking away from sin and back into spiritual restoration much more difficult. This is one of the many reasons we are commanded not to forsake the gathering of ourselves together (Heb. 10:25).

Those who are struggling in their faith need the prayers and encouragement of fellow believers.

Because sin is dark, it likes to be hidden. Have you wrestled with temptation to hide your sins? If so, what could your fellow believers in Christ do to help you through it? What can you do to help others when they are weak?

Call the presses – I neglect my yard! ☺

_____

I confess, I neglect my yard. I don't water, I don't fertilize, I don't control weeds, and I don't bag my grass. I know, that's a trivial confession that has nothing whatsoever to do with sin. But, the fact of the matter is, in doing so, I was open and honest with others concerning something I might find somewhat embarrassing to admit. In being vulnerable in that manner, I've allowed others who also neglect their yard to realize that I can fully relate to them in that. I've allowed you to see that I'm not the perfect "Ward Cleaver" and have hopefully

---

33   Walvoord and Zuck, *BKC NT*, p. 834

also let you know, through my confession, that I don't have high expectations of others concerning such things either.

As laughable as a confession about my yard is, it does give us a glimpse into the possible benefits of confession. When we share our vulnerabilities with others, we let others know that they are not alone in their own struggles and we allow them to see that we are human and relatable as well. It is in this way that those in the body of Christ can build one another up and be a soothing balm, a healing agent in one another's lives. No, this does not suggest that we need to share every private sin with the public, nor does it mean that we have to make regular confessions in front of an entire congregation. But, when there is an entrapment of sin consuming a believer to the extent of making him spiritually "ill," James instructs him to take it beyond his isolation and humbly ask for forgiveness and help.

When we share our vulnerabilities with others, we let them know they are not alone in their struggles.

Because our culture does not relate to the anointing of oil, the next part of James' instruction may seem obscure to us. The word used here for anoint, *aleíphō*, simply means "to rub with oil." This is not the same as the ceremonial or ritual anointing (*chrio*) that we see in other areas of Scripture. Rather, it is a mundane form of anointing, not used as a means of divine physical healing, but as a means of refreshment and encouragement.[34] A few other examples of this sort of anointing in Scripture are listed below:

Luke 7:38 – the woman "poured" (*aleíphō*) perfume on Jesus' feet

Luke 7:46 – a host "put oil" (*aleíphō*) on the head of his guest

aleíphō – to rub with oil as a means of refreshment and encouragement

Matt 6:17 – one who is fasting should not be sad and ungroomed, but should "put oil" (*aleíphō*) on his head and wash his face.

"Thus, James' point is that the 'weak' (*asthenei*) and 'weary' (*kamnonta*) would be refreshed, encouraged, and uplifted by the elders who rubbed oil on the despondents' heads and prayed for them."[35]

Verses 15 and 16 go on to say that the one who is weary from sin and defeated by spiritual discouragement, will be restored by the prayer offered in faith. If this verse were referring to physical healing, many a Christian with deep faith in God would wonder why his faith was not enough to claim the absolute assurance given here that *"the prayer offered in faith **will** restore the one who is sick."* (emphasis added) In fact, if physical healing was always assured to those who pray in faith, many would never die. But, James speaks of spiritual healing as he encourages the one trapped in sin to confess. Once a person is willing to humble himself enough to openly confess and seek the help of other Christians, he is willing to repent and seeks to do right. To this person, restoration and healing is assured.

James speaks of spiritual healing as he encourages those trapped in sin to confess.

According to James 5:16, fill in the blanks:

"The _____ prayer of a _____ man can accomplish much."

This verse has caused many Christians quite a bit of doubt and pain as they wonder why their prayers don't seem to get answered. When we pray in faith and nothing seems to get accomplished, what went wrong? Were we not "righteous" enough? Where is the fine line that makes us righteous enough for our prayers to be effective?

34   Daniel R. Hayden, "Calling the Elders to Pray," *Bibliotheca Sacra* 138. July–September 1981:264.

35   Walvoord and Zuck, *BKC NT*, p. 834-835

On Day Three of Week Three, we discussed three large words that we said were at the core of our Christianity: justification, redemption, and propitiation. We are going to revisit them today, and we'll hopefully see that understanding the concepts behind these words will help us understand many other areas of Scripture. If you recall, propitiation was what was required to appease the wrath of God. Christ's death propitiated God and paid our penalty (redemption). When Christ propitiated God, it was then possible for us to come to God and ask for the gift of salvation. When we do that, He (as sovereign Judge) pounds His gavel upon the courtroom bench and declares us justified. To be justified is to be declared **righteous**. In fact, righteous (*dikaios*) means "just in the eyes of God." You did **nothing** to become righteous, you can do **nothing** to become more righteous. You were **declared** righteous because the righteous Son of God stood in your place and paid the price for your sin. It is not your righteousness that God sees, but Christ's righteousness in you. Therefore, the righteous man is the saved man. The effective prayer of a **saved** man can accomplish much! If you're like us, that should bring a sigh of relief.

dikaios – Just in the eyes of God

Yes, we as Christians are able to walk in a "righteous lifestyle." We also know, from the example of the backslidden Christian referred to earlier, that we are able to choose to walk in an "unrighteous lifestyle." It is true, that when we have broken our fellowship with God, our prayers are inhibited. But, when you are walking in line with God's will and you feel that prayers are not being answered in the way you hoped, you need not fear this verse is telling you that you have not achieved a level of righteousness worthy of having effective prayers. As we've learned, even in the most trying times of our lives, it is not always God's will to remove our trials, but instead for us to endure and grow through them. Our suffering need not call into question our status as "righteous" in the sight of God.

Have you questioned whether or not the reason some of your prayers went unanswered was related to your lack of "righteousness?" How does seeing that the effective prayers that accomplish much come from the saved person encourage you?

The righteous man is the saved man. Therefore, the effective prayer of the saved man accomplishes much.

_____

_____

The other word we need to examine in this verse is "effective." If we aren't receiving the answers we want to our prayers and we know it isn't because we haven't achieved some perfect level of righteousness, could it be that we aren't praying "effectively?" The Greek word used here is *energeó*, which means "I am at work, am operative, accomplish." It is a word that involves action. You undoubtedly recognize the word "energy" in its root. It isn't a magic recipe for a perfect prayer; rather, it is saying that prayer is a work in action, an act of faith (James 1:6) that produces action. We are taking action in order to ask a God of action to move in our situation. So, the **active** prayer of a **saved** man can accomplish much. When we are living our life in fellowship with God, we can go to Him with confidence that our prayers can move mountains if it is in accordance with His will to act in that manner.

energeó – I am at work, am operative, accomplish

How active are you in your prayer life? If you are not actively going to God in prayer, should you expect Him to be active in answering?

_____

_____

Read James 5:17-18.

To illustrate the power of prayer, James invites one last Old Testament character to our study – Elijah. In doing so, he stays with his own context that has revolved around those who need spiritual healing due to sin. The drought brought on the nation of Israel by Elijah's prayer was due to their sin of idolatry under the evil king Ahab. Elijah prayed that the rains would cease, and they did. He further prayed that they would resume at a later date, and the skies opened up and poured down rain (1 Kings 17-18).

According to James 5:17, what kind of a man was Elijah?

_____

Elijah was only a man like the rest, yet he was a man of faithful prayer.

It was important for James to point out that Elijah's prayers were not more potent because he was a prophet. No, Elijah was a man with a sin nature, with emotions, with ups and downs in this life. He was only a man, yet he was a man of faithful prayer. We see in this verse that he prayed "earnestly." There again, we have a word that could cause us to fear when our own prayers seem unanswered. Did I perhaps not pray "earnestly" enough? The Greek words used for "prayed earnestly" are *proseuché proseuchomai*, which literally translate, he "prayed with prayer." "Here the point is not that Elijah put up a particularly fervent prayer, but that praying was precisely what he did."[36]

Prayer is to be our way of life. It is to be on our breath at all times as we walk through our day. God is not to be pulled out of the closet for random needs and shoved back in when we don't feel we care for any more of His input. He is with us always, and we are to include Him in our every moment, our every thought.

proseuché proseuchomai - prayed with prayer

Read 1 Thess. 5:17.

Praying without ceasing doesn't mean we are to be on our knees in prayer 24 hours a day, 7 days of the week. It means that as we go about our daily business, God should be included in it all. We are to be in constant communication with Him; considering Him in our every word, consulting Him in every action. Allowing Him to speak to us in every area of our lives is the way in which we take all that we have learned in His Word and LIVE it in an active life of faith. We cannot live that kind of active faith without inviting Him into our every action. We do not welcome Him into every action unless we proactively commit to communicate with Him in every moment.

Prayer is to be on our breath at all times.

Will you commit to do that today? Will you make a commitment to begin inviting God into every moment of your life? Will you invite Him into your smallest decisions? Will you commit your time to Him as you drive in your car instead of allowing your mind to wander every which way? Will you ask for His guidance **while** you're in the middle of conversations so He can direct your thoughts and words? The more we do this, the more readily His words are on our lips as we go throughout our day, and the more His words are on our lips, the more others are drawn to Him through the grace of our testimony. The ripple effects are mighty and wonderful, but it all begins with prayer. Will you be a man of prayer?

---

36 Adamson, *NICNT, James*, p. 201

Day Five — The Power of Prayer

It is hard to believe that we've arrived at the final day. You would not believe the extraordinary journey this has been for us! We hope and pray it has been a meaningful time for you as well. Let's dig in one more time and finish strong as we run through the finish line!

Just as we saw that the illustration of Elijah dealt with a <u>nation</u> that had fallen away in sin, the final two verses of the book of James flow directly from that idea and deal with <u>individuals</u> who had sinned and fallen away. Had the previous verses been talking about physical healing, these final two verses would have seemed disjointed from the rest of the chapter. We will see today, however, that because they dealt with spiritual weakness, they fit beautifully within their context.

For that context, read James 5:17-20.

Elijah knew his greatest option was prayer.

We briefly covered Elijah yesterday, but today, let's focus on the significance of some of the details of his story. Having read verses 19 and 20, we can now look back with a better understanding of the full surrounding context.

According to our homework yesterday, why did Elijah pray for drought?

_____

The nation of Israel had fallen into sin and needed spiritual restoration. Something needed to be done and prayer, imploring God to act, was Elijah's best option. About 3 ½ years into the drought, Elijah decided to confront Ahab and his false prophets, challenging them to a duel between the one true God and Baal. In the midst of presenting his challenge, he turned to the people of Israel and boldly rebuked them for being double-minded.

Read 1 Kings 18:16-21.

When Elijah confronted the people, what was their response? _____

These were God's chosen people! They'd personally experienced great miracles directly from the hand of their mighty God. Yet now, not only were they guilty of bowing before false gods, but when confronted with the truth – they stood silent. We do not have to be walking in overt sin to be spiritually "unwell." When we stand silent in the midst of a world that is blatantly turning their backs on God, our own spiritual apathy is contributing to the demise of the Christian faith in our world. These things ought not to be!

When we stand silent in the face of godlessness, we're contributing to the demise of the Christian faith.

Describe a time you stood silently when you probably needed to speak the truth in love. What were the results of your silence?

_____

_____

Read 1 Kings 18:22-37.

After the prophets of Baal utterly failed in their part of the challenge, Elijah called on God in order to demonstrate His power to the people.

According to verse 37, why did Elijah want God to answer his prayer?

_____

This question brings us to the heart of our lesson today. Elijah did not set up this elaborate plan in order to prove himself. In fact, his intentions were entirely selfless, for the life of a prophet was lonely, dangerous, and solely for the spiritual benefit of others. He was willing to live such a life because the people needed to be told of their God. His ultimate goal at this moment was the turning of their hearts away from sin and back to God. Oh how we need like-minded servants today.

Elijah's goal was to turn the heart of the people back to God.

Read James 5:19-20 once more.

We have already focused on the man who turns away in sin. Today let's focus on the one who prays for him and redirects his path back to the Lord. The primary focus of our study has been on **living** out our faith. Doing so is necessary to demonstrate the sincerity of our faith, and we have looked at many practical ways to do that in our lives. But, why does it matter? Has the basis for all we've learned been to solely benefit our own lives? No, like Elijah, our active faith is to bring glory to God and, in doing so, draw others to Him as we minister to them.

Our active faith is to bring glory to God and draw others to Him.

According to James, "live and let live" is just not an option for Christians. Just like Elijah, our goal should be to turn the hearts of others away from sin and back to God. The original Greek uses the word *planaó* for the one who strays from the truth. It literally means "to wander, lead astray, deceive." "It suggests one who has missed his path and is hopelessly lost. 'Planet' was taken from this Greek word to convey the idea that the luminaries were 'wandering stars,' not 'fixed' like the rest."[37] It is these wandering ones who need to be brought back into fellowship.

Are you willing to help restore a brother or sister who has wandered away from the faith? Have you benefited from a fellow believer lovingly helping you find your way back to the right path? If so, how?

planaó – to wander, lead astray, deceive

_____

_____

Verse 20 tells us the benefit of turning another back to the Lord. On the other side of that coin, what is the cost if in our selfishness we fail to do so?

_____

_____

The word used for death in verse 20 is *thanatos*, and is the same word used in James 1:15 that we previously discussed. It can refer to both spiritual and physical death. Because

---

37   Walvoord and Zuck, *BKC NT*, p. 835

verse 20 refers to a brother in Christ who has been turned back to the Lord, we know that the death he is saved from is not eternal death in hell. Rather, it is possibly either a "living death" that is indicative of a life lived outside of God's will, or a premature physical death due to the consequences of sin. Either way, the one who has made the effort to help restore him has done him a world of good.

On that same note, this restoration will cover a multitude of sins. When one confesses his sin and turns back to the Lord, his sins are covered. *Kaluptó* is a great Greek word that means "to cover, veil, hide, conceal, envelop." It is as if a veil covers the sin and frees the sinner to move forward without its haunting presence openly and consistently reminding him of his past sin. Have you had sin that has taunted you and held you tightly in its grasp? Wouldn't you be eternally grateful to anyone who would be willing to help you escape its torment? These verses tell us that through the power of prayer it is possible, and you are able to be that helpful agent in the life of another as well.

kaluptó – to cover, veil, hide, conceal, envelop

Let's take one more look at Elijah. When we left off, he was praying that God would act so the people would turn back to Him.

Read 1 Kings 18:38-45.

According to James 5:18, what happened when Elijah prayed for rain?

_____

When Elijah's prayers were answered, the barren land once again began producing fruit. Just before this, in 1 Kings 18:39, when God answered his prayer to send fire from heaven, the people fell on their faces and declared, *"The LORD, He is God!"* One of Elijah's prayers produced fruit from land, the other produced fruit from the people. When sin is repented of, the repentant life **will** produce fruit, and prayer for one another helps fertilize and water the roots. Hoarding our faith will not help others produce fruit; living for their advancement in the faith will.

Elijah's prayers produced fruit from the land and from the people.

When it all comes down to it, this concept returns us to our royal law – love your neighbor as yourself. We innately love ourselves enough to pray for God's best in our own lives, even when we are at our worst. Are we willing to take the time to do that for others? Are we willing to take time to share that prayer with them? Are we willing to give **all** of our "neighbors" that benefit and not only our closest friends? Aren't all of God's children equally worthy of unconditional love and a prayerful brother to help restore them to spiritual health?

Who are you willing to love unconditionally beyond their sin?

Let's look at verses 19-20 from the NASB one more time.

> *"My brethren, if any among you strays from the truth and <u>one turns him back</u>, <u>**let him know**</u> <u>that he who turns a sinner from the error of his way</u> will save his soul from death and will cover a multitude of sins."* (emphasis added)

As you can see, there is an emphasis in this passage on the brother who is restoring the wayward believer. Many non-literal translations of Scripture change the wording enough that it completely misses this important emphasis.

In these verses, James calls us to be sensitive to the spiritual needs of others. This is so hard to do. Therefore, James tells us to encourage those who have been instruments in restoring a wayward brother. There is no doubt that this process can be trying, emotional, and wearying to the one who is investing his life in another. If we see those around us doing this sort of ministry, we are to encourage them along the way, for as they give of themselves, they need our encouragement to "refill their cup." The writer of Hebrews tells us to consider how we can *spur one another on toward love and good deeds*" (10:24, NIV). Likewise, Paul reminds us to "*encourage one another and build each other up*" (1 Thess. 5:11, NIV). We are all called to be encouragers and, in essence, we should all be receiving encouragement and giving encouragement at all times.

In order to restore a brother in need, we must pay attention to those around us.

Who has been a consistent source of spiritual encouragement to you? Who do you know that cares for the spiritual needs of others? How can you be an encourager to them?

_____

_____

Before we can restore a brother, we must first recognize his need by paying attention to those around us, being sensitive to their needs. Again, this involves us taking our eyes off ourselves and focusing entirely on others. It can be the smallest things that make the biggest difference in someone's life. A person who may feel like no one would notice if they left the church might be profoundly moved by an email that simply lets them know they were missed. Someone whose head is hung low may be encouraged that you notice their hurt and care enough to extend a hand. One who shared a prayer request a few months ago may be blown away for you to follow up and check on them, because although they figure everyone had forgotten, maybe not **everyone** has.

Describe a time when someone displayed this type of care for you. What difference did it make to you at the time? Jot down the names of a few people you can minister to this week by expressing care and concern.

_____

_____

The words "I'll pray for you" should be followed by prayer.

Once we share that love and commit to pray for others, it is vital to keep that commitment. The words "I'll pray for you" should not be thrown around without follow-through. We need to be diligent to pray for those we've told we would. We've seen in our study that the power of prayer is nothing to take lightly; we must not just toss around such a powerful promise, it's quite a serious matter.

We have found that it is best to immediately pray for others as they come to mind. When the Lord allows someone to enter your thoughts, it's generally not a coincidence. Our minds are always busy, so when others come to mind, instead of just "thinking" about them, stop and pray for them. There's truly nothing better you could do for them. No matter who they are – struggling or solid, friend or foe, lift them up in prayer and it will benefit you both.

Are you in the habit of praying for others when you say you will? What can you do to become more consistent in praying for others?

_____

Finally, when we willingly consider the needs of others, we will begin to recognize their significance. We are quite a selfish lot, this human race. We assume each of our own sorrows are greater than the next person's. We even tend to compete concerning who's under the greatest amount of stress, who's endured the most pain, etc. We've all endured hurt that is unique to our own situation and the truth is, we all need one another's prayers. In order for that to happen, we need to consider each other's burdens as significant and lift them up as such. If we are **all** doing that, then **many** should be lifting our burdens while we lift other's as well.

The truth is, we all need prayer; each person's burdens are significant.

What is your reaction to the idea that other people's burdens are as great as yours? What benefits can you see in praying for the needs of others?

_____

_____

We can hardly believe our study has come to its conclusion. James has taught us that our faith needs to permeate every facet of our lives. He's challenged us with practical ways to do that, and has encouraged us by letting us know that the mighty Lord of Sabaoth is also the loving God of grace who walks with us every step of the way. Thankfully, He gives us one another for encouragement and strengthening through prayer. As we walk this life together, may we encourage each other to actively live this life of faith, **doing** the Word and not hearing it only. May we show ourselves approved when our Judge, who is standing at the door, finds us enduring patiently and obediently for His return. Lord, we pray that you will find us Living a Life of Faith!

Lord, we pray that you will find us living a life of faith!

JAMES – LIVING A LIFE OF FAITH

Leader's Discussion Guide

This leader's guide is intended to offer suggestions for facilitating seven sessions of *James – Living a Life of Faith* by Angie Smith and Dave Vitt. We believe that people of any level of Bible knowledge can, and will, benefit from this study.

To be an effective group facilitator, you do not need to be a Bible scholar, or even a gifted teacher. The most important "ability" is "availability," and the desire to lead men and see their faith in Christ, and knowledge of His Word, grow. Beyond that, all that is required is a little effort to promote the study within your church, and encourage the men to participate.

It is recommended that the study be conducted over a 7-week period of time, with each weekly session lasting 60 to 90 minutes. If you wish to offer the class time for prayer and fellowship, we certainly recommend 90 minutes; you will want a full hour for group discussion of the material. Alternately, you may choose to use the extended 13-session study plan found in Appendix A.

Session 1 is designed to be a time to introduce the men to the study and to one another. During this time, copies of the study should be handed out and introductions of each participant made. Many groups may like to complete an ice-breaker, or some activity, to get to know one-another. Further ideas to promote group interaction will be provided under Session 1.

Beginning in Session 2, (when using the 7-week schedule) the participants will begin digging deeply into God's Word. Chapter 1 of James will be covered during Sessions 2 and 3. Each of the remaining chapters of James (Ch. 2-5) will take one week each

(Sessions 4 - 7). Remember, these are suggestions only. It is your group – adapt the schedule to meet your individual needs.

Lastly, emphasize to your group the importance of completing each daily assignment. Remind them that it is "only 6 weeks" of actual study. However, after 40 days of any new activity, they will have developed a new habit, a godly habit of spending a significant amount of time in God's Holy Word. What an awesome role you can play in helping your friends develop such a vital spiritual discipline. Pray for them each week, and know that we have prayed for each of the faithful men who will lead them each week. Thank you for your willingness; may you, and your class, be incredibly blessed!

SESSION ONE – INTRODUCTION

Before the Session

- Have a copy of *James – Living a Life of Faith* available for each learner.

- Plan a welcoming, or ice-breaking, activity. For ideas, you may wish to visit one or more of the following sites: http://www.any-occasion-free-christian-game.com/christian-ice-breakers.html or

- http://christianicebreakergames.com

- Make a list of sports-related phrases (e.g., "Just Do It; No Pain No Gain; The Agony of Defeat; Quitters Never Win, etc) and hand one to each man. Because much of James focuses on changing our perspective, challenge the men to read their phrase with a different perspective and share a biblical truth that supports or refutes the phrase they have.

- Prepare an attendance sheet so members can have one another's names, phone numbers, and e-mail addresses. Consider the use of nametags for the 1st session or 2, if members aren't familiar with one another.

During the Session

- Welcome the men and hand out copies of the study.

- State that you believe groups learn better together if they know the people with whom they are studying. Invite the group to introduce themselves and then complete the icebreaker or activity of your choice.

- Have the group skim the introduction and Week 1, noting the 5-day format. **Encourage the men to read the introduction, as it is key to understanding the context of the book of James.** In fact, consider reading the introduction aloud to the group during the first session as it reads much like a narrative. Consider having one person read the body of the introduction and ask others to read the verses given in italics throughout the reading for group participation.

- **Further encourage them to complete each day of reading and be prepared to discuss the material during the next session.**

- Ask them what drew them to studying the book of James, and at least one thing they hope to gain from it over the next 6 weeks.

- Consider ending each session with a time of group prayer.

- Have FUN! The attitude of the leader sets the tone for the entire group. Enthusiasm for studying God's Word is contagious, and it can begin with you!

SESSION TWO – JAMES 1:1-12

Before the Session

- Have the class roster available for each member as they enter the room.

- Consider sending each man an email during the week encouraging them to remain on schedule with their reading, and remind them of the next class time and location.

- Pray for each class member by name.

- Select several questions from the list below to ask during the session in order to generate discussion. In addition, consider highlighting insights from the homework that you would like to further discuss.

During the Session

- Welcome the men and allow time for prayer requests and general comments about the content of the week's homework assignments. Consider having the group write prayer requests on a paper to be emailed to the entire group the next day as sharing requests verbally can take a considerable amount of time.

- Ask as many of the following questions as you deem appropriate and that time allows. Try to balance questions about actual Scripture passages (marked with an "S") with personal application questions (marked with an "A").

- S: Who was James writing to? (1:1)

- A: Does the answer to the above question impact how you'll respond to what you read?

- S: According to James 1:1-4, how should we consider trials that come our way?

- A: When trials actually come, what is your knee-jerk reaction to them?

- A: What prevents you from seeing God's perspective in your trials?

- S: What are we to let happen as we endure trials? (1:4)

- A: In what ways have you seen your endurance grow from previous suffering?

- S: What must accompany our request for wisdom? (1:6)

- A: What might cause you to doubt God when you ask for wisdom?

- S: According to James 1:12, the man who perseveres under trial is called what? What will this person receive?

- A: How might keeping your mind focused on the crown of life to come help you persevere today?

- A: What one truth from this week will you seek to implement?

SESSION THREE – JAMES 1:13-27

Before the Session

- Consider sending each participant an email during the week encouraging them to remain on schedule with their reading.

- Pray for each class member by name.

- Consider an outdoor activity if you feel it would improve the dynamics within your group.

- Select several questions from the list below to ask during the session in order to generate discussion. In addition, consider highlighting insights from the homework that you would like to further discuss.

During the Session

- Welcome the group and allow time for prayer requests and general comments about the content of the weeks' homework assignments.

- Ask as many of the following questions as you deem appropriate and that time allows.

- S: According to James 1:13-14, what is the source of our temptation?

- A: Have you ever tried to blame temptation on God or on others? Why?

- S: Temptation does not come from God. According to James 1:17, what does come from God?

- A: For what good things are you most thankful?

- S: According to 1:22, what should our response to the Word be?

- A: Would you consider yourself a hearer of the Word or a doer of the Word? What would others say about you concerning this question?

- S: According to 1:25, what type of person will be blessed in what he does?

- A: Absorbing God's Word is meant to change our hearts first and then our actions. Do your actions indicate that your heart is right with God?

- S: How does James describe pure religion in the sight of God? (1:27)

- A: Based upon that definition, how pure is your own religion? What changes might you need to make?

- A: What one truth from this week will you seek to implement?

SESSION FOUR – JAMES 2

Before the Session

- Keep ongoing communication with men throughout these weeks letting them know they are being prayed for as they study the book of James.

- Select several questions from the list below to ask during the session in order to generate discussion. In addition, consider highlighting insights from the homework that you would like to further discuss.

During the Session

- Welcome the men and allow time for prayer requests and general comments about the content of the weeks' homework assignments.

- Ask as many of the following questions as you deem appropriate and that time allows.

- S: According to James 2:1-7, what was not to be allowed within the church?

- A: In Day 1, 4 categories of people that Christ loves, but we may tend to avoid were described. They were: those of "questionable character," the "scary," the "awkward," and "the rude." Which are the most difficult for you to love? Why?

- S: To what is James referring when he mentions the "royal law?" (2:8-9)

- A: Loving others as ourselves is a very difficult calling. It requires us to love others at their worst and when our love is not returned. What have you found that helps you do that?

- S: What was the primary purpose of "the law?" (2:9-11)

- A: How can you remember from what you have been saved?

- S: James contends that faith without works is dead. (2:14-17) Do you agree?

- A: If others knew only what you did, and not what you said, what type of faith would they conclude you have?

- S: Who did James choose as examples of genuine faith? (2:20-26)

- A: Abraham was "the poster child" and Rahab, "the prostitute." Why do you think James chose them? Which do you relate to more? Why?

- A: What one truth from this week will you seek to implement?

SESSION FIVE – JAMES 3

Before the Session

- Is it time for some food and fellowship? Consider a cookout and do your study around a fire.

- This week's lesson is about the power of the tongue. Consider bringing an article that discusses the impact of positive and negative words to share with the group. Alternatively, prior to the class, enlist a volunteer to share the impact

someone's words (positive or negative) had on their life.

- Select several questions from the list below to ask during the session in order to generate discussion. In addition, consider highlighting insights from the homework that you would like to further discuss.

During the Session

- Welcome the group and allow time for prayer requests and general comments about the content of the weeks' homework assignments.

- Ask as many of the following questions as you deem appropriate and that time allows.

- S: With what warning does James begin Chapter 3? (3:1) Why?

- A: We are all teachers of someone somewhere. What are others learning from you by your words and actions?

- S: To what does James compare the tongue? (3:3-5) What's his point?

- A: On Day 2, you read, "Harsh words can crush a spirit, silence is impossible to interpret, but a kind word is seldom misunderstood." Share an example of when words crushed you or lifted you up? When has silence been deafening?

- S: James is stumped at how two opposing things can come out of the same mouth; what are they? (3:9-12)

- A: In what ways have you "cursed" your fellow believer who has been made in the likeness of God? What can you do to put an end to it?

- S: In James 3:13, two types of wisdom are mentioned; what were they?

- S: How would you describe the "gentleness of wisdom?"

- A: Based upon the amount of time you spend listening to each (the world and to God), which would you honestly say is your primary source of wisdom?

- S: What were the characteristics of the wisdom that comes from above? (3:17-18)

- A: Part of gentle and reasonable wisdom is to recognize whether or not the expectations you place on others are Scriptural or your opinion. When theological or moral principals are not involved, how good are you at extending freedom?

- A: What one truth from this week will you seek to apply?

SESSION SIX – JAMES 4

Before the Session

- You're nearing the end of your study, begin planning what your next move will be. Will you do another study? If so which one?

- James 4 includes teaching on conflict. Come prepared with news articles where conflict was a precipitating factor in what occurred. Discuss how the conflict may have been avoided.

- Select several questions from the list below to ask during the session in order to generate discussion. In addition, consider highlighting insights from the homework that you would like to further discuss.

During the Session

- Welcome the men and allow time for prayer requests and general comments about the content of the weeks' homework assignments.

- Ask as many of the following questions as you deem appropriate and that time allows.

- S: What does James say is the source of our quarrels and conflicts? (4:1-2)

- A: In what ways have envy and lust for pleasures caused conflict in your life?

- S: What does James call friendship with the world? (4:4)

- A: In what ways have you become too cozy with this world?

- S: What commands are we given by James in vs. 7?

- A: What does submit mean to you? Is submitting to God easy or difficult for you? Why?

- S: What are we not to do to one another? Why? (4:11-12)

- A: Speaking against includes gossip, slander, railing against, and talking down to. Which of these are you prone to? How might remembering that God is responsible for judging others help you cease "speaking against" them?

- S: To what does James compare our lives? (4:14)

- A: You are a mist, and He is your Maker; but do you have trouble leaving the planning to Him? Why?

- A: What one truth from this week will you seek to implement?

SESSION SEVEN – JAMES 5

Before the Session

- Contact each member, reminding them that they are in the home-stretch and to finish strong!

- If your group plans to continue with another study following James, have them bring ideas of what they would like to study next. Remember – after 6 weeks of studying God's Word, they have developed a new habit that you will want to help foster!

- Alternatively, consider taking another group of guys through the James study – it is always exciting to help more men start this new, fun, and life-changing pattern!

- Select several questions from the list below to ask during the session in order to generate discussion. In addition, consider highlighting insights from the homework that you would like to further discuss.

During the Session

- Welcome the men and allow time for prayer requests and general comments about the content of the weeks' homework assignments.

- THANK THEM for sharing the last 6 weeks with you. Encourage them to continue in their own Bible study or to join a new study soon!

- Ask them to think back over the prior sessions and identify 1 or 2 of the most significant things they learned and how they plan to apply it in their personal lives.

- Discuss the idea of forming small groups to encourage and hold one another accountable for those changes. Remind them that it's easy to be a "hearer" of the Word; it's much tougher to become a "doer" of the Word! Support from another brother can be the help they need.

- Ask as many of the following as you deem appropriate and that time allows.

- S: The rich had oppressed the poor, and the cries of poor had reached God, who was called what? (5:4)

- A: How does thinking of God as the Lord of all armies, seen and unseen, impact your willingness to call out to Him?

- S: What does James promise to those facing unfair, harsh oppression? (5:7-8)

- A: The Lord is coming "soon." How can keeping your focus on that promise help you through your current trials?

- S: Why should we, as Christians, not have to swear by any means? (5:12)

- A: Have you carelessly made promises without considering the impact if you don't/can't keep them? Describe a time when your "yes" was not a "yes" and the impact it had on those around you.

- S: T or F – James 5:13-18 promises physical healing? Support your answer.

- A: Have you prayed earnestly, and wondered why physical healing did not occur? What went through your mind as you watched a loved one lose their battle to illness?

- S: What are we to do when we encounter a brother or sister straying from the truth? (5:19-20)

- A: Caring for the spiritual well-being of others is hard, draining work. Think about those in your life who have been consistent sources of spiritual encouragement to you; how might you be an encourager to them?

- A: What one truth from this week will you seek to implement?

APPENDIX A

James – Living a Life of Faith

Alternate, 13-Session Study Plan

(Beginning with one introductory session, this alternate schedule then continues for 12 additional weeks of Bible study and discussion).

Introduction

<u>Session 1</u>: A Tried Faith*, Days 1-3

<u>Session 2</u>: A Tried Faith, Days 4-5

<u>Session 3</u>: A Tested and Triumphant Faith, Days 1-2

<u>Session 4</u>: A Tested and Triumphant Faith, Days 3-5

<u>Session 5</u>: An Active and Loving Faith, Days 1-3

<u>Session 6</u>: An Active and Loving Faith, Days 4-5

<u>Session 7</u>: A Controlled and Gentle Faith, Days 1-3

<u>Session 8</u>: A Controlled and Gentle Faith, Days 4-5

<u>Session 9</u>: A Peaceful and Humble Faith, Days 1-2

<u>Session 10</u>: A Peaceful and Humble Faith, Days 3-5

<u>Session 11</u>: A Prayerfully Patient Faith, Days 1-2

<u>Session 12</u>: A Prayerfully Patient Faith, Days 3-5

* Title of weekly sessions found in the Table of Content for easy reference.

as IAM ministries

The desire of as I AM ministries is to be a source of HOPE for the lost, PROVISION for the hungry, COMFORT for the broken-hearted, and INSIGHT for every Christian through the teaching of God's Word and the overflow of service that it inspires. At our root, as I AM is a Bible teaching ministry that produces Bible study curriculum and daily devotions. That is our root - but from every healthy root, there is growth and life. We believe that when we learn from God's Word, we should be inspired to be used as His hands and feet. Therefore, our ministry also creates opportunities for people to do just that. We want these to be hands-on activities where volunteers have a chance to look into the eyes of those they are serving and to show love through their own eyes and actions. Such opportunities include working in our community garden, which produces thousands of pounds of food for the hungry each year, and staffing weeks of summer camp that ministers to underprivileged children.

Jesus came to serve, and the masses were drawn to Him by His gentle and humble heart - the very heart He invites us to learn from (Matt. 11:29). We can teach for days, perhaps never being heard, but we can reach out in a moment of need, in order to make an eternal difference, and 'they will know us by our love.'

To support this work, or to schedule Angie and/or Dave to speak at your upcoming event, visit: www.asIAMministries.org

Notes: